W9-BLG-318

Christ Church
F R E D E R I C A
Cookbook

Published by
Episcopal Churchwomen
Christ Church, Frederica
St. Simons Island, Georgia

First printing	7,000 books	November 1992
Second printing	7,000 books	April 1995
Third printing	7,000 books	August 1997
Fourth printing	7,000 books	September 1999
Fifth printing	7,000 books	September 2001
Sixth printing	7,000 books	May 2003
Seventh printing	7,000 books	December 2005
Eighth printing	7,000 books	June 2008
Ninth printing	7,000 books	August 2011
Tenth printing	10,000 books	October 2013
Eleventh printing	10,000 books	December 2016

ISBN: 978-0-9644973-0-6

To order copies of *Christ Church, Frederica Cookbook*
please use the order forms provided in the back of the book or contact:
Christ Church, Frederica Cookbook
6329 Frederica Road
Saint Simons Island, GA 31522

WIMMER
cookbooks
wimmerco.com   800.548.2537
AN RR DONNELLEY COMPANY
"Cookbooks of Distinction"™

Contents

Compiled by
The Episcopal Church Women of Christ Church, Frederica

Cover Art: Betty Lowe
Photography: Dorothy McClain
Photography Assistants: Jerry Garrison
Martha Fitzgerald

Proceeds from the sale of
Christ Church, Frederica Cookbook
will be used for the glory of God in our
parish, community, nation and world.

⁓⟳⟳⟳⟳⟳⁓

Dedicated to Cam Caldwell

1920-1992

Her guidance and wisdom made a dream come true.

⁓⟳⟳⟳⟳⁓

Christ Church, Frederica
Episcopal Church Women

The Christ Church, Frederica ECW (Episcopal Church Women) sponsors two major projects each year: the annual Tour of Homes, which was begun in the mid 1950s, and the sale of the ever popular Christ Church cookbook. The combined proceeds of these projects are awarded each May through the grant process to deserving area charities benefiting women and children, so our community is the real winner.

The Tour of Homes, a one day event, attracts visitors from around the country each spring to enjoy a variety of architectural styles and fabulous interiors, ranging from vast island estates to welcoming beach cottages on St. Simons Island and Sea Island. Generous homeowners and guiding church docents welcome the guests through their homes, making the Tour one of the most celebrated events in the Golden Isles and throughout the Southeast. It takes over 400 community volunteers to accomplish the Tour each March, and a very grateful Christ Church thanks our many neighbors and volunteers for both their time and support of this most worthy effort.

The cookbook, first published in 1992, has become a most popular keepsake. It is prized for its recipes, its artwork and the special prayers and blessings throughout its pages. A highlight of this cookbook is the collection of beautiful photos which captures each stained glass window in the church and includes a cover page with an explanation of what that window depicts. This collector's item makes a wonderful souvenir of a visit to this beautiful worship space or a great gift for a friend; our brides love them as gifts and remembrances of their special day as well.

Please visit our website at www.christchurchtourofhomes.org for more information on all of our activities, to purchase tour tickets, or to see a list of grant recipients from recent years.

Episcopal Church Women's Prayer

Almighty God, our Heavenly Father, bless we pray, our work for the extension of your kingdom, make us so thankful for the precious gift of your Beloved Son, that we may pray fervently, labor diligently and give liberally to make Him known to all nations as their Saviour and their King, through the same Jesus Christ, our Lord.   Amen

In His Service,
Christ Church, Frederica ECW

Barbara Mueller

Christ Church, Frederica

Ministry under the oaks began in 1736
Christ Church incorporated in 1808, first church built in 1820
Current church building completed in 1884

Our mission is to make Christ known to our community and
the world through worship, fellowship, service and outreach.
We strive to be a clear and positive voice for Christian life, to
proclaim the Gospel message for all, and to preserve and cherish
our historical roots.

✌ Ministry at Christ Church ✌

Ministry of the gospel at Frederica began on March 9, 1736, with the arrival of an Anglican priest from England, The Reverend Charles Wesley, accompanying General James Oglethorpe as his Secretary of Indian Affairs and minister to the 116 settlers at the newly established Fort Frederica. Charles was here only a few short months but his older brother, The Reverend John Wesley, who was serving as pastor in Savannah, ministered to the local colonists for a longer period, returning to England in 1738. John made a total of five trips from Savannah to St. Simons during this two year period. Later services were conducted by additional clergy appointed by the Society for the Propagation of the Gospel until around 1766.

Following the Revolutionary War, the descendants of the early settlers petitioned for a charter and won incorporation from the Georgia state legislature on December 22, 1808, as *The Episcopal Church in the Town of Frederica,* called Christ Church. Worship continued under the oaks or in private homes until the first building was erected on this site in 1820.

The era of the Civil War was unkind to the small church. Plantation owners and islanders fled as the northern soldiers approached. The original church, decimated by the Union troops, was lovingly rebuilt by The Reverend Anson Green Phelps Dodge, Jr. as a memorial to his first wife, Ellen, who died in India from cholera during their around the world honeymoon. Ellen's casket was placed under the altar so that Anson could keep his promise never to leave her side as he preached. The church is the typical Anglican cruciform in shape and features a prized collection of stained glass windows depicting scenes from the life of Christ and other Biblical events, as well as the history of the area and the early church. A cemetery surrounding the church on three sides evokes the stories and lives of the parishioners through the years, whose trials and triumphs are woven into the fabric of this congregation. The oldest identified headstone dates back to 1803, and many of these older headstones convey the cause of death and age of those who lie here. A walking tour of these grounds reveals the worship and social life of this parish, demonstrated by the fact that many prominent Georgians, as well as former rectors and their families, are buried here.

Christ Church, Frederica remains an active, vibrant place of worship today. The congregation continues to thrive, and has the distinction of having had four sitting United States presidents worship with us during their time in office. The beauty of this place is an inspiration to those who live and worship here as well as to those who visit. The mission of the congregation remains: "to make Christ known to our community and the world through worship, fellowship, service and outreach." All are welcome in this house of worship. We invite you to come often and share the joy of Christian fellowship with us.

JOHN AND
CHARLES WESLEY

The ministry of John and Charles
Wesley at Frederica is depicted. The
brothers meet with settlers under the
shelter of live oaks, while the ship that
brought John from Savannah
waits at anchor.

The window was given in 1969 by
Mrs. Wylie Brown in memory of her
father and mother, "To the Glory of
God and in Loving Memory of Mr. and
Mrs. William Francis Kyle."

JOHN AND CHARLES WESLEY PREACHING UNDER LIVE OAKS AT FREDERICA, 1736

GENERAL JAMES OGLETHORPE

The window commemorates the found-
ing of Georgia. General James
Oglethorpe is shown with Indian Chief
Tomochichi and his nephew
Toonahowie. The strong friendship
between Oglethorpe and Tomochichi
proved extremely helpful when
Oglethorpe's army came into conflict
with the Spanish.

The window was given by Mrs. Edward
Postell King, Jr., in memory of her hus-
band, "To the Glory of God and
in Loving Memory of Edward Postell
King, Jr., Major General, United
States Army, Senior Warden,
Christ Church, Frederica.

Hot Artichoke Hors d'oeuvre

1   can artichoke hearts, drained and finely chopped

1   cup grated sharp Cheddar or Parmesan cheese

1   cup Hellmann's mayonnaise

Snipped fresh dill weed (optional)

- Mix together and bake 350° for 20 minutes.
- Serve with favorite crackers or Melba toast. This is good hot or cold.

SPECIAL NOTE: THIS RECIPE WAS GIVEN TO ME BY A GOOD FRIEND YEARS AGO. I THEN GAVE THIS RECIPE TO ANOTHER GOOD FRIEND AND SHE HAS MADE IT FOR ME EVERY TIME SHE COMES TO A RECTORY PARTY. WHAT A SMART MOVE TO GIVE HER THE RECIPE!

Serves 6-8   *Martha Fitzgerald*

Asperges Flamandes
Asparagus in the Flemish Style

Asparagus
Hard boiled eggs

Lemon wedges

- Boil asparagus slowly in small amount of salted water for 10 minutes or until asparagus is barely tender.
- While asparagus is cooking, chop hard boiled eggs, ½ egg per person.
- Cut lemon wedges, 2 per person.
- Arrange asparagus on individual plates, sprinkle chopped eggs on top, garnish with lemon.

SPECIAL NOTE: WHEN WE LIVED IN BRUSSELS, OUR BELGIAN COOK SERVED THIS AS A FIRST COURSE USING WHITE ASPARAGUS WHENEVER IT WAS AVAILABLE.

Serves any number   *Carolyn Mattingly*

*May the All Merciful bless my father,
my leader, the master of this house,
and my mother, my teacher, the mistress of this house.*

PRAYER A CHILD MAY GIVE IN A RELIGIOUS JEWISH HOME

BLACKEYED SUSANS

1 cup unsalted butter, room temperature
1 lb. sharp cheddar cheese, grated
2 cups all-purpose flour
Salt to taste
3 shakes cayenne pepper
1 lb. pitted dates, sliced lengthwise
Sugar

- Blend butter and cheese together.
- Mix with flour, salt and cayenne pepper to form dough. Chill.
- Roll out thinly and cut into small rounds with a biscuit cutter.
- Place date half on one side of dough round.
- Fold remaining dough over. Pinch edges together like a turnover.
- Bake on a non-stick cookie sheet at 250-300° for 30 minutes or until edges barely brown.
- Roll in sugar while warm.

SPECIAL NOTES: OPTIONALLY MAY CUT WITH 1½-2-INCH ROUND CUTTER. PUT CHOPPED DATE IN CENTER AND TOP WITH ANOTHER ROUND OF DOUGH. CRIMP EDGES AND BAKE AS ABOVE.

Davi Langston

CHEESE BISCUITS I

1 stick butter or margarine
1 cup flour
1 cup sharp cheese, finely grated
Pinch salt
Pinch sugar
2-3 drops Worcestershire sauce
Dash tabasco
⅓ cup chopped pecans
½ to ⅔ Rice Krispies

- Mix together butter, flour and cheese until fluffy, no lumps.
- Add a pinch of salt and sugar, few drops Worcestershire sauce and dash Tabasco. Blend.
- Add chopped pecans and Rice Krispies. Mix well.
- Shape dough into 1-inch balls.
- Bake 15-20 minutes on cookie sheet at 300°.
- Remove from oven and cover with foil. Pat flat.

Yields about 40 biscuits

Jill S. Cunningham

CHEESE BISCUITS II

½   lb. American cheese, sharp   Dash Tabasco
1   stick margarine or butter   Dash salt
2   cups flour

- Grate cheese.
- Cream margarine, adding cheese.
- Gradually add flour, Tabasco, salt.
- Combine into roll and slice.
- Bake in 350° oven 10 minutes.
- Sprinkle with granulated sugar while hot.
- May press ½ pecan in each biscuit before cooking if desired.

Can double recipe.

Ruth Backus

COCKTAIL SAUSAGES

1   cup currant jelly   Cocktail sausage, small wieners
¼   cup prepared mustard   or hot dogs cut diagonally in
                                 1-inch pieces

- Heat jelly and mustard in chafing dish or frying pan until jelly is melted. Add the hot dogs or whatever.
- Stir until hot. Serve with cocktail picks.

Jeanette Bessels

HANKY PANKY

1 loaf party rye	1 lb. Velveeta cheese
1 lb. hot sausage, bulk	

- Cook sausage.
- Add cheese until melted, cool.
- Spread on bread, broil until bubbly.

Anita Campbell

HANKY PANKS

2 loaves party bread	1 tsp. oregano
1 lb. ground beef	1 tsp. garlic salt
1 lb. sausage	½ tsp. red pepper
1 lb. Velveeta cheese	

- Cook meats in microwave, drain off as much fat as possible, then spread out on paper towels and pat to get out remaining fat.
- Return meats to bowl, place 1 lb. Velveeta cheese over meat and melt in microwave.
- Add oregano, garlic salt and pepper. Stir. Spread mixture on bread.
- Freeze on cookie sheet then store in plastic bag.
- To use: place on cookie sheet and bake 10 minutes at 350°.

Charlotte Raymond

Bless us, O Lord, and these Thy gifts,
which we are about to receive from Thy bounty,
through Christ Our Lord. Amen.

A CATHOLIC GRACE

MUSHROOM BITES

20 slices thinly sliced white
bread
2 tbsp. grated onion
¼ cup butter
¾ cup finely chopped
mushrooms

2 tbsp. flour
½ tsp. Tabasco sauce
1 tsp. salt
⅛ tsp. pepper
½ cup Half and Half
Butter and vegetable oil

- Cut each slice of bread with a 1¾-inch round cookie cutter into four rounds.
- Sauté onion in butter.
- Add mushrooms, sauté until all moisture is cooked out of the mushrooms.
- Add flour, stir until thick.
- Add Tabasco, salt, pepper and Half and Half. Cook until thickened.
- Spread 1 tsp. mushroom mixture on each round.
- Top with another bread round to make a sandwich.
- Repeat procedure until all ingredients are used up.
- Fry sandwiches in equal parts of butter and oil until brown and crisp, about 1 minute for each side. Drain thoroughly.
- Keep warm, uncovered in a 300° oven. Make ahead—freezes beautifully.

Davi Langston

NUTS AND BOLTS

1 10 oz. box Cheerios
1 box Rice Chex
1 box Corn Chex
1 box Wheat Chex
1 pkg. pretzel sticks
1 large can peanuts

3 sticks margarine
1½ cups bacon drippings
2-3 tbsp. Worcestershire
2-3 tbsp. Tabasco sauce
2-3 tbsp. garlic powder

- Place cereals, pretzels and peanuts in large roasting pan. Mix well.
- Melt margarine and bacon drippings, add seasonings and pour over cereal mix. Stir well to coat cereal.
- Cover, bake at 250° for 1 hour, stirring once after 30 minutes.
- Uncover and bake another hour, stirring every 15 minutes.
- Let cool. Store in tightly covered container.

SPECIAL NOTE: I HAVE MADE THESE FOR 40 YEARS FOR CHILDREN AND GRAND-CHILDREN, AND HAVE SELDOM BEEN WITHOUT THEM ON-HAND.

Martha Fitzgerald

ROASTED GARLIC AND BRIE

¼ cup olive oil
2 whole heads of garlic
1 2 lb. wheel of brie
½ cup Greek olives or ripe olives, pitted and quartered

Warm sour dough or French bread broken into small pieces

- Put oil in heavy saucepan and add the garlic. Cook and stir over medium heat for 5 minutes, or until garlic is soft. Remove and drain on paper towels, cool.
- To assemble: Carefully slice the thin rind from one flat side of the brie. Place on a baking sheet or suitable bake and serve dish, cut side up.
- Divide heads of garlic into cloves and peel. With a small sharp knife slice cloves diagonally, being careful not to cut through. Gently press garlic cloves into fans.
- Arrange garlic fans and olive pieces atop brie.
- Bake uncovered in a 400° oven for 10 to 12 minutes or until brie is softened.
- Sprinkle with parsley, if desired. Transfer to serving plate to serve wit the bread, apple slices, etc.
- Can be made ahead: Before baking it you can wrap the wheel in plastic and chill for as long as three days. Before serving, heat through as directed above.

SPECIAL NOTE: LOOKS PRETTY AND TASTES DELICIOUS! SERVE WITH FIRM CRACKERS, OR THE BREAD, OR CRISP BAKED PITA CHIPS.

Cam Caldwell

*Father, thank you for these
and all our many blessings; and forgive us for our sins.
May this food nourish our bodies that we
may more fully serve thee. Amen*

SPINACH SQUARES

4 tbsp. melted butter	½ cup chopped mushrooms
3 eggs	1 tsp. salt
1 cup flour	1 small onion, chopped fine
1 cup milk	
1 pkg. frozen chopped spinach, thawed then drained	

- Put melted butter in 9 x 13-inch baking dish.
- Mix other ingredients and spoon into baking dish.
- Bake at 350° for 35 minutes.
- Cut into bars. Serve hot or cold. Best if frozen then served later. Wrap individually to freeze then use as needed.

Serves 8-10   *Mary Walsh*

SWEDISH MEATBALL HORS D'OEUVRES

½ cup fine dry bread crumbs	2 tsp. salt
½ cup warm cream	½ tsp. pepper
½ lb. ground beef	⅛ tsp. allspice
¼ lb. ground veal	Parsley flakes, optional
¼ lb. ground pork	Parmesan cheese, optional
½ cup milk	Burgundy wine
2 egg yolks, slightly beaten	Consommé
2 tbsp. minced onion	

- Soak crumbs in cream, combine crumbs and meats; mix thoroughly and add milk.
- Add egg yolks, onion, and seasoning; form into tiny balls.
- Brown meatballs on all sides in butter or oil.
- Cover with Burgundy wine and marinate 2 to 4 days.
- Reheat meatballs in consommé to cover.
- Serve in chafing dish with small amount of consommé.
- Meatloaf mix may be substituted if it contains beef, veal and pork.

SPECIAL NOTE: SERVED TO 75 TO 150 GUESTS AFTER PENN STATE HOME FOOTBALL GAMES.

Serves 8-10   *Cornelia C. Ferguson*

VEGETABLE CANAPES

1	3 oz. pkg. cream cheese, softened	8	slices white bread
3	tbsp. sour cream	8	slices whole wheat bread
¼	tsp. garlic salt	1	cucumber, shredded
⅛	tsp. white pepper	1	carrot, shredded
½	tsp. dried dill		Thinly sliced squash or radishes
3	tbsp. frozen minced chives, thawed		Sliced cherry tomatoes
			Fresh dill sprigs

- Beat cream cheese until fluffy. Stir in next 5 ingredients, set aside.
- Cut two 1¾-inch rounds from each bread slice with a biscuit cutter.
- Spread each bread round with 1 tsp. cream cheese mixture. Top with assorted vegetables, mixing if desired.
- Garnish with a dill sprig. Makes 32 canapes.

Serves 8   *Becky Rowell*

ARTICHOKE DIP

1	can artichoke hearts, drained	4-5 tbsp. mayonnaise
1	pkg. dry Good Seasons Italian salad dressing mix	

- Mash artichoke hearts with a fork until cut in small pieces.
- Add dry salad dressing mix and mayonnaise. Mix well.
- Can be served hot in a chafing dish or cold. Best served with broken-in-half triscuits.

Jane Fann Sanders

O, He's been good to us.

PRESCHOOL BLESSING

Hot Artichoke Spread

1   14 oz can artichoke hearts, drain and chop
1   cup mayonnaise

1   cup grated parmesan cheese
½ tsp. garlic powder

- Combine all ingredients, mix well.
- Spoon into lightly greased 3 cup casserole.
- Bake at 350° for 20 minutes. Serve warm.
- Serve with crackers or thinly sliced toasted French bread.

SPECIAL NOTE: CAN BE MADE AHEAD. YOU MAY SUBSTITUTE LOW FAT MAYONNAISE.

Yields 2½ cups   *Brenda Hartsell*

Avocado Dip

1   avocado, mashed
1   8 oz. pkg. cream cheese, softened
2   tbsp. freshly squeezed lemon or lime juice

Dash Worcestershire sauce
⅓ cup minced green onion
½ tsp. salt, or to taste
2   green chilies, mashed

- Blend avocado into cheese until smooth.
- Add remaining ingredients, blend well, cover and chill.
- Serve with vegetables or chips.

SPECIAL NOTE: THIS DIP MAY BE PREPARED AHEAD OF TIME. SPREAD A THIN LAYER OF MAYONNAISE OVER SURFACE TO PREVENT DARKENING; STIR IT IN JUST BEFORE SERVING. CHECK FOR SEASONINGS.

Yield about 1½ cups   *Cam Caldwell*

O give thanks unto the Lord,
for He is good:
for His mercy endureth forever.

PSALMS 107:1

BEAN PESTO

1 can kidney beans, rinsed and drained
2 cloves garlic, mashed
1 jalapeña pepper, seeded and chopped (wear rubber gloves)
¼ cup water
1½ tsp. cider vinegar
½ tsp. paprika
½ tsp. black pepper
¼ tsp. chili powder
¼ tsp. salt
Dash hot sauce
½ cup salad oil

- Blend together for Mexican dip.

Davi Langston

CAVIAR PIE

1 8 oz. pkg. cream cheese
¼ cup mayonnaise
1 onion, chopped
6 hardboiled eggs, chopped
Dash Tabasco
1 tbsp. lemon juice
1 small jar caviar

- Mix all together, except caviar.

- Shape in a circle 1-inch deep on a plate and store in refrigerator until ready to serve.

- Drain a small jar caviar and soak up excess liquid with bits of paper towel.

- Spread on top of the cream cheese mixture.

- Serve with party pumpernickel.

Serves 8-10

Jeanne Alaimo

CHILI-CHEESE DIP

1 8 oz. pkg. cream cheese, softened
1 can chili, no beans (Hormel)
Chili powder and garlic salt to taste
Chopped onions
1 pkg. Monterey Jack cheese with Jalapeño peppers, grated

- Preheat oven to 350°. Layer ingredients in above order. Sprinkle chili powder and garlic salt over the chili.

- If you want it hotter, you may add additional chopped Jalapeño peppers.

- Bake at 350° for 15-20 minutes. Serve with corn chips or tortilla chips.

SPECIAL NOTE: THIS IS ALWAYS GOBBLED UP!

Nancy Sumerford

CURRY DIP WITH TORTELLINI

2   9 oz. pkgs. fresh or frozen
    cheese or spinach-filled
    tortellini
Dip:
1½ cups mayonnaise or salad
    dressing

½   cup dairy sour cream
¼   cup apple juice
¼   cup chopped green onions
½   tsp. curry powder

- Cook tortellini to desired doneness as directed on package; drain.
- Cover and refrigerate 2-3 hours or overnight until well chilled.
- Combine all dip ingredients; blend well.
- Cover and refrigerate 2 to 3 hours or overnight to blend flavors.
- To serve, spoon dip into bowl and arrange tortellini around dip.

SPECIAL NOTE: DIP MAY ALSO BE SERVED WITH FRESH VEGETABLES.

Yields 25 servings (2 to 3 each)   *Betty Link*

FOUR CHEESE PATÉ

1   8 oz. pkg. cream cheese
2   tbsp. milk
2   oz. sour cream
¾   cup chopped pecans, toasted
2   8 oz. pkgs. cream
    cheese,softened

1   4 oz. pkg. camembert,
    softened
1   4 oz. pkg. crumbled blue
    cheese
1   cup Swiss cheese, shredded
Pecan halves

- Line 9-inch pie plate with plastic wrap.
- Combine 1st three ingredients in mixing bowl. Beat at medium speed.
- Spread over plastic wrap then spread with pecans.
- Combine other cheese. Spoon on top of above.
- Cover with plastic wrap. Chill for one week.
- Serve with crackers or Melba toast.

Helen W. Loughlin (from Jean Sucher)

SPINACH DIP

1 pkg. frozen spinach, thawed, drained well
2 tbsp. fresh parsley or 1 tbsp. dried parsley
1 tsp. salt

Mayonnaise, enough to hold mixture together (¼ cup)
2 tbsp. chopped onion
1 tsp. black pepper (that's right!)

- Mix all ingredients well, refrigerate.
- May be made a day ahead. Serve with crackers.

SPECIAL NOTE: THIS IS A PRETTY DIP AND MEN LIKE IT AS MUCH AS WOMEN. LOWFAT MAYONNAISE MAY BE SUBSTITUTED.

Yields 1½-2 cups   *Brenda Hartsell*

TACO DIP

1½ can Frito Bean dip
1 large or 2 small avocados, mashed
Juice of ½ lemon
1 16 oz. container sour cream
2 pkgs. taco seasoning
¼ cup chopped spring onions

¼ cup chopped ripe olives, drained
2 large tomatoes, seeded and chopped
1 cup extra sharp cheddar cheese, grated

- Spread beans in large bowl
- Spread avocado with lemon juice over beans.
- Mix taco mix with sour cream; spread over avocado mix.
- Top with onions, olives, tomatoes, cheese.
- Serve with Tostito chips.

Mary Jane Flint

*Give us grateful hearts, our Father
for all thy mercies, and make us mindful
of the needs of others; through Jesus Christ our Lord.
Amen.*

THE BOOK OF COMMON PRAYER

THREE LAYER MEXICAN DIP
OR THE MAYOR'S CHOICE

Bean pesto (recipe in this section)
1½ cup guacamole
½ cup sharp cheddar cheese, grated
½ cup tomatoes, seeded, diced
½ cup chopped black olives
2 green onions

Mix for sour cream mixture:
1½ cup sour cream
½ tsp. garlic powder
¼ tsp. chili powder
¼ tsp. cumin
¼ tsp. each salt and pepper

- In 10-inch baking dish, layer in order:
  Bean pesto, Guacamole, sour cream mixture, cheese.
- Sprinkle top with tomatoes, olives and green onion (white and 3-inches of stem chopped).
- Bake at 350° for 15 minutes until hot.

Davi Langston

CLAM DIP

1 12 oz. pkg. cream cheese, softened
1 small can minced or chopped clams, with juice

¼ tsp. lemon pepper
Juice of ½ lemon
¼ tsp. garlic powder

- Combine all ingredients including clam juice. (Add more seasonings if desired.)
- Serve with mexican style chips or raw vegetables.

Serves 25 plus   *Eileen B. Hutcheson*

*Bless us, O Lord and these Thy gifts
which we are about to receive
from Thy bounty, through Christ our Lord.
Amen*

A ROMAN CATHOLIC BLESSING

CRAB MOUSSE

½ can cream of
    Mushroom Soup
1 8 oz. pkg. cream cheese
1 pkg. plain gelatin
⅛ cup cold water

1½ cup crabmeat (fresh or
    canned)
1 small white onion, diced
½ cup mayonnaise
½ cup finely diced celery
Dash salt

- Heat soup, add cream cheese. Stir until combined.
- Dissolve gelatin in ⅛ cup cold water, add to soup, let cool.
- Add onion, mayonnaise, salt, celery and crabmeat.
- Pour into a greased mold and chill to set.
- Unmold and serve with crackers.

SPECIAL NOTE: A REALLY GOOD, GOOD APPETIZER!

Serves 6-8　　　　　　　　　*Mrs. Jennings Head (Mrs. Robert Allen)*

COCKTAIL CRAB SPREAD

½ cup (plus) real mayonnaise
    (Hellmann's)
1 lb. fresh crabmeat
Dash garlic powder

Dash salt
Dash Beau Monde
Dash dill weed

- Mix together to taste and enjoy.

Serves 6-8　　　　　　　　　　　　　*Peggy Sullivan*

SHRIMP BUTTER

1½ sticks butter
2 tbsp. onion (dried flakes)
1 8 oz. pkg. cream cheese

Juice of 1 lemon
1 4 oz. can shrimp (drained)
4 tbsp. mayonnaise

- Blend in blender or by hand.
- Use as a dip or a sandwich spread.

Frances Burns (Mrs. Allen)

SHRIMP MOUSSE

1   can tomato soup
1   large pkg. cream cheese
2   pkgs. Knox gelatin
1   cup cold water
2   cans shredded shrimp

1½ cups celery, chopped
1   green pepper, chopped
1   small onion, grated
1   cup mayonnaise

- Heat tomato soup and cream cheese in double boiler until cheese melts.
- Dissolve Knox gelatin in cold water and add to soup mixture while cooling.
- Chop and mix rest of ingredients. Add to mixture.
- Pour into ½ qt. mold. Serve on lettuce.
- Make a day ahead.

SPECIAL NOTE: THIS IS AN OLD RECIPE FROM ATLANTA.

Serves 10   *Sarah B. Jones*

SHRIMP DIP

1   4 oz. can small shrimp
     (preferably Orleans brand)
1   8 oz. jar mayonnaise

1   5 oz. jar Kraft cream-style horseradish

- Drain shrimp and mash.
- Add mayonnaise.
- Add horseradish to taste (about ¾ jar). Serve with favorite crackers.

Donna and George Dunbar

HOT SHRIMP DIP

2 lbs. cream cheese
1 medium onion, chopped
1 medium tomato, seeded and chopped
2 cloves garlic, chopped
1½ banana pepper, chopped
1 toreta pepper, chopped
1½ lbs. shrimp, cooked, coarsely chopped

- Combine in container over hot water on stove, do not boil water.
- When warm, fold in 1½ lbs. shrimp chopped (not too finely).
- Dilute with milk to desired consistency.
- This can be made ahead and reheated.

SPECIAL NOTE: KEEPS SEVERAL DAYS IN REFRIGERATOR. RECIPE CAN EASILY BE CUT IN HALF OR LESS. ADD AS MUCH SHRIMP OR LOBSTER AS DESIRED.

Serves 30-40   *Hazel Crowley*

SPICY SHRIMP SPREAD

1 8 oz. pkg. cream cheese, softened
¼ cup mayonnaise
5 green onions, finely chopped
½ tsp. horseradish
½ tbsp. dry mustard
Garlic salt or powder to taste
½ lb. cooked shrimp, ground in blender or processor

- Mix all ingredients together, adding shrimp last.
- Chill for at least 6 hours or overnight. Serve with crackers.

Serves 12   *Becky Rowell*

FRUIT PUNCH

3 small cans frozen orange juice concentrate
3 small cans frozen lemonade juice concentrate
2½ qts. water
1 large can pineapple juice
3 cups sugar (scant)
1 small bottle almond extract
1 large bottle of Ginger ale

- All ingredients can be mixed together in advance and chilled in refrigerator.
- Pour in punch bowl with fruit ice ring.
- Add ginger ale just before serving.

SPECIAL NOTE: THIS RECIPE IS OFTEN ENJOYED AT CHRIST CHURCH.

Serves 50   *Mary Evelyn Cook*

PINK FRUIT PUNCH

3 46 oz. cans pineapple juice
1 46 oz. can grapefruit juice

2 46 oz. cans red Hawaiian
   punch
1 large bottle ginger ale

- Mix juices together in advance and chill.
- Add ginger ale just before serving.

Serves 50   *Kathy Palmer*

SPICED CRANBERRY JUICE

1 qt. water
6-8 cloves
1 cinnamon stick

1 tea bag
1 qt. cranberry cocktail

- Simmer water and spices until water is amber-colored and kitchen is fragrant.
- Add tea bag and steep for 5 minutes, then add cranberry cocktail. Heat to serve.

SPECIAL NOTE: THIS IS VERY FLEXIBLE. SOMETIMES I USE CIDER OR APPLE JUICE AND LEMON JUICE TO TASTE.

Serves 10-12   *Carolyn Mattingly*

The following beverages contain alcohol.

AGGRAVATION

1½ oz. Scotch
1 oz. Kahlua

Milk
Ice

- Fill a glass with ice.
- Pour Scotch and Kahlua over ice.
- Fill with milk and blend well.
- May be put in blender.

SPECIAL NOTE: THIS IS A VERY GOOD MILK PUNCH. SERVE IT INSTEAD OF THE USUAL BLOODY MARY.

Nancy Krauss

AMERICAN GROG

1   jigger light rum
Juice of ½ lemon

1   lump sugar soaked in
    angostura bitters
Hot water

- Place silver spoon in heavy highball glass and fill half way with very hot water.
- Add remaining ingredients. Stir well.

Lucy Vrooman

BORDER BUTTERMILK

1   6 oz. can frozen lemonade
    concentrate

1   lemonade can tequila

- Put into blender. Fill with crushed ice and blend at high speed until smooth, frothy and milky looking.

SPECIAL NOTE: THE NAME SOUNDS AWFUL, BUT YUM-YUM GOOD!

Serves 4-6

Nancy Krauss

CAMPBELL'S IRISH CREAM

1¼ cups whiskey
2   tsp. instant coffee
1   tsp. almond extract
2   tbsp. chocolate syrup

1   can Eagle Brand milk
1   cup whipping cream
4   eggs
1   tsp. vanilla

- Mix all ingredients except whipping cream in blender until well blended.
- Add whipping cream, just until mixed—or cream will curdle.

Anita Campbell

COFFEE ALEXANDER

1 oz. coffee flavored brandy   1 oz. cream
1 oz. brandy

- Shake with ice and strain into champagne glass.
- Dust with powdered coffee.

Nancy Krauss

CREME DE MENTHE

4 cups sugar   1½ tsps. peppermint flavoring
4 cups water   Few drops green food coloring
2 cups 180 proof alcohol

- Bring sugar and water to boil.
- Add coloring and peppermint.
- Cool a bit and add alcohol. Enjoy.

Mrs Robert W. Peters

IRISH COFFEE

1 jigger Irish whiskey   Sugar
Hot coffee   Hot water
1½ tsp. whipped cream

- Make coffee.
- Heat whiskey and warm Irish whiskey mug.
- Dip rim of mug into very hot water, then into sugar to coat rim.
- Immediately pour warm whiskey into hot mug and tilt over flame for ½ minute.
- Drop whipped cream into flaming whiskey.
- Fill with hot coffee.

Cam Caldwell

KAHLUA

4 cups sugar
¼ cup instant coffee
1 large vanilla bean

2 cups boiling water
2 cups vodka (spill a little)

- Dissolve sugar and instant coffee in boiling water.
- Put in ½ gal. glass jug.
- Cool a bit, add vanilla bean and vodka.
- Store in a cool, dark place for one month.
- Shake jug once a week.

SPECIAL NOTE: CANNOT TELL DIFFERENCE FROM STORE BOUGHT!

Mrs. Robert W. Peters

LONDON FOG

2 qts. black coffee
2 qts. vanilla ice cream

1-2 qts. bourbon

- Combine lukewarm coffee and ice cream in punch bowl.
- Add bourbon and let blend.
- Refrigerate for at least 8 hours.

SPECIAL NOTE: SERVE DURING THE HOLIDAYS IN EGGNOG CUPS.

Serves 24

Lucy Vrooman

*Would that you could live on the fragrance
of the earth and like an air plant be sustained by the light.*

*But since you must kill to eat, and rob the newly
born of its mother's milk to quench your thirst,
let it then be an act of worship.*

*And let your board stand as an altar on which the pure
and the innocent of the forest and plain are sacrificed
for that which is purer and still innocent in man.*

FROM *THE PROPHET* BY KAHLIL GIBRAN

MINT JULEP

Simple syrup or granulated sugar   Crushed ice
12   or more tender mint leaves   Water
Bourbon

- First chill silver mint julep cups.
- For each julep place 1 tbsp. simple syrup in bottom of pitcher. Add the tender mint leaves.
- Bruise the mint gently with a muddler and blend ingredients by stirring and pressing gently for a few minutes. DO NOT CRUSH the mint, for this releases a bitter, inner juice.
- Pack the pitcher with crushed ice and add bourbon to cover.
- Stir with a long bar spoon, up and down. Add more bourbon if necessary.
- Pour mixture into individual silver, chilled julep cups.
- Place in refrigerator for 5 minutes to frost glass.
- Serve with a sprig of mint.

Cam Caldwell

NEW YEAR PUNCH

6   lbs. loaf sugar
3   gals. sweet Catawba wine
2   gals. Rhine wine
2   gals. Claret wine

1   gal. brandy or whiskey
4   cans sliced pineapple
4   doz. oranges, sliced
2   doz. lemons, sliced

- Put above ingredients together in a large crock or similar vessel. Let stand a few hours
- Place a large ice mold in the center of a large punch bowl. Decorate the top of the ice with fruits in season.
- Fill the bowl with mixture. Serve in punch or Champagne glasses.
- Just before serving, Champagne may be added.

SPECIAL NOTE: OFTEN SERVED AT WEDDINGS AND CHRISTMAS PARTIES.

Yields 10 gals.

Sally McCauley

PAIN KILLERS

3 cups orange juice
1 cup pineapple juice
1 cup rum

1 8 oz. can Coco Lopez (cream
of coconut)
Grated nutmeg

- Mix in blender.
- Serve over ice with freshly grated nutmeg.

SPECIAL NOTE: A VARIATION OF AN OLD FAVORITE "ISLAND" RECIPE.

Yields 1½ qts. *Nancy Sumerford*

SPECIAL EGGNOG

4 eggs, separated
3 jiggers of bourbon
1 jigger rum

½ pint whipping cream
4 tsp. sugar
Nutmeg

- Separate eggs.
- Mix liquors gradually with yolks.
- Beat whites until stiff. Whip cream.
- Mix sugar and yolk mixture together.
- Blend mixture into beaten whites gently.
- Fold in whipped cream.
- Sprinkle with nutmeg (if desired).

Serves 6 *Cam Caldwell*

THE FEEDING OF
THE FIVE THOUSAND

Jesus, standing on the hillside, confronts
the lad who was found to have a basket
containing loaves and fishes. Nearby are
three disciples who have brought the
boy to Jesus. The multitudes, soon to be
miraculously fed, wait on the hillside.
(Matthew 15: 29-39)

The window was given to the glory of
God by the Episcopal Churchwomen
of Christ Church, Frederica
and installed for Easter, 1969.

SOUPS, BREADS, SANDWICHES

ANSON GREENE PHELPS DODGE
ESTABLISHED AND MAINTAINED DODGE
HOME FOR BOYS 1895-1956
ESTABLISHED GEORGIA MISSION FUND 1886
ENDOWED ALL SAINTS CATHEDRAL
ALLAHABAD INDIA 1884

THE MINISTRY OF
ANSON GREEN PHELPS DODGE

In one of the two windows located in
the vestibule of the church, The
Reverend Anson Green Phelps Dodge,
Rector of Christ Church, Frederica from
1884 until 1898, holds the hand of a
small boy who signifies the Dodge
Home for Boys which The Reverend
Dodge founded on St. Simons Island in
memory of his son. The symbols
in the side panels signify the Corporal
Acts of Christian Mercy. An inscription
on this window reads, "Anson Green
Phelps Dodge. Established and maintained Dodge Home for Boys 1895-
1956. Established Georgia Mission
Fund 1886. Endowed All Saints
Cathedral, Allahabad, India, 1884."

CAULIFLOWER HAM CHOWDER

2 cups sliced cauliflower
1 13¾ oz. can chicken
  broth1¾ cups)
1 cup light cream
1 can condensed cream of potato soup

¼ cup water
2 tbsp. cornstarch
⅛ tsp. pepper
2 cups diced cooked ham

- In large saucepan, cook cauliflower, covered, in chicken broth til almost tender, about 10 minutes. (Do not drain.)
- In mixing bowl, gradually stir cream into potato soup.
- Blend water, cornstarch and pepper; stir into potato soup mixture. Pour over cauliflower; cook and stir until thickened and bubbly.
- Stir in ham; simmer over low heat for 10 minutes. Garnish with parsley.

Serves 5-6   *Betty Ford (Mrs. Gerald R. Ford)*

COLD CUCUMBER SOUP

1 cucumber peeled and
  seeds cut out
1 medium or small onion, cut
  in half
1 cup chicken broth
1 can cream of chicken soup

¾ cup sour cream (yogurt or
  buttermilk may be
  substituted)
Dash Tabasco and
Worcestershire sauce
½ tsp. curry powder

- Place all ingredients in blender and blend until smooth.
- Taste and adjust seasonings to your taste.
- Chill at least one hour.
- Will keep in refrigerator for several days.

SPECIAL NOTE: AMOUNT OF INGREDIENTS ARE SLIGHTLY FLEXIBLE. IT GETS THICKER WHEN CHILLED WHEN HOME COOKED CHICKEN BROTH IS USED. I SUBSTITUTE BUTTERMILK ONLY WHEN I HAVE HOMEMADE BROTH.

Serves 4-5   *Lindsay Lowe Owens*

CREAM OF CAULIFLOWER

1	head cauliflower, chopped coarse	4	cups chicken stock (3 14½ oz. cans)
2	medium potatoes, peeled and chopped coarse	1	tsp. salt
2	tbsp. butter	¼	tsp. white pepper
3	ribs of celery, minced	1	cup Half and Half
2	onions, chopped		Parsley
			Carrot grated

- Melt butter in a heavy, large saucepan over medium heat.
- Add onion, celery and stir until translucent, about 5 minutes; do not brown.
- Remove from pan and set aside in a small bowl.
- To same pan add stock, cauliflower, potato and bring to a boil.
- Reduce heat, cover and simmer for 15 minutes, or until potatoes are tender. Do not drain.
- Add onion-celery mixture.
- Puree soup in batches in processor until smooth.
- Return to saucepan. Stir in half and Half and grated carrot if desired.

Heat through. Season with salt and pepper. Garnish with parsley.

SPECIAL NOTE: I USE A LARGE FOOD PROCESSOR ALL THE WAY THROUGH WHICH LEAVES ONE WORK BOWL. THIS IS A FAVORITE!

Yield 1 qt. *Cam Caldwell*

COLD CUCUMBER AND SPINACH SOUP

1	bunch scallions (sliced)	½	cup peeled sliced potato
2	tbsp. butter	½	tsp. salt
4	cups diced cucumber		Dash of white pepper
3	cups chicken broth		Lemon juice to taste
1	cup spinach (chopped) or 1 pkg. frozen chopped and squeezed dry	1	cup Half and Half cream
			Thin slices cucumber (garnish)

- Cook scallions in butter until softened.
- Add cucumber, chicken broth, spinach, potato, salt and pepper. Simmer until potatoes are tender.
- Transfer to blender and puree in batches. Transfer puree to bowl and stir in lemon juice 1 cup and Half and Half cream.
- Chill for several hours. Garnish with thin slices of cucumber.

Serves 6 *Virginia Petretti*

COLD SQUASH SOUP

2	chicken bouillon cubes		White pepper
2	cups water	¼	tsp. dill weed
1	lb. yellow squash		Tabasco to taste
1	onion chopped	½	cup sour cream
½	tsp. salt		

- Dissolve 2 chicken bouillon cubes in hot water.
- Add ½ cup bouillon mix to yellow squash and chopped onion. Cook until tender.
- Put in electric blender to blend adding remaining 1½ cup bouillon. Add salt, pepper, dill weed and Tabasco. Cool.
- Stir in ½ cup sour cream. Chill at least 4 hours before serving. Keeps for several days.

SPECIAL NOTE: GREAT FOR CALORIE COUNTERS.

Serves 6-8 *Nancy Krauss*

CONSOMME MADRILENE

2	cans beef consomme	1	tsp. chopped tarragon
3	large tomatoes peeled	4	tbsp port wine
2	tbsp. chopped fresh parsley		Salt and pepper to taste
2	tbsp. chopped chives		

- Puree tomatoes and add to consomme, heat 5 minutes.
- Add salt and pepper to taste, and port wine.
- When ready to serve, sprinkle top of consomme with chives, parsley and tarragon.

Serves 6 *Mary Frances Gould*

COUNTRY CRAB SOUP

1   lb. crabmeat, fresh or
    pasteurized
⅓   cup finely chopped onion
¼   cup finely chopped celery
¼   cup finely chopped green
    pepper
1   clove garlic, minced
1   tbsp margarine or butter
1   13¾ oz. can condensed
    chicken broth, undiluted

1   12 oz can tomato juice
1   tsp. basil
1   tsp. salt (or less)
¼   tsp. thyme
¼   tsp. pepper
3-4 drops liquid hot pepper sauce
1   10 oz. pkg. frozen mixed
    vegetables

- Remove any pieces of shell or cartilage from crabmeat.

- In 3 qt saucepan, cook onion, celery, green peppers, and garlic in margarine until tender but not brown.

- Add broth, tomato juice, basil, salt, thyme, pepper and liquid hot pepper. Bring to a boil. Reduce heat and simmer 10 minutes.

- Add mixed vegetables. Cover, simmer 10 minutes.

- Add crab and continue cooking until vegetables are tender and crabmeat is heated.

SPECIAL NOTE: RECIPE CAN BE DOUBLED.

Serves 6   *Jeannie Wade*

CURRIED CRABMEAT,
CUCUMBER AND ZUCCHINI SOUP

1   lb. lump crabmeat
1   large cucumber, peeled, seed-
    ed
2   large or 4 small zucchini,
    unpeeled
2   stalks celery
18 fresh basil leaves, 1 tsp. dried

2   8 oz. containers plain yogurt
Juice of 1 lemon
¼   cup olive oil
10 drops Tabasco Sauce
2   tsp. curry powder
Salt to taste
2-3 radishes, chopped

- Reserve 18 lumps of crabmeat.

- Cut up vegetables coarsely.

- In the bowl of a food processor fitted with a metal blade, add cut vegetables and all other ingredients except chopped radish.

- Puree the mixture until very smooth.

- Using a fine mesh sieve, strain soup into large serving bowl. Chill .

- Divide soup into 6 well-chilled soup bowls, and garnish each with 3 lumps of crabmeat and chopped radishes.

SPECIAL NOTE: THIS IS A FAVORITE AT NEW YORK CITY'S SEA GRILL
RESTAURANT—A WONDERFUL BEGINNING TO AN ELEGANT DINNER PARTY!

Serves 6   *Judi E. Morgan*

FRENCH ONION SOUP

¼ cup olive oil
5 cups yellow onion, thinly sliced and punched into rings
2 tbsp. flour
3 10¾ oz. cans beef broth diluted with 2 cans of water
½ tsp. salt
¼ tsp. pepper
¼ cup sherry
6 slices French bread, toasted
6 slices Swiss or gruyere cheese, sliced
¼ cup parmesan cheese

- Heat oil over low heat and saute onions until golden.
- Stir in flour and brown.
- Add broth and water. Cover and cook for 30 minutes.
- Add sherry and simmer for a few minutes.
- Divide into ovenproof bowls. Top with toasted French bread, cover with sliced Swiss or gruyere and sprinkle with parmesan cheese.
- Place on cookie sheet and run under broiler until cheese is melted and golden.

Cooking time: 1 hour

Serves 4   *Becky Rowell*

HEARTY SHRIMP GAZPACHO

1 lb. tomatoes, seeded, chopped (2 cups)
1 15 oz. can garbanzo beans, drained
1 7 oz. can whole kernel shoe peg corn, drained
1 green bell pepper, chopped
1 small cucumber, peeled, diced
¼ cup chopped green onion
2 garlic cloves, minced
1 tbsp. fresh lime juice
18 oz. V-8 juice
1 cup water
¼ cup prepared hot salsa
½ tsp. sugar
Salt and pepper to taste
½ lb. cooked medium shrimp. peeled and deveined

- Combine first 7 ingredients in large bowl. Sprinkle with lime juice. Combine vegetable juice, water, salsa and sugar in medium bow. Season with salt and pepper. Cover mixtures and refrigerate for 1 hour.
- Stir salsa mixture into tomato mixture. Add shrimp.
- Ladle soup into bowls. Garnish with lime wedges.

SPECIAL NOTE: A FEW DASHES OF HOT PEPPER SAUCE OR CAYENNE MAY BE ADDED.

HEPBURN'S ZUCCHINI SOUP

¼ cup butter
2 lbs. small zucchini, thinly sliced
5 tbsp. finely chopped shallots (about 3)
4 cups chicken broth
1½ tsp. curry powder
⅛ tsp. salt

⅛ tsp. cayenne pepper

Garnish (if served hot):
⅓ cup croutons

Garnish (if served cold):
2 tbsp. chopped fresh chives

- Melt butter in large skillet. Add zucchini and shallots; cover and cook 10 to 15 minutes, stirring often, until zucchini is soft but not browned.

- Combine half of the zucchini mixture, 2 cups of chicken broth, the curry powder, salt and cayenne in food processor or blender. Puree. Pour into saucepan if serving hot, or into large bowl, if serving cold.

- Repeat pureeing with remaining ingredients. Combine batches.

- If serving hot, heat soup and garnish with croutons. If serving cold, chill 2 hours, garnish with chives.

SPECIAL NOTE: 123 CALORIES PER SERVING.

Serves 6   *Betty Link*

LENTIL SOUP

¼ cup vegetable oil
3 cups diced cooked ham
½ lb. Polish sausage, ½-inch slices
2 cups chopped onion
3 cloves garlic, chopped
2 cups chopped celery with leaves

1 large tomato, cut in wedges
1 lb. dried lentils
3 qts. water
½ tsp. hot pepper sauce
1½ tsp. salt
1 pkg. frozen chopped spinach, thawed

- In large kettle heat oil, add ham, sausage, onion and garlic. Cook 5 minutes.

- Add celery, tomato, lentils, water, hot pepper sauce, salt. Heat to boiling, cover, simmer 2 hours. Stir once or twice.

- Add spinach and cook 10 minutes.

- Taste and add additional salt and several twists of freshly ground pepper if desired.

SPECIAL NOTE: RECIPE CAN BE FROZEN. MAKES A GOOD LIGHT SUPPER WITH FRENCH BREAD AND SALAD.

Cooking time: 2 hours

Serves 12 easily   *Lotta M. Hunt*

OKRA VEGETABLE SOUP

1 cup chopped onion
2 tbsp. vegetable oil
½ tsp. each dried oregano, thyme, basil, celery seed
1 tsp. ground cumin
2 bay leaves
2 celery stalks, finely chopped
1 green or red bell pepper, chopped
1 medium carrot, diced

1 cup chopped potatoes
2 cups chopped fresh tomatoes
3 cups chicken stock
1 cup niblet corn
1 cup sliced fresh okra or 10 oz. frozen
1 tbsp. cider vinegar
Tabasco to taste
1 tsp. Worcestershire sauce

- Saute onions in oil until translucent.
- Add herbs, celery, bell pepper, carrot, and potatoes and cook for about 10 minutes on medium heat, stirring to prevent sticking.
- Add tomatoes and stock and simmer for 10 minutes.
- Add corn, okra, vinegar. Simmer until okra is tender.
- Add remaining seasonings to taste.

Cooking time: 1 hour unattended

Serves 4   *Becky Rowell*

PEA SOUP

2 10 oz. pkgs. frozen peas
2 cups shredded lettuce (iceberg)
2 cups chicken stock
2 tbsp. oleo
½ tsp. curry

¼ tsp. salt
¼ tsp. pepper
1 cup Half and Half
Chopped mint for garnish (optional)

- Combine lettuce, peas, chicken broth in sauce pan. Simmer 10 minutes.
- Add butter, curry, salt and pepper. Puree in blender.
- Return to sauce pan. Add Half and Half. Cover, cook on medium heat until heated through. Do not boil.
- Garnish with mint.

SPECIAL NOTE: EASY AND DELICIOUS!

Cooking time: 10 minutes

Serves 6   *Lotta M. Hunt*

PISTOU SOUP

8   cups chicken broth
1   cup each diced potatoes, car-
    rots, celery, onion, zucchini,
    string beans and lima beans
    (small)
3   slices of bacon diced
1   cup chopped tomatoes
½   cup fresh or 1½ tsp. dry basil

¼   cup olive oil
Garlic Tomato Butter (mix the
    following):
½   cup mayonnaise
¼   cup butter
¼   cup tomato paste
4-5 cloves garlic, mashed

- To the chicken broth add the bacon and vegetables except tomatoes.
- Cook for 1 hour.
- One half hour before serving add tomatoes, basil and olive oil and boil 15 minutes.
- Serve with garlic tomato butter on toasted bread.

Cooking time: 1 hour, 15 minutes

Serves 8   *Jacqueline G. Curl*

POTATO-CORN CHOWDER

3   slices bacon, diced
1   medium onion, chopped
Water
1   14½ oz. can chicken broth
8   ox. potatoes, peeled, diced

3   ears corn
½   cup light cream
½   tsp. pepper
2   thsp. chopped parsley
Salt to taste

- Cook bacon in large saucepan until bacon is browned and crisp. Drain on paper towel.
- Pour off all but 1 tbsp. of fat from pan. Add onion and sauté until tender.
- Add water to chicken broth to measure 3 cups. Pour into pan. Add potatoes. Bring to boil. Lower heat; cover and simmer 15 minutes.
- Cut corn kernels from cobs (about 2 cups of kernels). Add corn to saucepan. Cook 3-5 minutes until corn is tender.
- Add the cream, pepper and parsley. Heat soup to serving temperature.

YANKEE (NEW ENGLAND) CLAM CHOWDER

1	qt. juicy fresh clams	¼	lb. diced salt pork
1	qt. fresh milk, scalded	2	tbsp. butter
2	cups raw sliced potatoes	½	tsp. salt
2	medium sliced onions		Dash black pepper

- Sauté pork until rich brown.

- Add onion until brown and tender.

- Add potatoes, salt, pepper and barely cover with water. Let simmer 20 minutes.

- Add juicy clams and boil until potatoes are very well done.

- Scald milk with butter and simmer about 2 minutes.

- Mix together and serve at once in soup cups or bowls with crisp buttered croutons or oyster crackers.

SPECIAL NOTE: ONE OF THOSE FINE OLD RECIPES. THIS ONE DATES BACK TO SLAVE-TRADE DAYS, BROUGHT TO FLORIDA BY YANKEE SEA CAPTAINS.

Cooking time: Approximately 1 hour

Serves 6   *Elizabeth Lewis McCartney*

DOROTHY'S ANGEL BISCUITS

4	cups self-rising flour	1	cup shortening
⅓	cup sugar	1¼	cup sweet milk

- Measure 4 cups self-rising flour into large mixing bowl. Add ⅓ cup of sugar to flour and mix together well.

- Take 1 cup shortening and use a pastry blender to cut small ½-inch lumps into the dry mixture.

- Pour 1¼ cup sweet milk over the flour/sugar mix and gently work together.

- Spread flour onto kitchen counter as base for wet dough. Keep flour on hands and press out dough. Sprinkle dough surface with flour and fold half mixture over itself, then roll out ¾-inch thick.

- Cut with biscuit cutter and place on ungreased cooking sheet.

- Bake in 450° oven 10-12 minutes until golden brown. Makes about 20-24 biscuits 2½-inch round by 1¼-inch high.

SPECIAL NOTE: FOR ALL FAMILY GATHERINGS AND ANNUAL REUNIONS, I MUST FURNISH AT LEAST 2 BATCHES OF THESE DELICIOUS BISCUITS.

Serves 10-20   *Dorothy Paulk McClain*

SMYRNA HIGH RISE BISCUITS

3 cups all purpose flour
2 tbsp. sugar
1 tbsp. plus 1½ tsp. baking powder
¾ tsp. cream of tartar

¾ cup shortening
¾ tsp. salt
¾ cup milk
1 egg

- Mix dry ingredients.
- Cut in shortening. Add egg mixed with milk.
- Knead dough on floured board 8-10 times. Roll out 1-inch thick.
- With a cookie cutter cut into biscuits.
- Bake at 450° approximately 15 minutes.

Serves 16   *Martha Russell*

FRIED CORN BREAD

1 cup self rising corn meal
1 egg
1 tsp. salt

½ cup oil
Enough ice water to make a pancake like consistency

- Mix ingredients.
- Heat oil in black iron skillet and drop batter by spoonful.
- Cook small number of patties at a time.
- Let brown on both sides until crisp and drain well on paper towels.

SPECIAL NOTE: THIS IS A GOOD CRISP BREAD TO HAVE WITH SOUPS, VEGETABLES AND TO SERVE UNDERNEATH CREAMED TUNA AND CHIPPED BEEF.

Serves 2   *Charlotte Parker Harris (Mrs. Walter D.)*

MEXICAN CORN BREAD I

1½ cups self-rising cornmeal
Dash salt
1 cup buttermilk
½ green pepper, chopped fine
1 small can green chilies, chopped fine

1 can Mexicorn
1 cup grated New York sharp cheese
3 eggs, beaten
¾ cup corn oil

- Mix together first seven ingredients.
- Add eggs and oil, mix well.
- Pour into greased 8 x 8-inch pan.
- Bake 350° for 40 minutes.

Aunt Frances-Charlotte Marshall

MEXICAN CORN BREAD II

1 cup self-rising flour
1 cup self-rising corn meal
1 cup cream style canned corn
4 ozs. grated American cheese

1 large onion, chopped
2 jalapeño peppers, chopped fine
1 cup buttermilk

- Combine all ingredients and mix well.

- Pour into a hot greased 10-inch iron skillet or greased pyrex dish. Bake in a 425° oven until golden brown and firm.

Serves 8   *Brenda Hartsell*

PECAN CORN STICKS

¾ cup crushed pecans
2 cups corn meal
1 cup white flour
3 tsp. baking powder
1 tsp. salt

¼ cup sugar
1 cup buttermilk
1 tsp. soda
2 eggs well beaten
¼ cup melted shortening

- Sift dry ingredients together.

- Blend with the beaten eggs and milk.

- Add melted shortening and pecans.

- Pour into oiled corn stick molds or waffle iron, level full.

- Bake in a 450° oven for 12-15 minutes.

SPECIAL NOTE: IN THE COOL OF A SOUTHERN EVENING, WHEN THE YOUNG FOLKS GATHER TO SING OR TO PLAN—OR TO DREAM—CUPID IS HELPED ALONG BY THE SERVING OF THESE DELICIOUS MORSELS. HANDED DOWN FROM GENERATION TO GENERATION IN ALABAMA.

Mrs. Elizabeth Rhodes McCartney

CORN BREAD

1½ cups white corn meal
¾ cup plain flour
2 tsp. baking powder
1 tsp. salt

½ cup butter Crisco, melted
1½ cups milk
1 large egg

- Preheat oven to 400°. Sift dry ingredients together

- Add milk and stir until mixed.

- Add egg and mix well. Add melted Crisco, mix well.

- Melt 2 tsp. Crisco in 6½- x 10-inch pan for 1 minute in oven.

- Put batter in hot pan and bake 25-30 minutes or until browned on top.

Serves 6-8   *Martha L. Veal*

SOUTHERN CORN BREAD

1   cup self-rising corn meal
1   cup self-rising flour
1   tbsp. sugar

1   egg, beaten
2   cups buttermilk

- Mix all ingredients very well. Batter should be fairly thin. If not, add more buttermilk.
- Put 3 tbsp. shortening in iron skillet and heat on range top.
- When melted and hot pour 2 tbsp. of shortening into batter, stirring it in well.
- Pour batter into hot pan.
- Bake at 450° until crispy brown on sides and top.

SPECIAL NOTE: MY MAMA SAYS YOU CAN'T MAKE GOOD CORN BREAD OR BIS-CUITS WITHOUT BUTTERMILK AND SHE'S RIGHT!

Serves 6   *Brenda Hartsell*

BACON-CHEESE CORN MUFFINS

8   strips bacon
1   egg
1   cup milk
4   tbsp. (½ stick) melted mar-
     garine
1   can (8¾ oz) creamed corn
1   cup all purpose flour

1   cup yellow corn meal
3   tbsp. sugar
3   tsp. baking powder
½   tsp. salt
2   dashes hot pepper sauce
1½   cups (6 ozs.) grated cheddar
     cheese

- Preheat oven to 400°.
- Cut bacon into small pieces and cook until crisp. Drain.
- In a medium bowl, whisk egg, milk, margarine until blended.
- Stir in corn, flour, corn meal, sugar, baking powder, salt.
- Add pepper sauce, cheese and bacon, stirring until blended.
- Spoon batter into greased muffin tins, mini or regular, filling ¾ full.
- Bake 20-25 minutes until toothpick inserted in center comes out clean and tops are lightly browned.
- Cool 10 minutes and remove from tins. Serve warm.

SPECIAL NOTE: FREEZES NICELY.

Davi Langston

BLUEBERRY MUFFINS

2   cups self-rising flour
1½ cups sugar
2   eggs, slightly beaten
1   tsp. vanilla
½   cup vegetable oil
½   cup whole milk
1   cup blueberries

- Combine sifted flour and sugar, make a well in center. Set aside.

- Combine eggs, vanilla, oil and milk. When mixed pour liquid ingredients into well of dry ingredients, and mix gently.

- Add the cup of blueberries; stir one minute.

- Spoon batter into sprayed muffin tins, filling half full.

- Bake in 375° oven for 25 minutes.

Yield 15-16 muffins   *Cam Caldwell*

BRAN MUFFINS

2½ cups whole wheat flour
2½ cups all bran cereal
1¼ tsp. salt
2   tbsp. sugar
1   tbsp. baking powder
2   cups skim milk
½   cup canola oil or other vegetable oil
5   large eggs beaten or egg substitute
1   cup pecans or walnuts chopped
1   cup honey
2   tsp. vanilla
¾   cup raisins
2   cups grated carrots
1   cup crushed pineapple, drain
2   apples chopped coarsely
¾   cup chopped dates
12   prunes cut into small pieces

- Preheat oven to 350°. Mix milk, raisins, and bran together and let soak for 15 minutes to soften.

- Combine rest of liquids and add to bran mixture.

- Mix all dry ingredients, fruit and nuts and add to bran mixture. Do not over mix. Fill greased muffin cups or muffin papers to top.

- Bake for 30-40 minutes. Don't worry if you do not have all the dried fruits or nuts, just use what you have.

Mrs. George Bush

HERB TOAST

1   tsp. dried thyme
1   tsp. dried basil
½   tsp. dried marjoram
1   stick butter, softened

- Mix butter with herbs. Spread on sliced buns and bake at 225° until crisp and lightly browned.

SPECIAL NOTE: GOOD SERVED WITH BARBEQUE.

Martha L. Veal

BREAKFAST MUFFINS

2	cups all purpose flour			walnuts
¾	cup bran cereal (All-Bran, etc.)		½	cup margarine
			1	cup sugar
½	cup coconut		¼	cup packed brown sugar
2	tsp. baking powder		3	eggs
1	tsp. cinnamon		¾	cup (2 mashed) ripe bananas
3½	oz. jar macadamia nuts, chopped, or ½ cup chopped dates and ½ cup chopped		2	tsp. vanilla
			8	oz. can crushed pineapple, drained

- Heat oven to 350°. Line with paper baking cups or grease muffin cups of 22 regular or 12 large muffin cups.
- In a large bowl, combine flour, cereal, coconut, baking powder, cinnamon, nuts and dates if used. Mix well.
- In another bowl, combine margarine and sugar. Cream well.
- Add eggs, blend.
- Stir in vanilla, bananas and pineapple. Mix. Add to dry ingredients all at once. Stir until just moistened.
- Fill muffin cups ⅔ full. Bake at 350° 20-30 minutes or until golden brown and toothpick inserted in center comes out clean.
- Cool in pan 2 minutes and turn out to rack to cool.

SPECIAL NOTE: THESE INGREDIENTS CAN BE VARIED. USE RAISINS INSTEAD OF DATES. IF YOU WANT TO ELIMINATE THE NUTS, INCREASE DATES AND/OR RAISINS.

Davi Langston

CARROT(!) MUFFINS

2	cup flour		½	cup raisins
1¼	cup sugar		½	cup coconut
2	tsp. baking soda		1	apple, peeled, cored and grated
2	tsp. cinnamon			
½	tsp. salt		3	eggs
2	cups grated carrots		1	cup oil
½	cup nuts		2	tsp. vanilla

- In a large bowl, mix flour, sugar, baking soda, cinnamon and salt.
- Stir in carrots, nuts, raisins, coconut and apple.
- In a separate bowl beat together eggs, oil, and vanilla; add to batter.
- Spoon into well greased muffin tins, filling almost to the top.
- Bake in a 350° oven for 20 minutes.

SPECIAL NOTE: SERVED WITH HALF A GRAPEFRUIT THIS GIVES YOU A COMPLETE BREAKFAST.

Serves 14-18 muffins

Davi Langston

CRANBERRY MUFFINS

4	cups plain flour	2	eggs
2	cups sugar	1½	cups orange juice
3	tsp. baking powder	2	tsp. grated orange peel
2	tsp. salt	1	cup nuts (pecan or walnut)
1	tsp. baking soda	2	cups chopped cranberries
½	cup shortening		

- Grease and flour 2 muffin tins, 6 cup size.
- Set oven to 350°.
- Sift dry ingredients into large bowl.
- Cut in shortening.
- Combine eggs, orange juice and orange peel. Add to dry ingredients.
- Mix just until moist. Fold in nuts and cranberries.
- Place in muffin tins and bake in a 350° oven 20-25 minutes or until toothpick comes out clean. Cool on racks or serve warm with butter or cream cheese.

SPECIAL NOTE: VERY GOOD FOR BREAKFAST OR BRUNCH.

Serves 12

Mrs. Robert Allen

SESAME CORN MUFFIN

¼	cup flour	¼	cup sesame seeds
3	tbsp. sugar	½	cup wheat germ
½	tsp. salt	1	egg beaten
¾	tsp. soda	1	cup buttermilk
1	cup corn meal	⅓	cup salad oil

- Combine flour, sugar, salt, soda, corn meal, sesame seeds and wheat germ in a mixing bowl, set aside.
- Combine egg, buttermilk and oil, stir into flour mixture.
- Spoon batter into greased muffin cups, filling 2/3 full.
- Bake at 350° for 20 minutes.

Serves 1 dozen

Kathy Palmer

CHEDDAR-CUMIN ROLLS

1¼ tsp. active dry yeast	3½ cups bread flour (divided)
1 tsp. sugar	1½ tsp. salt
1¼ cup warm water	1½ tsp. ground cumin
½ lb. cheddar cheese (chilled and cubed)	1½ tsp. corn meal

- In a glass mixing cup combine yeast, sugar and water—set aside until it bubbles (approximately 10 minutes).
- Process cheese with ½ cup flour, mix well.
- Add remaining flour, salt, cumin and process, mix thoroughly.
- Stir yeast mix with dried ingredients—dough forms a shaggy mass—put dough in warm bowl and cover—set aside until it triples its size (3-3½ hours).
- Work dough on lightly floured board.
- Cut in half. Cut each half into 6 pieces, shaped into a ball, pinch in one spot.
- Sprinkle baking sheet with corn meal. Place dough 2-inches apart on prepared baking sheet.
- Cover with floured cloth and let rise 1½-2 hours.
- Place on lowest rack of the oven.
- Spray with cold water. Bake in a 450° oven for 20 minutes.

Yields 12 rolls   *Martha Russell*

ORANGE NUT BREAD

4-5 oranges	1 cup sugar
1 cup water	2 eggs, lightly beaten
1 tsp. baking soda	1 cup milk
Bread:	2 tbsp. melted butter
3 tsp. baking powder	1 cup sugar
3½ cups flour	½ cup water

- Cut orange peel into small pieces. Boil 5 minutes in 1 cup water and baking soda. Rinse and drain. Return to saucepan with ½ cup water and 1 cup sugar. Cook 10 minutes. Cool.
- Bread: Mix dry ingredients. Add milk, butter and eggs.
- Add nuts and half orange mixture. Pour into 2 sprayed loaf pans.
- Bake in a 350° oven for 1 hour.

Makes 2 loaves   *Janet Daniel*

APRICOT WALNUT BREAD

1 cup dried apricots	¼ tsp. cinnamon
1½ cup boiling water	¼ tsp. nutmeg
1 cup chopped walnuts	1 egg
2½ cup sifted flour	1 tsp. vanilla
3 tsp. baking powder	1 cup sugar
½ tsp. salt	¼ cup salad oil

- Cut dried apricots in small pieces.
- Place in mixing bowl. Add boiling water. Let cool.
- Chop walnuts.
- Sift flour, baking powder, salt, cinnamon and nutmeg together.
- Combine apricots, nuts, egg, vanilla, sugar and salad oil. Add flour mixture all at once. Stir well.
- Bake in well greased loaf pan in 350° oven for 65 minutes.
- Cool in pan for 30 minutes, then remove to wire rack.
- When completely cool wrap in foil and store in refrigerator 12 hours before using.

SPECIAL NOTE: SLICED THIN MAKES DELICIOUS TEA SANDWICHES WITH CREAM CHEESE.

Lucy Vrooman

BUNDT PAN BREAD

3 cans of biscuits	2 tsp. sesame seeds
1 stick of oleo	

- Melt stick of oleo. Put half in bottom of bundt pan.
- Put 1 tsp. of sesame seeds in the oleo in the bottom of pan.
- Stand biscuits on their edges in bundt pan (all 3 cans).
- Pour remaining oleo over biscuits.
- Sprinkle with 1 tsp. sesame seeds. Bake 350° for 25-30 minutes.

SPECIAL NOTE: THIS DOESN'T LOOK VERY PROMISING BEFORE IT IS BAKED, BUT IT BECOMES A VERY PRETTY SHAPE. A LOT OF PEOPLE HAVE COMMENTED TO ME ON THE DELICIOUS "HOMEMADE" BREAD.

Ann Jarrett

MONKEY BREAD

¾	oz. yeast or 1 pkg. dry yeast	3½	cup flour
1	to 1¼ cups milk	6	oz. butter, room temperature
3	eggs	½	lb. melted butter
3	tbsp. sugar	2	9" ring molds
1	tsp. salt		

- In bowl, mix yeast with part of milk until dissolved. Add 2 eggs, beat.
- Mix in dry ingredients. Add remaining milk a little at a time, mixing thoroughly. Cut in butter until blended.
- Knead dough, let rise 1-1½ hours until double in size.
- Knead again, let rise 40 minutes.
- Roll dough onto floured board, shape into a log. Cut log into 28 pieces of equal size.
- Shape each piece of dough into ball, roll in melted butter.
- Use half of the pieces in each of buttered, floured molds. Place 7 balls in each mold, leaving space between. Place remaining balls on top, spacing evenly.
- Let dough rise in mold. Brush tops with remaining egg.
- Bake in preheated oven at 375° until golden brown. Approximately 15 minutes.

Nancy Reagan

NO-BEAT POP OVERS

2	eggs	1	cup flour
1	cup milk	½	tsp. salt

- Break eggs into bowl, add milk, flour and salt.
- Mix well with spoon (disregard lumps).
- Fill greased muffin tins ¾ full.
- Put in oven, set controls to 450°. Turn on heat.
- Bake 30 minutes and don't peek!
- You may want to fork them to release the steam and let them cook 5-10 more minutes.

Yields 6 popovers

Jeanette Bessels

PESTO SWIRL BREAD

Bread:
1 pkg. Pillsbury hot roll mix
1 cup water heated to 120-130°
2 tbsp. margarine, softened
1 egg

Filling:
¼ cup olive oil
2 cloves garlic, crushed

½ cup chopped fresh basil or
¼ cup dried basil leaves
½ cup freshly grated Parmesan cheese

Topping:
1 egg, slightly beaten
1 tbsp. coarse salt
1 tbsp. chopped fresh basil or 1 tsp. dried basil

- Lightly grease large cookie sheet.
- In large bowl, combine flour mixture with yeast from foil packet; blend well.
- Stir in hot water, margarine and 1 egg until dough pulls away from sides of bowl.
- Turn dough out onto lightly floured surface.
- With greased or floured hands, shape dough into a ball.
- Knead dough for 5 minutes until smooth.
- Cover dough with large bowl; let rest 5 minutes.
- Divide dough in half; roll each half into 14 x 9-inch rectangle.
- In small bowl, combine oil and garlic. Brush half of oil mixture on each rectangle.
- In medium bowl, combine ½ cup basil and Parmesan cheese. Sprinkle each rectangle.
- Starting at long side, roll up each rectangle, pinch each seam to seal.
- Place loaves, seam side down on greased cookie sheet.
- Lightly brush with egg; cover with greased plastic wrap. Let rise for 30 minutes.
- In small bowl combine salt and 1 tbsp. basil, sprinkle over tops of loaves. Bake 350° for 20-30 minutes.

SPECIAL NOTE: PREPARE DAY BEFORE TO BLEND FLAVORS AND MAKE SLICING EASIER.

Makes 2 loaves   *Betty Link*

SWEDISH TOAST

1	cup butter or oleo	2	tsp. baking powder
1½ -2	cups sugar	½	tsp. salt
2	eggs	1	cup chopped almonds
1	(8 oz) sour cream	1	tsp. ground cardamon
3½	cup flour		

- Cream butter, sugar and eggs.
- Stir in sour cream.
- Blend in dry ingredients.
- Stir in nuts and cardamon.
- Spread batter into greased foil-lined 9 x 13-inch baking pan. Bake 350° oven until cake tests done (about 40-45 minutes).
- Cool in pan 15 minutes, loosen edges and turn out on cooling rack.
- Cool. Cut into 3 lengthwise strips, wrap in foil and refrigerate several hours.
- Cut into ½-inch slices.
- On baking sheet bake at 300° 20 minutes.
- Turn bake until golden brown (10-15 minutes).
- Store in airtight container.

SPECIAL NOTE: WONDERFUL FOR BREAKFAST DUNKING OR EATING PLAIN.

Lucrece Truax

Lord, our God, You love life:
You feed the birds of heaven and clothe the
lilies of the field.
We praise and thank You for all Your creatures
and for the food we are about to receive: we pray that no
one may be left without nourishment and care.
Through Christ our Lord. Amen.

POPE PAUL VI

CORN BEEF SANDWICHES

1 12 oz. can corn beef, crumbled
1 stick melted butter
½ cup sweet pickle juice
1 tbsp. Worcestershire sauce
½ cup chopped celery
2 chopped medium onions
1 tsp. chili sauce
Hamburger buns

- Sauté all ingredients, except buns, together in skillet until onions are soft.
- Fill buns very full. Wrap each in foil.
- Heat in oven at 350° for 20 minutes.

SPECIAL NOTE: CAN BE FROZEN. IDEAL FOR HOT SANDWICHES ON A PICNIC.

Nancy Krauss

HAM AND CHEESE ROLLS

sliced Swiss cheese
sliced boiled ham
1 pkg. dinner rolls (pre-cooked)
1 stick margarine
1 tbsp. prepared mustard
1 tbsp. grated onion or onion juice
1 tbsp. poppy seed

- Heat the last four ingredients (margarine, mustard, onion and poppy seed) together.
- Split the whole package of rolls crosswise.
- Spread both sides with the margarine mixture.
- Lay sliced Swiss cheese and sliced boiled ham on the bottom half.
- Place top half over bottom half of rolls.
- Heat in 350° oven till cheese melts. Cut the rolls apart.

SPECIAL NOTE: I USUALLY DOUBLE THIS WHEN CARRYING IT TO A COVERED DISH AFFAIR.

Ann Jarrett

SOFT-SHELL CRAB SANDWICHES

8 live soft-shelled crabs (2-3 oz. each)	2 tbsp. fresh lemon juice
⅓ cup vegetable oil	2 tbsp. minced fresh parsley
2 garlic cloves, sliced	1 tbsp. minced shallot
1 tsp. Old Bay Seasoning	8 English muffins, split in half and flattened with rolling pin
1 stick unsalted butter	

- Rinse the crabs under running cold water.
- With scissors, cut off the heads about ¼-inch behind the eyes and cut off the white gills.
- Peel back the aprons, cut them off and rinse the crabs again. Pat the crabs dry.
- In a dish combine the oil, garlic, Old Bay Seasoning and salt and pepper to taste.
- Add the crabs, turn them to coat them with the mixture and let them marinate, covered and chilled for at least 2 hours.
- In a small saucepan combine the butter, lemon juice, parsley, shallot and salt and pepper.
- Heat the mixture over moderately low heat, stirring until the butter is just melted; remove from heat.
- Drain the crabs, put them in a grill basket or directly on the grill; cook over glowing coals for 3-5 minutes on each side, or until they turn red.
- Brush muffins with the herbed butter, grill.
- Serve crab between 2 muffin halves.

Betty Link

Almighty God, our Heavenly Father, bless we pray, our work for the extension of your Kingdom, make us so thankful for the precious gift to us of your Beloved Son, that we may pray fervently, labor diligently and give liberally to make Him known to all nations as their Saviour and their King, through the same Jesus Christ, our Lord. Amen

EPISCOPAL CHRUCHWOMEN'S PRAYER

THE MINISTRY OF
ANSON GREEN PHELPS DODGE

One of two windows in the vestibule, this one depicts Old Church Frederica which stood on the site of the present church until is was desecrated and made untenable during the Civil War. To the left is the original Seal of the Diocese of Georgia. The seal incorporates the Seal of the Society for the Propagation of the Gospel which was founded in 1701 to promote Christianity in foreign lands.

To the right is the Seal of the Presiding Bishop of the Protestant Episcopal Church.

The windows, originally in the sanctuary of the church, were reworked and placed in the vestibule in 1969.

The dedication of theses windows is as follows: "A grateful congregation dedicates these windows to the Glory of God and in memory of Anson Green Phelps Dodge, Rector of this Parish, 1884-1889, who rebuilt and endowed Christ Church Frederica, 1885-1886."

THE OLD CHURCH FREDERICA

A GRATEFUL CONGREGATION DEDICATES
THESE WINDOWS TO THE GLORY OF GOD AND IN
MEMORY OF ANSON GREENE PHELPS DODGE
RECTOR OF THIS PARISH 1884-1898.
WHO REBUILT AND ENDOWED
CHRIST CHURCH FREDERICA 1885-1886

LO, I AM WITH YOU ALWAYS

Following His Resurrection, Jesus
appeared to His disciples on a mountain
in Galilee. He is shown here with five of
the disciples. After commissioning them
to go into the world baptizing and
teaching all nations, Jesus promises to be
with them until His Kingdom is established on Earth. (Matthew 28: 16-20)

The window is dedicated
"To the Glory of God and in memory
of Harry Wentworth Young
and Louisa King Young."

APRICOT NECTAR SALAD

1	8 oz. pkg. orange Jello	1	small can crushed pineapple
1	8 oz. pkg. cream cheese	½	cup chopped pecans
1	can apricot nectar		

- Heat nectar to boiling.
- Crumble cheese in dry Jello.
- Pour hot nectar over Jello mixture and stir to dissolve.
- Add pineapple and mix some more.
- Chill and add pecans after the mixture has thickened.
- Pour into a mold of your choice and allow to congeal.

Serves 6   *Beegie Searcy*

Elephant Stew

1 Elephant (medium size)
2 Rabbits (optional)
Salt and pepper to taste

Cut elephant into bite-size pieces (this takes about 2
months). Add enough gravy to cover. Cook over kerosene
fire for 4 weeks at 465°. This will serve about 3,800 people.
If more come than expected, the 2 rabbits may be
added…but do this only if necessary. Most people don't like
hare in their stew!

ASHEVILLE SALAD

1	can tomato soup	1	cup chopped nuts
1	cup mayonnaise	½	cup chopped olives
1	tbsp. gelatin	½	cup chopped celery

- Heat soup; add mayonnaise.
- Dissolve gelatin in water and add to soup mixture.
- Refrigerate.
- When it begins to gel stir in nuts, olives, and celery. Pour into
  mold and refrigerate.

Serves 8-10   *Jane Roebuck*

BEET HORSERADISH SALAD

1	No. 2 can beets (mashed with fork)	½	tsp salt
3	tbsp. vinegar	2	tbsp. onion juice
1	3 oz. pkg. lemon jello	2	tbsp. horseradish, or to taste
		¾	cup diced celery

- Drain liquid from beets into measuring cup and add water to make 1½ cups liquid.
- Heat liquid and add vinegar and gelatin. Stir to dissolve.
- Add salt and onion juice. Chill until partially set.
- Add beets, horseradish and celery. Mix.
- Fill an 8-inch ring mold, sprayed with vegetable oil.
- When ready to serve, top with homemade mayonnaise or ½ cup sour cream mixed with 2 tbsp. horseradish.

SPECIAL NOTE: WHEN DOUBLING RECIPE ADD 2 OR 3 ENVELOPES OF GELATIN FOR SAFE MEASURE. THIS SALAD IS ESPECIALLY GOOD WHEN SERVED WITH BEEF. THIS IS A VESTRY PARTY RECIPE.

Serves 6-8

Martha Fitzgerald

"THE BEST"
EASY CRANBERRY SALAD

1	3 oz. pkg. lemon jello	1	small can crushed pineapple, with juice
1	can whole cranberry sauce		
1	cup boiling water		

- Dissolve jello in boiling water. Add cranberry sauce and pineapple. Mix.
- Refrigerate until firm.
- Top with a dressing made of sour cream and any fruit juice mixed together.

SPECIAL NOTE: MAKES A NICE CHRISTMAS SALAD.

Serves 6

Nancy Krauss

BLACK BEAN AND CORN SALAD

1   15 oz. can black beans, drained
1   16 oz. can niblet corn
2   tomatoes, peeled, seeded and diced
1   bell pepper, red or green, diced
4   green onions, sliced

3   tbsp. minced cilantro or parsley
2   tbsp. red wine vinegar
½   tsp. ground cumin
⅛   tsp. red pepper flakes
3   tbsp. olive oil
Salt and pepper to taste

- Mix black beans, corn, tomatoes, bell pepper, onions and cilantro.

- Mix remaining ingredients and pour over bean and corn mixture.

- Chill 4 hours or overnight.

Serves 6   *Becky Rowell*

BLUEBERRY SALAD

2   3 oz. pkgs. blackberry jello
2   cups hot water
1   can blueberries
1   small can crushed pineapple
1   8 oz. pkg. cream cheese

1   cup sour cream
1   tsp. vanilla
½   cup sugar
½   cup chopped walnuts or pecans

- Dissolve Jello in hot water; cool.

- Add blueberries, and pineapple with juice.

- Pour into a 9 x 12-inch sprayed mold. (This makes a large salad.)

- Place in refrigerator to congeal.

- Topping: Mix together cream cheese, sour cream, sugar and vanilla.

- Spread over Jello mixture.

- Sprinkle walnuts or pecans on top. Cut into squares if you wish.

Serves 12   *Mary Evelyn Cook*

BROCCOLI SALAD I

2 heads raw broccoli, broken
   into pieces
8 slices crisp bacon, crumbled
1 cup raisins
1 medium onion, chopped

Dressing:
1 cup mayonnaise
⅓ cup sugar
⅓ cup lemon juice

- Combine first 4 ingredients.

- Mix the next 3 ingredients for dressing.

- Pour on salad and toss.

Serves 8

Betty Link

BROCCOLI SALAD II

1 bunch fresh broccoli
1 cup grated mozzarella cheese
½ medium purple onion
8 slices bacon, fried and
   crumbled

Dressing:
½ cup mayonnaise
¼ cup sugar
1 tbsp. red wine vinegar

- Wash broccoli and break into pieces.

- Peel tender stalks and slice.

- Add remaining three ingredients and mix with dressing.

- Dressing: Heat vinegar to dissolve sugar. Add to mayonnaise.
  Refrigerate.

- Pour over salad and toss.

Martha Pate

*Father, we thank you
for this meal,
for our lives, for other people,
for beautiful things,
for goodness, and for you.
Amen*

CAESAR SALAD

2-3 cloves of garlic
½ cup olive oil
4 cups bread cubes, ¼-inch
4 qts. assorted lettuce greens
1 cup grated parmesan cheese
1 tsp. salt

½ tsp. pepper
12 tsp. olive oil
½ cup crumbled blue cheese
1 egg
7 tbsp. lemon juice
2 tbsp. worcestershire sauce

- Cut garlic into quarters and let sit in ½ cup olive oil overnight (out of refrigerator).
- Put bread cubes into shallow pan. Toast them in a slow oven (300°) for 30 minutes until golden brown—turning with a fork. After cooling, wrap them in wax paper until needed.
- Sprinkle lettuce greens with parmesan cheese, blue cheese, salt and pepper.
- Add olive oil (not the oil treated with garlic.)
- Mix together one egg, lemon juice and Worcestershire sauce. Pour over salad and toss.
- Add croûtons (flavored with garlic and oil mixed beforehand) to salad and toss. Do this at the last moment as the croûtons get soggy.

Serves 8   *Barbara Bush (Mrs. George Bush)*

CALICO SALAD

1 16 oz. can of shredded sauerkraut, rinsed and drained
1 medium chopped onion
1 small chopped bell pepper
2 canned chopped pimientos
½ cup vinegar

¼ cup salad oil
½ tsp. pepper
1 tsp. celery seed
½ cup sugar
1 tsp. salt
½ tsp. garlic salt

- Combine first 4 ingredients.
- Combine the next 7 ingredients and pour over vegetables.
- Stir well.
- Cover and store in refrigerator for at least 24 hours. Drain to serve. Will keep for weeks.

Serves 8-10   *Kathy Palmer*

CHRISTMAS CRANBERRY SALAD

1 large pkg. raspberry gelatin	1 cup heavy cream, whipped
2 cups hot water	½ cup chopped pecans
2 tbsp. lemon juice	1 16 oz. can of whole
1 8 oz. pkg. cream cheese	cranberry sauce

- Dissolve gelatin in hot water. Stir 2 minutes.
- Add cranberry sauce. Stir until sauce is dissolved.
- Add lemon juice.
- Pour into 9 x 13-inch casserole. Refrigerate until firm.
- Soften cream cheese at room temperature and mix on medium speed until fluffy.
- Fold whipped cream and nuts into cream cheese.
- Spread over top of congealed salad.
- When firm, cut in squares and serve on a bed of lettuce leaves.

SPECIAL NOTE: MY NIECES HAVE REQUESTED THIS SALAD FOR YEARS ON THANKSGIVING AND CHRISTMAS.

Serves 12

Angie Burns

CONGEALED ASPARAGUS SALAD

2 envelopes Knox gelatin	½ cup chopped pecans
½ cup asparagus juice	1 cup chopped celery
1 cup boiling water	1 No. 2 can cut green
¾ cup sugar	asparagus
½ cup vinegar	1 tbsp. grated onion
Juice of ½ lemon	1 small jar pimiento
½ tsp. salt	

- Mix gelatin in asparagus juice.
- Dissolve in cup of boiling water.
- Add sugar, salt, vinegar and lemon juice.
- Allow to thicken slightly before adding remaining ingredients.
- Pour into a sprayed mold or oblong glass dish. Refrigerate until set.

SPECIAL NOTE: PRETTY FOR A CHRISTMAS BUFFET WITH THE RED AND GREEN COLORS.

Serves 12

Janet Daniel

CONGEALED FRUIT SALAD

2 3 oz. pkgs. lemon Jello
1¾ cups boiling water
1 16 oz. can crushed pineapple
   in syrup
1 6 oz. bottle of cherries, cut
   in half

½ cup cottage cheese
¼ cup mayonnaise
½ cup nuts, chopped
1 tsp. lemon juice
1 cup whipping cream,
   whipped

- Dissolve gelatin in boiling water, cool and place in refrigerator until thick, but not firm.
- Stir well. Add pineapple, cherries, cottage cheese, mayonnaise, nuts and lemon juice. Mix well.
- Fold in whipped cream.
- Spray a 8 x 12-inch baking dish with vegetable oil.
- Pour in filling. Refrigerate overnight. Serve on lettuce.

Serves 24   *Cam Caldwell*

CRANBERRY MOLD

2 3 oz. boxes cherry Jello
2 cups boiling water (scant)
1 16 oz. can whole-berry
   cranberry sauce

⅓ cup chopped walnuts
½ cup diced celery
1 cup sour cream

- Dissolve Jello in the water and chill until thick, not firm.
- Add all other ingredients and pour in a 4 cup mold.
- If it will sit out for more than an hour, add 1 tsp. knox gelatin mixed in a little warm water when first mixing to make it firmer.

Serves 8-10   *Jeanne Alaimo (Mrs. Anthony Alaimo)*

CRANBERRY SALAD

1   lb. cranberries
1   6 oz. pkg. strawberry gelatin
1   cup sugar
1   cup boiling water

1   8 oz. can crushed pineapple,
    with juice
Juice of 1 orange

- Wash cranberries and grind finely, set aside.
- Dissolve gelatin and sugar in boiling water. Cool.
- Add cranberries and remaining ingredients, stir well.
- Spoon mixture into individual or 5 cup mold. Refrigerate.
- 1 cup pecans or almonds, orange sections, and or diced celery may be added.

Serves 6-8

Gerda B. Brown

Lord, warm all the kitchen with Thy love,
And light it with Thy Peace,
Forgive me all my worry, and make my grumbling cease.

CURRIED CHUTNEY SPREAD

2   8 oz. pkgs. cream cheese,
    softened
¾   cup finely chopped pecans

½   cup commercial chutney
½   tsp. curry powder

- Combine all ingredients in a small mixing bowl, beat at medium speed until blended.
- Spoon into serving container. Cover and chill at least 8 hours.
- Serve with crackers.

SPECIAL NOTE: A GREAT "MAKE AHEAD" APPETIZER.

Yields 2-2½ cups

Nancy Krauss

FESTIVAL SALAD

¾ cup sugar	1 small can chopped pimientos
½ cup vinegar	1 #2 can asparagus, chopped
1 cup water	Juice of ½ lemon
3 tbsp. gelatin	2 tsp. grated onion
½ tsp. salt	½ cup stuffed green olives,
1 cup chopped pecans	chopped

- Boil together sugar, vinegar and water for at least 2 minutes.
- Dissolve gelatin in ½ cup cold water. Set 5 minutes. Add to boiled vinegar mixture.
- Let cool and put in the refrigerator until the consistency of unbeaten egg whites.
- Add remaining ingredients and pour into a 1½ qt. mold until set (four to six hours).
- Serve with mixture of equal parts sour cream and mayonnaise.

SPECIAL NOTE: THIS MAKES A PRETTY CHRISTMAS SALAD.

Serves 6-8   *Patricia H. Collins*

GREEN BEAN-ZUCCHINI SALAD

½ lb. fresh green beans, trimmed and snapped	1 small zucchini (4 oz.) cut into matchstick strips
2½ tsp. olive oil	1 small red onion, sliced thin and punched into rings
1 clove garlic, minced	1½ tsp. tarragon vinegar
½ tsp. dried tarragon crumbled	
⅛ tsp. black pepper	

- In a small saucepan with enough boiling salted water to cover, cook the green beans until tender but still crisp, 3 to 5 minutes.
- Drain in a colander, rinse under cold running water to stop the cooking and drain again.
- In a medium-size bowl, combine the olive oil, garlic, tarragon and pepper. Add the green beans, zucchini and onion and toss well.
- Cover and chill for 2-3 hours, tossing occasionally.
- Just before serving add the vinegar and toss again. (Vinegar may be added with the olive oil mixture.)

Serves 2   *Becky Rowell*

GREEN BEAN SALAD

Fresh green beans
Vidalia or spring onions
Boston or leaf lettuce
(any sweet lettuce)

Blue cheese
1   pkg. Italian dressing
Minced garlic

- Boil green beans 5 minutes. Drain and plunge into ice water.(This may be done ahead of time and refrigerated in the ice water.)
- Make salad with the lettuce, onion and drained beans.
- Sprinkle with blue cheese, as desired.
- Dressing: Prepare Italian dressing as directed on the package. Add minced garlic, shake and refrigerate.

SPECIAL NOTE: USE QUANTITIES TO SUIT YOUR OWN TASTES AND NEEDS.

Nancy Sumerford

JACKSON SALAD

2   qts. (8 cups) packed mixed
    greens
1   cup hearts of palms, cut up
1   cup artichoke bottoms, cut up
⅓   cup chopped hard-boiled egg
⅓   cup fried bacon, drained and
    crumbled
⅔   cup bleu cheese or smoked
    gouda, shredded
⅓   cup fresh chives

Dressing:
1   egg yolk
1½ tsp. dry mustard
⅓   cup red wine vinegar
1   cup salad oil
1   tbsp. lemon juice
½   tsp. salt
¼   tsp. white pepper
½   tsp. Worcestershire sauce

- Rinse, dry and crisp the greens in the refrigerator. Prepare French dressing: put egg yolk and dry mustard in a stainless steel mixing bowl. Add vinegar and gradually whisk in oil.
- Sprinkle in salt and pepper, then add lemon juice and Worcestershire sauce. Mix thoroughly, cover the bowl and allow dressing to stand at room temperature about 30 minutes before serving.
- Toss the greens, hearts of palm and artichoke bottoms in a large salad bowl with dressing. Put salad into 6 individual bowls, and sprinkle each with 1 tbsp. chopped egg. 1 tbsp. bacon, 2 tbsp. cheese and 1 tbsp. chives.

SPECIAL NOTE: FROM BRENNAN'S RESTAURANT IN NEW ORLEANS.
AN EXCELLENT SALAD.

Serves 6

Becky Rowell

JEWELED GRAPE AND MUSHROOM SALAD

2 cup sliced fresh mushrooms	Vinaigrette Dressing:
1 cup red seedless grapes, halved	¼ cup oil
	2 tbsp. red wine vinegar
¼ cup chopped scallions	1 tbsp. lemon or lime juice
2 tbsp. chopped parsley	1 tsp. salt
	¼ tsp. dry mustard
	⅛ tsp. each basil and oregano
	¼ tsp. sugar
	Dash pepper

- Combine first 4 ingredients.
- Combine and mix well Vinaigrette ingredients.
- Pour dressing over salad mixture. Toss and serve.

Serves 5-6 *Virginia Leveau*

MARTHA'S LAYERED SALAD

1 pkg. fresh spinach, cleaned and dried	salt and pepper and sugar sprinkled on peas
1 lb. bacon, cooked and crumbled	several small sliced sweet onions (Vidalias are ideal)
6 hard boiled eggs, sliced	1 pt. mayonnaise with enough lemon juice added to make the mixture a little runny
1 large head (or 2 small) iceberg lettuce, broken up	
1 pkg. frozen small peas, thawed, well-drained, uncooked	Lots of grated Swiss cheese

- Place ingredients in salad bowl in layers in order given.
- Make the day before serving and refrigerate overnight, tightly covered (Saran Wrap is best).
- The original recipe was copied from a newspaper and instructed to "dig deep" for serving to get some of each layer. I prefer to toss at the last minute because I almost always double or triple (or more), depending on number being served.

SPECIAL NOTE: I HAVE SERVED THIS SALAD SO MANY YEARS AND FOR SO MANY OCCASIONS. I AM ALMOST ALWAYS ASKED FOR THE RECIPE. IT'S WONDERFUL BECAUSE IT IS MADE THE DAY BEFORE AND RELIEVES THE HOSTESS OF LAST MINUTE PREPARATIONS.

Serves 8-10 *Martha Fitzgerald*

MINCEMEAT JELLO

1 pkg. mincemeat (dry pkg.
   like Nonesuch)
½ cup water

2 3 oz. pkgs. cherry Jello
2 cups boiling water
1½ cups pineapple juice

- Break up mincemeat, add ½ cup water and cook until almost dry, cool.
- Dissolve Jello in boiling water, add pineapple juice.
- Pour small amount of clear jello in bottom of mold and let set.
- Stir prepared mincemeat into remaining Jello and pour over clear set layer.

SPECIAL NOTE: WONDERFUL AT CHRISTMAS TIME.

Serves 8-10   *Lucrece Truax*

MUSTARD RING

1 envelope unflavored gelatin
1 tbsp. cold water
4 eggs, beaten
¾ cup sugar
2 tbsp. dry mustard

⅔ cup vinegar
⅓ cup cold water
¼ tsp. salt (optional)
1 cup whipped cream

- Soak gelatin in cold water.
- Place beaten eggs, sugar, mustard, vinegar, water and salt in top of double boiler; add gelatin and cook over hot water until mixture is creamy.
- Cool by beating over ice water.
- Fold into ring mold. Chill until firm.
- Unmold and fill center with pickled peaches, olives, etc.

SPECIAL NOTE: ESPECIALLY NICE SERVED WITH BAKED HAM.

Serves 8   *Eugenia J. Jossman*

Blessed are You, O Lord God, King of the Universe,
for you give us food to sustain our lives
and make our hearts glad;
through Jesus Christ our Lord. Amen

BOOK OF COMMON PRAYER, 1979

ORANGE ALMOND SALAD

Dressing:
½ cup oil
2 tbsp. vinegar
½ tsp. salt
2 tbsp. sugar or to taste
1 tbsp. parsley, minced
Dash pepper

Salad:
¼ head lettuce
1 head romaine
1 red onion, thinly sliced
1 can mandarin oranges, drained

Garnish:
¼ cup almonds
1 tbsp. plus 1 tsp. sugar

- Sauté almonds and sugar. (Start on medium heat, reduce to low.)
- Cool almonds on wax paper.
- Prepare dressing.
- Combine salad ingredients. Toss with dressing.
- Garnish with almonds.

Serves 8   *Hazel Crowley*

ORANGE SALAD MOLD

2 small cans mandarin oranges
1 large can crushed pineapple
3 3 oz. pkgs. orange jello
1 small can frozen orange juice, thawed

- Drain oranges and pineapple, saving juices.
- Add enough water to juices to make 3½ cups liquid.
- Heat 2 cups of this liquid and dissolve gelatin in it. Add remaining liquid.
- Chill until slightly thickened; add fruit and undiluted orange juice.
- Chill until firm. If you use a large rectangular glass casserole dish, which has been sprayed, you can cut in squares to serve on lettuce.

Serves 8-10   *Cam Caldwell*

RASPBERRY ELITE

1 pkg. raspberry Jello
1 pkg. lemon Jello
1½ cups boiling water
1 10 oz. pkg. frozen raspberries

1 cup cranberry-orange relish
1 7 oz. bottle or 1 cup lemon-lime soda

- Dissolve both Jellos in boiling water.
- Stir in frozen raspberries.
- Add cranberry relish.
- Chill until cold, but not set.
- Slowly add soda and stir with an up-and-down motion.
- Chill until partially set. Then pour into a 6 cup mold and chill 6 hours. Unmold and serve with mayonnaise.

SPECIAL NOTE: WONDERFUL WITH PORK OR HAM.

Serves 6-8

Mrs. Robert Allen

THE SAPPHIRE

3 cups drained canned crushed pineapple (save juice)
1 6 oz. pkg. lime flavor gelatin
2 cups finely chopped walnuts

4 tbsp. lemon juice
½ tsp. salt
1 cup chopped celery
2 cups cold evaporated milk

- Drain pineapple. Reserve crushed pineapple.
- Add water to juice to make 2½ cups. Bring to a boil. Remove from heat.
- Add lime gelatin and stir until gelatin is dissolved.
- Add lemon juice and salt.
- Chill mixture until slightly thickened.
- Stir in evaporated milk, walnuts, celery, and reserved pineapple.
- Pour into 2 qt. mold. Chill until firm. Unmold.

SPECIAL NOTE: THIS RECIPE CAN EASILY BE HALVED.

Serves 24

Mary Jo Cochran

SPICED PEACH SALAD

1   jar spiced peach pickle
1   small pkg. cream cheese
    (softened)

Suitable amount of chopped nuts
6   oz. pkg. jello
    (orange or lemon)

- Remove seed from peaches.
- Stuff with cream cheese and nut mixture.
- Place in individual molds.
- Cover with jello made according to pkg. directions. Refrigerate until firm.
- Unmold on lettuce leaves and enjoy.

Martha Lokey

SPINACH SALAD

Dressing:
⅓   cup vinegar
⅓   cup sugar
3   tsp. prepared mustard
1   tsp. celery salt
Freshly ground pepper to taste
½   tsp. salt
1   cup salad oil
1   medium onion, chopped

Salad:
1   bag fresh spinach, usually ½ lb. plus
½   cup crumb stuffing from Pepperidge Farm
2-3   hard-boiled eggs
6   slices crisply fried bacon, crumbled

- Mix dressing ingredients in a blender.
- Combine ingredients for salad and toss.
- Add dressing as needed and toss again.

SPECIAL NOTE: THE SALAD INGREDIENTS MAY BE VARIED, BUT ALWAYS USE DRESSING EXACTLY. THIS DRESSING IS DELICIOUS ON ALL SALAD GREENS.

Betty Sumey

Blessed are You, O Lord God, King of the Universe,
for You give us food to sustain our lives
and make our hearts glad;
through Jesus Christ our Lord. Amen

BOOK OF COMMON PRAYER, 1979

SWISS SALAD

1   cup each of the following:
    Grapes, cut in half
    Beets, cooked and chopped
    Swiss cheese, in small cubes
    Apple, chopped
    Celery, thin sliced
    Fennel, thin sliced
    Walnuts or pecans
    Belgian endive, cut up

Salt and pepper
Olive oil and vinegar (2 to 1 proportions)

- Mix all salad ingredients.
- Add oil, vinegar, salt and pepper. Mix well.
- Serve cold as a salad or as an entrée.

Serves 6   *Jacqueline G. Curl*

TOMATO ASPIC

1   envelope gelatin
1   can tomato soup
2   cups cocktail vegetable juice
1   3 oz. pkg. lemon jello
1   tsp. hot sauce

⅛   tsp. salt
½   cup chopped green pepper
½   cup chopped celery
½   cup chopped stuffed olives

- Stir gelatin in 2 tbsp. cold water and 2 tbsp. hot water until dissolved.
- In large bowl add tomato soup to dissolved gelatin. Stir well.
- Heat cocktail vegetable juice to boiling and stir in lemon jello. Add hot sauce and salt. Mix well.
- Very slowly spoon into tomato soup mixture. Be careful not to leave lumps.
- Refrigerate until thickened.
- Stir in green pepper, celery and olives.
- Pour into mold. Refrigerate

SPECIAL NOTE: VERY GOOD MADE WITH OLIVES ONLY.

Serves 6-8   *Virginia Leveau*

TOMATO AND ONION SALAD

4	large tomatoes	½	tsp. oregano
1	large onion	½	tsp. salt
¼	cup salad oil	½	tsp. pepper
1	tbsp. lemon juice	1	tbsp. parsley

- Cut tomatoes in ¼-inch slices.
- Peel onion, slice into ⅛-inch slices, separate rings.
- Arrange half the tomatoes and half the onions. Repeat layers.
- Combine remaining ingredients.
- Pour over tomatoes and onions.
- Cover and refrigerate. Serve on lettuce leaves.

Serves 8   *Kathy Palmer*

Lifetime Recipe

2 heaping cups of Patience

2 handfuls of Generosity

1 pinch of Understanding

3 Tablespoons of Love

1 dash of Laughter

Sprinkle generously with kindness, adding plenty
of faith and mix well.

Spread over a period of a Lifetime, and serve to
everyone you meet. It doesn't fail!

CATCH-ALL PASTA SALAD

1 pkg. rotini, cooked and drained	3-4 pkgs. sliced pepperoni, sautéed and drained
2 cups broccoli florets	2 jars marinated artichoke hearts, drained
3 carrots, sliced	
1 pkg. frozen peapods, thawed	1 lb. shrimp, boiled and peeled
1 small can sliced black olives	(marinated optional)
3-4 green onions, chopped	Vinaigrette dressing
1 red bell pepper, sliced	¼ cup basil pesto (see sauces)
1 small zucchini, sliced	

- To pasta, add remainder of ingredients.
- Mix with vinaigrette dressing mixed with basil pesto.
- To make vinaigrette mix as follows: ¼ cup wine vinegar, 1 tsp. salt, ½ tsp. sugar, ¼ tsp. freshly ground pepper. Whisk in ¼ cup vegetable oil and ½ cup good olive oil (preferably extra virgin or light).
- For a main dish salad you may add 2 lbs. shrimp or pepperoni, sautéed and drained to remove any fat.
- Marinate at least 12 hours.

SPECIAL NOTE: THE INGREDIENTS CAN BE SUBSTITUTED FOR WHATEVER YOU HAVE AVAILABLE, SUCH AS GREEN OLIVES INSTEAD OF BLACK, GREEN PEPPER FOR RED, VIDALIA INSTEAD OF GREEN ONIONS, ETC. BROCCOLI WILL TURN YELLOW IF ADDED MORE THAN ONE DAY AHEAD.

Serves 12-20   *Davi Langston*

ELEANOR'S PASTA SALAD

1 lb. box vermicelli	2 large or 3 small tomatoes
1 16 oz. bottle Italian dressing	1 medium purple onion
1 large bell pepper	1 2¾ oz. jar McCormick Salad
1 large cucumber	Supreme

- Take a few vermicelli strands at a time and break into 1-inch pieces. Cook as directed, drain well, cool.
- Add bell pepper, cucumber, tomatoes and onions. Toss.
- Then add Italian dressing and Salad Supreme.
- Mix well several hours before serving. Refrigerate.

Serves 8   *Mrs. Richard Wilkins*

COLE SLAW

1	large head cabbage, grated	1	tsp. prepared mustard
1	large onion, chopped	1	tsp. celery seed
1	large green pepper, chopped	1	tbsp. salt
1	cup sugar	½	cup salad oil
¾	cup cider vinegar		

- Mix cabbage, onion and green pepper in a bowl.
- Sprinkle sugar over this mixture.
- In sauce pan mix vinegar, salad oil, salt, celery seed and mustard.
- Bring to a boil and pour over the cabbage. Do not stir.
- Let it sit in refrigerator for 8 hours, then stir.

SPECIAL NOTE: THIS WILL KEEP 2 WEEKS OR MORE IN THE REFRIGERATOR.

Serves 10-12   *Jeanne Alaimo*

Thank you for the world so sweet
Thank you for the food we eat
Thank you for the birds that sing
Thank you God for everything.

AN OLD SCOTCH TABLE GRACE

A FAVORITE SLAW

½	head cabbage, shredded	½	tsp. mustard seed
1	tbsp. sugar	½	tsp. celery seed
1½	tbsp. cider vinegar	2-3	tbsp. mayonnaise
¼	tsp. salt		

- Mix sugar, vinegar, salt and seeds.
- Let stand 5 minutes.
- Add mayonnaise to taste.
- Add cabbage. Stir. Keep refrigerated.

SPECIAL NOTE: GRATED CARROT MAY BE ADDED. REDUCED CALORIE MAYON-
NAISE WORKS WELL.

Davi Langston

Everlasting Slaw

3 lbs. cabbage, grated
1 small can pimiento, chopped fine
1 pint sweet pickles, chopped fine
2 green peppers, chopped fine
1 pt. canned tomatoes, chopped
½ cup sugar
½ cup vinegar
1 tbsp. salt
Dash red pepper

- Mix all ingredients well. Refrigerate. Flavor improves after 2 hours. Keeps a long time in the refrigerator.
- If using a food processor, chop the pimiento, pickles, peppers and tomatoes at the same time with blade, then use grating attachment for cabbage. It cuts the preparation time in half.

SPECIAL NOTE: WE USE THE SLAW AS AN ACCOMPANIMENT TO BARBEQUED PORK, NORTH CAROLINA STYLE, BUT IT IS GOOD ANYTIME.

Yields 3 qts.   *Brenda Hartsell*

Oriental Spicy Slaw

Dressing:
¼ cup sugar
¼ cup rice or cider vinegar
2 tsp. each salt and pepper
¾ cup vegetable oil
¼ cup dark oriental sesame oil
1½ tbsp. hot chili oil or to taste

2¼ cups green cabbage, shredded
1⅓ cups chopped green onions
3 3 oz. pkgs. chicken-flavor oriental noodles with seasoning packets
1 cup toasted slivered almonds
¼ cup toasted sesame seeds

- Dressing: Mix sugar, vinegar, salt and pepper until sugar dissolves. Whisk in oils until blended.
- Add cabbage and green onions, toss to mix. Cover and refrigerate overnight.
- About 4 hours before serving, crumble uncooked noodles over cabbage mixture. Sprinkle with seasonings (from packets) and toss to mix well.
- Cover and refrigerate; Noodles will soften as they moisten.
- Just before serving add almonds and sesame seeds and toss.

SPECIAL NOTE: START THIS SALAD A DAY AHEAD AS THE UNCOOKED NOODLES NEED TIME TO ABSORB MOISTURE AND BECOME SOFT.

Yields 10 cups   *Betty Link*

SMITTY'S SLAW

1	medium head cabbage, shredded	⅓	cup salad oil
1	medium onion, chopped fine	1	cup sugar
⅓	cup white vinegar	2	tbsp. poppy seeds

- Mix ingredients together and let stand in refrigerator 3 hours or overnight. (Will keep in refrigerator 3 weeks.)

Serves 6-8 *Joan Heller*

MOLDED CORN BEEF SALAD

1	can corned beef, chilled	2	cups celery, chopped fine
1	3 oz. pkg. lemon Jello	⅓	onion, chopped fine
1½	cup boiling water	3	hard boiled eggs, sliced
1	cup mayonnaise		
½	cup green pepper, chopped fine		

- Dissolve Jello in boiling water and chill slightly.
- Pour into mixing bowl and beat with mixer.
- Add mayonnaise and continue beating.
- Shred corned beef and add to celery, pepper and onion.
- Add to Jello mixture.
- Pour into 9 x 9-inch oiled dish.
- Place sliced eggs on top.
- Chill until firm and cut into squares.

Serves 8 *Hazel Crowley*

SPICY BEEF SALAD

1	tbsp. red wine vinegar	1	clove garlic, minced
1	tsp. dijon mustard	2	cups cubed cooked beef
¼	tsp. salt	2	ribs celery, chopped
Pinch black pepper		¼	cup onion, finely chopped
¼	cup olive oil	2	medium red or green bell peppers, chopped
1	tbsp. minced parsley		
1	tsp. ground cumin	2	medium tomatoes, chopped

- In a small serving bowl, combine the vinegar, mustard, salt, pepper, oil, parsley, cumin and garlic.
- Add the beef, celery, onion, pepper and tomatoes. Toss well. Chill 30-60 minutes.

Serves 4 *Becky Rowell*

HOT CHICKEN SALAD

1   can cream of chicken soup
¾   cup mayonnaise
1½ tbsp. lemon juice
½   cup chopped onion
1   cup diced celery (not too small)
1   can water chestnuts

3   hard boiled eggs, finely chopped
1   cup fresh mushrooms sliced and sautéed in butter
4   cups cooked chicken breasts, cut in chunks (3 whole breasts)
Salt and pepper to taste

- Combine and mix first 3 ingredients.
- Add remaining ingredients.
- Top with ½ of 8 oz. package of Pepperidge Farm herb seasoned stuffing moistened with butter.
- Bake in 350° oven for 30-35 minutes.

SPECIAL NOTE: PREPARE AHEAD AND ENJOY YOUR GUESTS.

Eugenia Jossman

HAM BUFFET MOLD

1   can tomato soup
¾   cup water
2   envelopes unflavored gelatin
½   cup cold water
3   oz. cream cheese
2   tbsp. lemon juice

1   tbsp. grated onion
½   cup mayonnaise (Light is O.K.)
2   tsp. prepared mustard
2   cups finely chopped ham

- Combine soup and ¾ cup water and bring to boil.
- Soak gelatin in ½ cup cold water for 5 minutes. Stir into hot soup.
- Add cream cheese and beat until smooth. Cool until slightly thickened.
- Stir in remaining ingredients.
- Pour into lightly oiled 6 cup mold.
- Chill 4 hours or until firm.
- Unmold and garnish with variety of salad greens, egg slices, stuffed olives.

SPECIAL NOTE: SERVED THIS OLD PIRATES HOUSE RECIPE AT A GEORGIA LUNCHEON FOR MY INTERNATIONAL CLUB IN WASHINGTON. BARBARA BUSH NOT ONLY PARTOOK OF IT BUT ALSO POPPED INTO THE KITCHEN TO HELP, THE GROUP BEING SO LARGE THAT NOT ONE OTHER SOUL WOULD FIT INTO OUR HOUSE. EVEN HER SECURITY MEN WERE FORCED OUTSIDE BECAUSE THEIR EARPHONES WERE OF NO USE ABOVE OUR CHATTER.

Serves 8-10   *Carolyn Mattingly*

PASTA CRAB SALAD

1½ lbs. imitation king crab	3 tbsp. sliced black olives
¼ cup mayonnaise (light)	¼ cup chopped celery
4 oz. cream cheese (light)	½ lb. pasta (any small pasta
3 tbsp. finely chopped onion	shells or twists)
½ tbsp. dill weed	Salt and pepper to taste

- Cook pasta according to pkg. directions and set aside.
- Cream mayonnaise and cream cheese together.
- Add all other ingredients.
- Stir in pasta. Chill and serve.

Serves 6   *Linda Allen*

SHRIMP AND RICE SALAD

¾ lb. fresh mushrooms, chopped	3¼ cups cooked rice (half white, half wild)
2 tbsp. salad oil	2 hard boiled eggs, chopped
2 tbsp. lemon juice	1 green pepper chopped
1 tsp. salt	1½ lbs. shrimp, cleaned and cooked

- Sauté mushrooms in oil. Add lemon juice and salt.
- Mix rice, eggs, green pepper, mushrooms and shrimp together. Refrigerate overnight.
- Toss with Garlic Mayonnaise before serving.
- Garlic Mayonnaise: Blend 1 clove garlic, ¼ tsp. dry mustard, ⅛ tsp. pepper, 1 tsp. warm water and ¾ cup mayonnaise together well. Toss with shrimp and rice mixture.

Serves 10   *Rosemary Lokey*

KING SALAD

1 lb. king mackerel fillet, or any similar fish	¼ minced onions
Juice of one lemon	¼ cup Durkee dressing
2 cups chopped celery	½ cup mayonnaise
	Salt and lemon pepper to taste

- Season fish with juice of ½ lemon.
- Cover loosely with foil. Bake 30 minutes at 350° or until done.
- Cool, flake fish into a large bowl and toss with juice of ½ lemon.
- Add remaining ingredients and mix well.
- Serve on lettuce or as filling for a sandwich.

Serves 8   *Angie Burns*

FRENCH DRESSING

1 cup sugar	1 tsp. ground onion (or more)
½ cup vinegar	1 clove garlic (optional)
1 cup salad oil	Catsup (to color)
1½ tsp. salt	Paprika
1 tsp. Worcestershire sauce	

- Blend sugar with vinegar.
- Add oil and blend.
- Add remaining ingredients and beat well.
- Bottle and refrigerate. Keeps well. Shake well before using.

Beegie Searcy

DELICIOUS SALAD DRESSING

1 qt. mayonnaise	2½ tsp. salt
1 qt. buttermilk	½ tsp. garlic powder
2 tsp. parsley flakes	2 tsp. Accent
2 tsp. chives	¾ tsp. coarse pepper
2 tsp. onion salt	

- Beat all together with egg beater or whisk, store in refrigerator.

SPECIAL NOTE: THIS IS A HOMEMADE RANCH DRESSING RECIPE FROM MY VERY DEAR FRIEND FROM GRADUATE SCHOOL, MARY BRIDGE (NOW DECEASED).

Yields ½ gallon   *Susan Shipman*

THIS WOMAN WAS
FULL OF GOOD WORKS.

Dorcas, a woman "full of good works
and acts of charity," was raised from the
dead by Peter. He is shown with friends
of Dorcas who are displaying garments
she had made. (Acts 9: 36-42)

The window is dedicated
"In Memory of Rebecca Holmes
Dangerfield. Born Dec. 17, 1815.
Died July 19, 1885. R.I.P."

THE GOOD SAMARITAN

The parable of The Good Samaritan is
depicted. The wounded traveler is being
assisted and treated with healing oils by
the Samaritan. The other panel show
the priest, busily reading with eyes avert-
ed from the wounded man, and the
Levite, passing "on the other side."
(Luke 10: 29-37)

The window is dedicated "In memory
of William Earl Dodge. Born Sept. 4,
1805. Died Feb. 9, 1883. R.I.P."

CRAB ENTREE

1   lb. crab meat
3   slices of bread crumbed
½   cup mayonnaise (Blue Ribbon)
½   tsp. mustard

2   tbsp. Worcestershire sauce
½   cup of cream
½   green pepper chopped and sauteed in butter

- Mix ingredients in bowl and spoon into a large shell or ovenproof dishes.
- Bake 15 minutes in 400° oven

Serves 4-6   *Cornelia C. Ferguson*

CRAB IMPERIAL

1   tbsp. chopped pimiento
1   tbsp. chopped green pepper
2   tbsp. mayonnaise
1   tbsp. Worcestershire sauce

6   saltines
1   egg
1   lb. crabmeat
Dash Accent

- Combine all in casserole.
- Mix ⅓ cup mayonnaise plus 1 egg yolk. Pour over mixture.
- Bake 425° for 15 minutes until brown.

Serves 6-8   *Peggy Sullivan*

DEVILED CRAB I

3   cups dry bread crumbs
⅓   cup chopped onions
⅓   cup chopped celery
Green pepper if desired
½   stick margarine

1   tbsp. prepared mustard
2-3 tbsp. Worcestershire sauce (more or less if desired)
1   lb. crabmeat, either white meat or claw meat

- Mix bread crumbs, mustard and worcestershire sauce together.
- Saute onions and celery in margarine, add to bread crumbs. Add a little water to make it moist.
- Add crabmeat last and mix lightly to avoid making crab meat mushy.
- Make into patties or put in shells. Put cakes on a sheet pan sprayed with Pam.
- Bake in 350° oven for about 30 minutes or until lightly brown.

Serves 12   *Elizabeth Wright*

DEVILED CRAB II

1	lb. fresh crab	1	cup canned milk
½	cup chopped celery	½	cup mayonnaise
¼	cup chopped peppers	¼	cup butter
½	cup chopped onion	1½	cups bread crumbs
1	tsp. lemon juice		Prepared mustard
1	tsp. salt		Dash Worcestershire Sauce
¼	tsp. black pepper		

- Combine all ingredients and place in 12 x 8-inch casserole that has been sprayed with Pam.
- Bake at 400° approximately 20-30 minutes or until golden brown.

SPECIAL NOTE: IF PREFERRED, PLACE MIXTURE IN INDIVIDUAL SHELLS. THIS FREEZES WELL.

Serves 8   *Mary C. Freeman*

DEVILED CRAB ISLAND STYLE

4	tbsp. butter	¼	cup sauteed celery chopped fine
2	tbsp. flour		
1	cup Half n' Half cream	1	tbsp. finely chopped parsley
1	tsp. prepared mustard	2	cups flake crabmeat
¼	cup Pepperidge Farm dry dressing mix	2	tbsp. sherry wine
			Dash Tabasco
¼	cup sauteed onions chopped fine		Dash salt to taste

- Make a rich cream sauce with butter, flour and cream.
- Add all ingredients.
- Add crabmeat and wine last.
- Put in crab shells (or scallop shells.)
- Top with buttered toast crumbs or crushed soda crackers.
- Bake 350° oven for 30 minutes. This fills 6 large shells.

SPECIAL NOTES: ALWAYS PICK THROUGH CRABMEAT TO REMOVE SMALL SHELLS. TO BOIL CRABS: DROP LIVE CRABS IN LARGE POT OF BOILING WATER WITH 3 TBSP. VINEGAR AND SALT. VINEGAR MAKES CRAB EASY TO PICK. BOIL FOR 25 MINUTES. REFRIGERATE SHELLS UNTIL USED.

Serves 6   *Mickey McBride*

ISLAND SHRIMP AND CHEESE PASTA

2 lbs. shrimp boiled and peeled
8 oz cream cheese
8 oz sour cream
4 oz saga blue cheese
4 oz Velveeta Cheese
1 tsp. garlic powder
3 tbsp. fine chopped parsley
4 tbsp. dry white wine
12 oz. egg noodles

- Heat and blend together cheeses and sour cream, til mixture is smooth and even.
- Add garlic and parsley.
- Add wine, adding more or less to keep mixture from being too thin.
- Add shrimp and heat well.
- Spoon mixture over cooked egg noodles (pasta).

Serves 8   *Mickey McBride*

HOT CRABMEAT DIP

1 large package Philadelphia Cream Cheese
1 can (8 oz) crabmeat and its juice
3 scallions (sliced) using some
of the green part
¼ tsp. curry
1 tbsp. chopped chives

- Soften cheese with juice from crabmeat
- Mix all together. Put in small ovenproof dish.
- Sprinkle with paprika.
- Bake at 350° til bubbly. Serve with crackers or vegetables.

Serves 10

CRAB QUICHE DELUICHE!

Pastry for deep dish pie
½ cup mayonnaise
2 tbsp. flour
2 eggs beaten
½ cup milk

½ lb. crab (thawed and drained)
½ lb. Monterey Jack cheese (cut in small cubes)
⅓ cup chopped onion

- Bake crust and cool.

- Combine mayonnaise, flour, eggs and milk. Mix thoroughly.

- Stir in crabmeat, cheese and onion.

- Spoon into shell. Bake at 350° for 30-40 minutes or until firm in center.

- Garnish with parsley.

SPECIAL NOTES: MY FRIENDS EXPECT THIS FOR SUMMER LUNCH AT MY HOUSE. WE CATCH OUR OWN CRABS AND FREEZE THE MEAT IN MILK.

Serves 6

Angie Burns

CRAB CASSEROLE

¼ cup butter
3 tbsp. flour
2 cups milk
2 tbsp. minced onion
¼ tsp. celery salt
⅛ tsp. orange rind
1 tbsp. minced parsley
1 tbsp. chopped green pepper

1 minced pimiento
  dash Tabasco
2 tbsp. sherry
4 cups deluxe lump crabmeat
1 egg , beaten
1 tsp. salt
Dash of pepper

- Make white sauce with first 3 ingredients.

- Add remaining ingredients to white sauce.

- Remove from heat. Add sherry.

- Stir some of mixture into beaten egg and return to hot mixture.

- Add 1 tsp. salt, dash pepper and deluxe lump crabmeat.

- Put in buttered 8 x 12-inch casserole, top with 1 cup buttered bread crumbs, dust with paprika and bake at 350° for 12-20 minutes.

SPECIAL NOTES: CAN BE MADE IN ADVANCE OF SERVING. INCREASE COOKING TIME IF REFRIGERATED BEFORE COOKING.

Serves 6

Mrs. William J. Hull

VILLAGE CREEK
CRABMEAT CASSEROLE

8	slices of white bread	3	cups milk
2	lbs. of select crabmeat	4	beaten eggs
¾	cup mayonnaise	1	tsp. salt
1	medium onion chopped fine	1	can mushroom soup
1	medium green pepper chopped fine	1	cup grated American cheese
1	cup celery chopped fine		Paprika and white pepper to taste

- Grease a 13-inch casserole and put in half the bread diced.
- Mix the crabmeat, mayonnaise, onion, green pepper, celery and place on diced bread in casserole.
- Trim crust from the remaining bread and place in slices on top of crabmeat mixture.
- Mix beaten eggs, milk, salt and pepper and pour over all.
- Let stand overnight in refrigerator. Next day pour on undiluted soup but DO NOT MIX.
- Sprinkle with cheese and paprika. Bake for 1 hour in 325° oven.

Serves 8   *Marge Amme*

CRAB QUICHE

3	eggs slightly beaten	1	3½ oz can french fried onions
1	cup sour cream	1	cup coarsely shredded Swiss cheese
½	tsp. Worcestershire sauce		
¾	tsp. salt		Pastry shell, 9-inch lightly baked
½	lb. crabmeat		

- Combine all ingredients and pour into shell. Bake 55-60 minutes in 300° oven.

SPECIAL NOTES: TASTE APPEAL, EASY PREPARATION, VERSATILE. MAY BE SERVED FOR BRUNCH OR LUNCH, ADAPTABLE FOR PARTY OR FAMILY.

Serves 6-8   *Alice Bradford*

SHERRIED CRABMEAT

1	lb. fresh crabmeat	1	tsp. sugar
2	8 oz package cream cheese	¾	tsp. salt
7	tbsp. mayonnaise	½	grated white onion
4	tbsp. good white wine	⅓-½	cup good sherry
2	tsps Dijon mustard		

- Pick over crabmeat.

- Over low heat in double boiler, mix all ingredients. If mixture is too thick, add a little cream.

- Transfer to chaffing dish. Warm and serve with toast points.

SPECIAL NOTES: SO DELICIOUS FOR COCKTAILS.

Serves 8-10

Mrs. Robert Allen

SOUFFLE SANDWICH WITH CRABMEAT

16	slices buttered bread, crust removed		Parmesan cheese
8	slices Swiss cheese	2	tsp. salt
5	eggs	1	large can crabmeat, shredded
3	cups milk		watercress or parsley for garnish

- Butter a large, shallow rectangular baking dish. Place half the bread slices into pan, buttered side down.

- Lay cheese slices on bread. Sprinkle crab on cheese.

- Beat together eggs, milk, salt in mixer bowl.

- Place remaining 8 slices of bread on top of crabmeat.

- Pour beaten egg mixture over all. Top with parmesan cheese generously.

- Refrigerate overnight or at least 8 hours.

- Bake for one hour at 325°. Cut carefully and remove with spatula to serve.

Serves 8

Sally McCauley

SHIPMAN'S DEVILED CRABS

1   lb. crabmeat
1   cup bread crumbs (plain or seasoned)
2   eggs, well beaten
1-2 tbsp. mayonnaise
Worcestershire sauce to taste
Tabasco to taste
Juice of 1 lemon or
1   tbsp. cider vinegar

1   tbsp. or 1 tsp. Creole seasoning (to your taste)
1   clove garlic, diced finely
2-3 ribs celery, diced
1   small bell pepper, diced
1   onion, diced
⅔   stick butter or margarine
Paprika
Salt and pepper to taste

- Sauté celery, onion, bell pepper and garlic in butter. Mix crabmeat, bread crumbs, eggs, mustard, mayonnaise, Worcestershire, Tabasco, lemon juice, salt, pepper and creole seasonings in large mixing bowl.

- Add sautéed vegetables and mix well. Spoon into crab shells, garnish with paprika.

- Cook at 350° for 10-12 minutes. Mixture may also be spooned into casserole, topped with grated cheese and baked uncovered for 24-30 minutes at 400°.

Susan Shipman

CLAM AND CORN SOUFFLE

1¼ cups crushed saltines
1   cup milk
2   eggs, beaten
1   can minced or chopped clams, undrained
1   cup frozen or canned corn, uncooked

3   tbsp. melted butter or margarine
2   tbsp. minced onion
½   tsp. Worcestershire sauce
½   cup shredded sharp cheese

- Soak crackers in eggs and milk until soggy, about ½ hour.

- Then add all ingredients but the cheese. Mix gently and refrigerate (overnight is fine).

- When ready to bake, place in 1½ qt casserole.

- Bake uncovered at 300° for 50 minutes.

- Sprinkle cheese on top and allow to bake just to melt cheese (about 10 minutes).

SPECIAL NOTES: 2 CANS OF CLAMS MAY BE USED BOTH MINCED AND CHOPPED. SODA CRACKERS INSTEAD OF SALTINES AND ADD ¼ TSP. SALT.

Serves 4   *Sally McCauley*

SCALLOPS WITH MUSHROOMS IN SHELL

½ cup butter, at room temperature
1 cup thinly sliced mushrooms
3 tbsp. finely chopped shallots
1 tbsp. finely chopped garlic

1 lb. fresh scallops
½ cup finely chopped parsley
½ cup soft bread crumbs
Salt and pepper

- Preheat oven to 450°

- Melt ¼ cup of the butter in a small skillet and add mushrooms. Cook, stirring often, until the mushrooms are wilted.

- Add the shallots and garlic and cook briefly.

- Spoon the mushroom mixture into a mixing bowl. Let cool briefly.

- Add 2 tbsp. of the remaining butter, the scallops, bread crumbs, parsley, salt and pepper to taste. Blend well.

- Use the mixture to fill 6 seafood shells.

- Arrange filled shells on baking or cookie sheet. Melt the rest of the butter and pour over the mixture in the shells. Place in the oven and bake 10 minutes.

- Run the shells under the broiler until nicely browned on top, about 1-2 minutes.

Serves 6

Jeannie Wade

SHRIMP DE JONGHE

3 lbs. cooked shrimp
¾ cup butter
1 large clove garlic
1 tsp. salt

Chopped parsley
Pinch marjoram
Pinch tarragon
1 cup fine bread crumbs
½ cup dry sherry

- Mash garlic until it is almost a paste, then add to it butter softened, salt, tarragon and marjoram. Cream well until blended.

- Add bread crumbs and sherry. Blend well. In a fairly large buttered baking dish place alternate layers of shrimp and bread mixture. Sprinkling parsley over top each layer.

- Bake in 400° oven for 20-25 minutes and serve immediately.

SPECIAL NOTES: CAN BE USED AS APPETIZER OR AS ENTREE. SERVED AT THE CLOISTER HOTEL MANY YEARS AGO.

Serves 6

Julia C. Rose

GOLDEN SHRIMP PUFF

10	slices white bread	½	tsp. salt
6	eggs	2	cups (8 oz) shredded sharp
3	cups milk		American cheese
2	tbsp. minced parsley	2	cups cleaned, cooked shrimp
¾	tsp. dry mustard		

- Preheat oven to 325°.

- Remove crusts from bread; cut slices into cubes.

- Beat eggs, milk and seasonings. Stir in bread cubes, cheese and shrimp.

- Pour into oblong baking dish. Bake uncovered for 1 hour, or until center is set. Serve immediately.

Serves 8   *Sally McCauley*

BEER BOILED SHRIMP

5	lbs. raw shrimp in shells	½	cup salt
1	qt cider vinegar	¼	cup black pepper
2	12 oz cans beer	⅛	cup red pepper

- Divide shrimp into two equal portions (2½ lbs. each).

- In large pot bring to boil vinegar, beer and seasonings. When brew reaches hard rolling boil, drop in shrimp. Let it just return to boil and remove shrimp.

- Cook remaining shrimp in same manner.

- Serve with drawn butter. Everyone peels their own!

Cooking time: About 4-5 minutes

Serves 6   *Gwen Mayberry*

OYSTERS IN PORT

1	pt. oysters, fresh or frozen	36	sesame crackers
8	ozs. port wine cheese		

- Drain thawed oysters. Remove any shell particles. Place in single layer in well-greased 12- x 8- x 2-inch baking dish, Dot with port wine cheese.

- Bake in 350° oven for 15-20 minutes or until edges of oysters curl and cheese melts. Remove each cheese-topped oyster with a fork and place on a cracker.

Yield about 36 canapes   *Susan Shipman*

CREAMY SHRIMP DIP

1   can (10 oz) frozen cream of shrimp soup thawed
8   oz cream cheese, softened, or you can substitute an 8 oz carton cottage cheese (if using cottage cheese do not add lemon juice)

2   tbsp. chopped green onion
1   tsp. lemon juice
¼   tsp. curry powder
4   drops hot pepper sauce
    dash of garlic powder

- To really be super, add a few chopped boiled shrimp or a small can of shrimp, drained and chopped to the dip.
- Gradually blend soup and other ingredients with electric mixer. Do not over-beat or dip will be too thin.
- Chill and serve with raw vegetables. Makes 2 cups.

Ann Fendig's recipe submitted by Jane Ledbetter

SHRIMP CREOLE

2   tbsp. olive oil
2   cups chopped onion
2   cups chopped fresh parsley
1   cup chopped bell pepper
1   cup chopped green onion
6   cups chopped fresh tomatoes, peeled and seeded
8   oz tomato sauce

1   tbsp. garlic, chopped
1   tbsp. Worcestershire Sauce
½   tsp. red pepper (optional)
1   cup chablis or dry white wine
3   lbs. shrimp, peeled and deveined
Salt and pepper to taste

- Heat olive oil in a dutch oven. Add onion, parsley, bell pepper and green onion. Cook until vegetables are tender.
- Add remaining ingredients, except shrimp. Cover and simmer over low heat, stirring occasionally, until thickened. an hour or more.
- Add shrimp just prior to serving and cook until just done. Serve over rice.

SPECIAL NOTES: FREEZES WELL—JUST ADD FRESH SHRIMP (DON'T FREEZE WITH COOKED SHRIMP OR BECOMES MEALY).

Cooking time: 90 minutes

Serves 8   *Becky Rowell*

ENCHILADAS VERA CRUZ

6 oz. flaked crabmeat
6 oz. bay shrimp (tiny)
6 oz. sour cream
4 green onions
1 4 oz. can mild green chilies, chopped

6 small flour tortillas
Monterey Jack Cheese, shredded
Avocado (guacamole)
Sour cream
Black olives (pitted)

- Mix crabmeat, shrimp, chilies and onion together with sour cream. Spread on tortilla and roll up. Place in baking dish and set aside.

Spanish Sauce

1 onion, finely chopped
1 clove garlic, minced
1 small can tomato sauce
2 green bell peppers, finely chopped
2 stalks celery, chopped

Dash Tabasco
2 tbsp. vegetable oil
1 cup water
Salt and pepper to taste
1 bay leaf

- In saucepan, sauté onion and garlic in 1 tbsp. oil until onion is transparent. Add tomato sauce. Simmer 10 minutes.

- In separate saucepan, cook celery and green pepper in remaining 1 tbsp. oil several minutes to soften slightly. Add to tomato mixture.

- Stir in 1 cup water, Tabasco, salt and pepper to taste, and 1 bay leaf.

- Heat, stirring occasionally. Mix 1 tbsp. cornstarch in ¼ cup cold water. Add to tomato mixture, stirring constantly, until thickened.

- Warm tortillas in 350° oven. Pour half sauce over top, sprinkle with shredded Monterey Jack cheese. Return to oven until cheese melts.

- To serve: Spoon sour cream, then avocado, black olives over each tortilla. Add more sauce if desired.

SPECIAL NOTE: USE SOFT FLOUR TORTILLAS FROM DAIRY CASE. USE A FOOD PROCESSOR TO CUT DOWN PREPARATION TIME. GUACAMOLE MAY BE USED FOR GARNISH INSTEAD OF AVOCADO SLICES.

Serves 6   *Sally McCauley*

SHRIMP CREOLE CASSEROLE

1 medium onion, chopped	Dash Tabasco
1 bell pepper, diced	2 cups wild rice (cooked)
1 bay leaf	2 cans stewed tomatoes
1 tbsp. lemon juice	3 lbs. (about 100 medium)
¼ cup margarine	shrimp, deveined
1 tsp. garlic powder	2 cups grated sharp cheddar
1 tsp. dry mustard	cheese
½ tsp. white pepper	

- Saute onion, bell pepper, bay leaf and lemon juice in margarine. Add garlic powder, dry mustard, white pepper and Tabasco.

- Stir mixture into stewed tomatoes.

- Add cooked rice (or rice may be cooked in stewed tomatoes with 1 cup water added.)

- Spoon in shrimp.

- Refrigerate mixture overnight, if desired.

- Bring to room temperature. Layer mixture with grated cheese in 3 qt casserole.

- Bake in 400° oven for 30 minutes.

SPECIAL NOTES: WILD RICE MAKES THIS RECIPE SPECIAL FOR COMPANY. SUBSTITUTE TOMATO SOUP OR TOMATO SAUCE FOR STEWED TOMATOES, IF NECESSARY.

Serves 8-10   *Mrs Royce (Bootie) Wood*

SAVORY SHRIMP CREOLE

1 medium onion, chopped	1 tbsp. Worcestershire sauce
½ cup green pepper, chopped	1 tbsp. sherry wine
½ cup celery, chopped	1 cup sharp cheddar cheese
1 tbsp. butter	1 small bottle stuffed olives
¾ cup water	1 tsp. sugar
1 small can tomato paste	Salt and pepper to taste
1 small can tomato sauce	2 lbs. shrimp, cooked, peeled
1 16 oz can tomatoes	and deveined

- Saute onions, green pepper and celery until softened. Add tomato paste, tomato sauce, can tomatoes, Worcestershire sauce and water and wine.

- Simmer together about 20 minutes.

- Add seasonings and grated sharp cheese. Add olives that have been sliced in half, and lastly, add the already cooked shrimp. Serve over hot rice.

SPECIAL NOTE: SOMETIMES I SPICE THIS RECIPE UP BY ADDING A DASH OF HOT SAUCE OR CREOLE SEASONING.

Serves 8   *Jane F. Ledbetter (Mrs. W.S., Jr.)*

SHRIMP FRIED NOODLES

1 16 oz pkg. spaghetti
1 lb. large shrimp, peeled and
   deveined
1 medium sized head bok choy,
   cut crosswise into 2-inch
   pieces
4 large green onions, cut into
   1-inch pieces
2 medium red peppers, cut
   into ¼-inch strips
2 tbsp. cornstarch

3 tbsp. soy sauce
1½ tsp. sugar
Salad oil
Salt
1 15 oz can straw mushrooms
   or two 7 oz cans whole
   mushrooms drained
¼ tsp. ground ginger
¼ tsp. crushed red pepper
2 tbsp. dry sherry

- Prepare spaghetti as label directs, drain well and cool while preparing shrimp and vegetables.
- In small bowl mix cornstarch, soy sauce, sugar and 1½ cups water.
- In nonstick 12-inch skillet over medium heat, in 1 tbsp. hot oil, arrange cooked spaghetti to form a 12-inch round "pancake". Cook 5-10 minutes until golden on bottom. Carefully invert onto platter.
- Heat 1 tbsp. oil in skillet. Slide "pancake" into skillet, cook 5-10 minutes until golden. Remove to warm platter.
- Heat 1 tbsp. oil and cook bok choy, green onions and ½ tsp. salt, stirring constantly, until vegetables are crisp-tender; remove to bowl.
- Heat 1 tbsp. oil, cook peppers until crisp-tender. Add bok choy mixture and mushrooms to peppers in skillet; add cornstarch mixture.
- Cook until mixture thickens and coats vegetables. Spoon vegetable mixture onto noodle pancake.
- Heat 1 tbsp. oil, stir-fry shrimp, ginger, crushed red pepper and ¼ tsp. salt until shrimp turn pink.
- Add sherry, stirring constantly. Spoon shrimp mixture over vegetables.

Cooking time: 30 minutes

Serves 6

Becky Rowell

HAR CHOW FON
(FRIED RICE WITH SHRIMP)

4	cups cooked rice	1	lb. shrimp shelled, cleaned
4	tbsp. salad oil		and coarsely chopped
3	eggs	3	onions chopped
1	tsp. salt	¼	lb. mushrooms
½	tsp. pepper	3	tbsp. soy sauce
		1	tsp. sugar

- Heat oil in heavy skillet. Beat eggs and cook quickly until firm. Cut them into thin shreds and remove.

- Return pan to heat and add onions, shrimp, mushrooms, salt and pepper. Cook on low heat about 5 minutes stirring often.

- Add rice, soy sauce and sugar, cook on medium heat stirring constantly.

- Serve on platter and pile egg shreds over the top.

SPECIAL NOTE: THIS IS A FRIEND'S RECIPE, SHE LIVED IN THAILAND FOR SEVERAL YEARS.

Cooking time: 10 minutes

Serves 6   *Jeanette Bessels*

SHRIMP LOUISIANA

1½	cups large shrimp cut in thirds	½	tsp. salt
2	cups cooked rice (¾ cup raw)	4	tbsp. catsup
2	cups Half and Half	1	tsp. Worcestershire sauce
3	tbsp. butter or oleo	½	tsp. Tabasco
1	tbsp. grated onion	½	cup buttered bread crumbs

- Add seasonings and butter to cooked HOT rice.

- Gradually add 1½ cups of the cream.

- Pour into 1½ qt baking dish (8 x 12 x 2-inch).

- Let stand in warm place for several hours, then add shrimp and rest of cream.

- Put buttered crumbs on top.

- Bake at 325° for about 40 minutes until hot and slightly browned on top.

SPECIAL NOTE: BE SURE TO HAVE HOT RICE WHEN ADDING CREAM OR IT WON'T BE ABSORBED PROPERLY. AN OFTEN REQUESTED RECIPE—SO SIMPLE AND TASTY!

Cooking time: 40 minutes

Serves 8   *Peggy Manley*

SHRIMP MOUSSE

¾ lb. cooked shrimp
½ cup celery
3 tbsp. chopped pimiento
⅓ cup chili sauce
⅓ cup lemon juice
8 oz sour cream
8 oz pkg. softened cream cheese
½ tsp. salt
½ cup mayonnaise
½ tsp. lemon seasoning
½ tsp. pepper
½ tsp. liquid hot pepper sauce
1 tbsp. Worcestershire sauce
1 tbsp. instant minced onion
1 tbsp. instant minced green pepper
1½ envelopes unflavored gelatin
3 tbsp. cold water

- Place all ingredients in blender except gelatin and blend well. It may be necessary to stop blender occasionally to stir ingredients so mixture will blend.
- Soften gelatin in cold water for five minutes. Dissolve over hot water.
- Add gelatin to blender mixture slowly.
- Place in oiled mold. Chill until firm.

Mrs. Katherine K. Perry

SHRIMP MOUSSE MOLD

1½ lbs. cooked, peeled, deveined shrimp fresh or frozen (about 1½ cups finely chopped shrimp)
1 can (10¾ ozs) condensed tomato soup
1 pkg. (8 oz) cream cheese
2 tbsp. unflavored gelatin
1 cup mayonnaise or salad dressing
¾ cup finely chopped celery
½ cup finely chopped green onion
¼ cup finely chopped green pepper
1 tsp. Worcestershire sauce
1 tsp. lemon juice

- Thaw shrimp if frozen and chop.
- Heat tomato soup and cream cheese in the top of double boiler until cream cheese melts. Cool slightly.
- Stir in gelatin, mix well.
- Add shrimp, mayonnaise, celery, green onion, green pepper, Worcestershire sauce, and lemon juice. Mix well.
- Pour into a well-greased 1½ qt mold (fish mold if you have one).
- Cover and refrigerate at least 8 hours. Serve with crackers. Makes about 5½ cups.

SPECIAL NOTE: IF CONDENSED TOMATO SOUP AND CREAM CHEESE ARE LUMPY, BEAT WITH MIXER UNTIL SMOOTH; THEN ADD GELATIN AND CONTINUE WITH THE RECIPE.

Jeannie Wade

SHRIMP PIERRE

1 lb. large shrimp, shelled and deveined
2 cloves garlic, minced
1 medium onion, finely chopped
¼ cup fresh parsley, chopped

1 tsp. dried basil
1 teaspoon dry mustard
1 tsp. seasoned salt
½ cup olive oil
Juice of 1 lemon or lime

- Combine all ingredients, except shrimp and mix well. Add shrimp and let marinate in the refrigerator for 3-4 hours.
- Thread shrimp onto skewers. Grill over charcoal or in a preheated broiler for 4-6 minutes until the shrimp are just cooked through, turning once.

Serves 2-4   *Becky Rowell*

BLACK IRON POT SHRIMP STEW

1 cup flour
½ cup salad oil
½ cup olive oil
3 large yellow onions, chopped
1 bunch green onions, chopped
2 green peppers, chopped
½ cup Worcestershire sauce
Dash Tabasco
1 8 oz can tomato sauce
1 10¾ oz can condensed cream of mushroom soup
1 10 oz can tomatoes with chilies

Salt and pepper
Dash oregano
Dash thyme
2 8 oz cans sliced mushrooms or ½ lb. fresh mushrooms
4 ribs celery, chopped
1 lb. smoked sausage, sliced and par boiled
6 bay leaves
¾ cup sauterne
5 lbs. raw shrimp, shelled and deveined
½ cup fresh parsley, minced

- Make a rich brown roux by stirring flour and oil in iron pot, cook over low heat. Do not let it burn!
- Add onions and peppers to roux, and cook over very low heat for 45 minutes.
- Add remaining ingredients except shrimp and parsley. Cover and simmer about 1 hour, stirring occasionally. Add shrimp, cover and cook 30 minutes. Keep low heat constant, and stir frequently.
- Before serving, add parsley. Serve over buttered and fried rice.

SPECIAL NOTE: THIS IS AN ALL-TIME FAVORITE IN OUR FAMILY—SPICY AND DIVINE! IT'S WELL WORTH THE EFFORT.

Cooking time: 3 hours

Serves 10   *Judi E. Morgan*

SHRIMP AND WILD RICE

½ cup thinly sliced onion
¼ cup thinly sliced green
    pepper
½ cup mushrooms sliced thin
¼ cup butter
1 tbsp. Worcestershire sauce

Dash Tabasco
2 cups cooked wild rice
1 lb. cooked shrimp
2 cups thin cream sauce (use
    chicken broth in place of
    milk)

- Saute the onion, green pepper and mushrooms in butter until soft.
- Add seasonings, rice, shrimp and cream sauce.
- Place in buttered casserole and bake at 350° until thoroughly heated approximately 30 minutes.

SPECIAL NOTE: IF USING UNCLE BEN'S WILD RICE USE ONLY 2 CUPS WATER.

Serves 6   *Jane Roebuck*

SPANISH OLIVE ZARZUELA

¼ cup olive oil or salad oil
1 medium onion, chopped
½ cup slivered blanched
    almonds, toasted
½ cup dry white wine
3 garlic cloves
3 parsley sprigs
⅓ cup pimiento-stuffed olives
1 16 oz. can whole tomatoes
    with liquid

1 lb. fresh or frozen king crab
    legs, cut into chunks or 1
    pkg. (6 oz.) frozen crabmeat
½ lb. fresh or frozen shelled
    deveined shrimp
½ lb. fresh or frozen scallops
1 lb. fresh or frozen cod
    fillets, cut in chunks
1 cup pimiento-stuffed olives,
    halved
1 tsp. salt and ¼ tsp. pepper

- Heat olive oil in 5 qt. Dutch oven. Sauté onions until tender (about 3-5 minutes.
- In blender, blend almonds, white wine, garlic, parsley and ⅓ cup stuffed olives until smooth.
- Add puréed olive mixture and undrained tomatoes to onions and heat to boiling. Cook 1 minute, stirring constantly.
- Add clams and crab and return to boil. Reduce heat, cover and cook 5 minutes, stirring occasionally.
- Add shrimp, scallops, cod fillets, 1 cup olives, salt and pepper. Cover and cook 5 minutes more, stirring occasionally, until cod flakes easily when tested with fork. Serve in soup bowls.

SPECIAL NOTE: OLD SPANISH STEW PROVIDED TO US BY A BELGIAN SEA CAPTAIN.

Serves 6-8   *Sally McCauley*

SHRIMP BOAT STEW

1 lb. shelled and deveined shrimp	1 large can chopped tomatoes
4 medium potatoes, diced	1 clove garlic minced fine
1 large onion	Salt and pepper

- Cook tomatoes, onion, salt, pepper and garlic on low heat about 30 minutes.
- Then add diced potatoes and allow to cook until tender.
- When all is thick, put in the shrimp and cook only until the shrimp is pink. If not thick enough, add 1 tsp. instant potato flakes.
- Serve with fried corn bread and fresh fruit.

SPECIAL NOTE: THIS IS POPULAR ABOARD THE SHRIMP BOATS THAT FISH IN THE ST. SIMONS SOUND.

Cooking time: 1 hour

Serves 4   *Charlotte Parker Harris (Mrs. Walter D.)*

BAKED GROUPER PIQUANT

¾ lb. grouper fillets	1 tbsp. Dijon mustard
Juice of ½ lemon	Coarse, dry bread crumbs
1 tsp. olive oil	Melted butter or margarine

- Preheat the oven to 400°. Place the fillets in a flat, lightly greased baking pan.
- Sprinkle the fish with lemon juice and rub on olive oil. Spread mustard evenly over fish.
- Sprinkle the bread crumbs over the fish, then drizzle lightly with melted butter. Do not moisten heavily.
- Add a little water to the pan.
- Bake 12-18 minutes, depending on the thickness of the fish.

SPECIAL NOTE: EVEN GOOD WITHOUT THE MELTED BUTTER.

Serves 2   *Becky Rowell*

BAKED GROUPER SPANISH STYLE

¾ lb. grouper or snapper
1 medium onion, thinly sliced and punched into rings
1 green pepper, sliced in ¼-inch rounds

¾ cup orange juice
6 cloves garlic, minced
1 16 oz. can tomatoes, crushed
Salt, pepper and paprika

- Preheat oven to 350°. Arrange fish in a lightly greased pan.
- Place onion rings, pepper rings and tomatoes on top of fish.
- Mix garlic and orange juice together and pour over fish. Season with salt and pepper. Sprinkle with paprika.
- Bake 20-30 minutes or until fish is just done.

SPECIAL NOTE: VERY LOW IN FAT.

Serves 2   *Becky Rowell*

BLACKENED REDFISH

3 lbs. redfish, fileted
Melted butter or margarine
1 tbsp. paprika
2½ tsp. salt
1 tsp. onion powder
1 tsp. red pepper

1 tsp. garlic powder
¾ tsp. white pepper
¾ tsp. black pepper
½ tsp. dry thyme
½ tsp. oregano

- Dip fish in melted butter or margarine and then in mixture of seasonings.
- Cook in cast iron skillet, preheated until pan is very hot.
- Cook 2 minutes on one side, turn, and cook for another minute.

SPECIAL NOTE: THIS DISH IS VERY SMOKY TO PREPARE; IT COOKS WELL OUTSIDE ON A GRILL OR CAMP STOVE.

Barbara Bush (Mrs. George Bush)

DEVILED FISH FILLETS

3 cups soft bread crumbs
1½ tbsp. parmesan cheese
½ tsp. salt
½ cup melted butter or oleo, divided

1½ tbsp. Worcestershire sauce
½ tsp. prepared mustard
2 lbs. white fish fillets, (grouper, flounder, etc.)

- Preheat oven to 325°. In a medium bowl, mix bread crumbs, parmesan cheese, salt, half of the melted butter and the Worcestershire sauce and mustard.
- Place fish fillets in a single layer in a greased shallow pan. Spoon bread crumb mixture evenly over fillets.
- Dribble remaining butter over bread crumbs. Add water to barely cover the bottom of the pan (about ½ cup).
- cover with greased foil. Bake until fish flakes when tested with a fork, about 15 minutes.
- Remove cover and lightly brown under hot broiler.

COOKING TIME: 15-20 MINUTES

Serves 4-6   *Davi Langston*

SALMON CROQUETTES

1 6 oz. can salmon
1 tbsp. chopped onion
1 egg
1 tbsp. bread crumbs

1 tsp. instant potato flakes
Dash paprika
Enough oil to fry crisp

- Fork salmon and add onion, crumbs, egg, salt and pepper.
- Mix together until a small ball is formed.
- Press into patties and fry in oil until brown on both sides.
- Drain on paper towels and serve with lemon sauce or tartar sauce.

COOKING TIME: 10 MINUTES

Serves 2   *Charlotte Parker Harris (Mrs. Walter D.)*

SALMON ON A BED OF LEEKS

1	bunch leeks (3 to 4)		Salt and white pepper to taste
2	tsp. margarine	2	tbsp. grated gruyere cheese
½	cup dry white wine		(optional)
2	8 oz. salmon steaks or fillets		

- Trim green tops and root ends from leeks, slit vertically into quarters. Separate sections and wash under running cold water. Drain well.

- Melt butter in a 10-inch saute pan over medium heat. Add leeks and cook 2-3 minutes, stirring often, until leeks are wilted.

- Stir in wine, arrange salmon on leeks, sprinkle with salt and white pepper.

- Reduce heat to low, cover and cook 5 minutes.

- Sprinkle cheese over salmon, cover and cook another 3-5 minutes or until salmon is opaque around edges and firm and cheese is melted.

- Transfer fish and leeks to a warm dinner plate and serve immediately.

COOKING TIME: 15 MINUTES

Serves 2   *Becky Rowell*

K.C.'S JELLIED
SALMON MOUSSE

1	cup cottage cheese	4	envelopes gelatin, unflavored
½	cup mayonnaise	1-2	tbsp. hot sauce
3	oz. cream cheese	1-2	tbsp. lemon juice
15	oz. can salmon	3	tbsp. chopped dill

- In a blender, blend cottage cheese, mayonnaise and cream cheese. If too thick, add juice from salmon.

- Add salmon, gelatin, hot sauce and lemon juice. If too thick add a little milk.

- Add 3 tbsp. chopped dill.

- Refrigerate until ready to serve.

Serves 6-8   *Martha Russell*

SALMON LOAF

1	lb. can red salmon (2 cups)	1	tsp. lemon juice
1	cup bread crumbs	4	tbsp. melted butter
1	cup milk	½	tsp. salt
2	eggs, well beaten	¼	tsp. pepper
2	tbsp. chopped onions		
¼	cup sliced stuffed olives		

- Mix thoroughly all ingredients.
- Pour into 1½ qt. loaf pan. Bake 1 hour in 350° oven.

SPECIAL NOTE: I DIVIDE THIS RECIPE INTO TWO PANS AND FREEZE ONE.

Ann Jarrett

BAKED SEAFOOD SALAD

1	small green pepper, chopped	1	cup mayonnaise
1	small onion chopped	½	tsp. salt
1	cup celery, chopped		Pepper to taste
1	lb. crabmeat		Seafood seasoning
1	lb. raw shrimp, peeled and deveined	1	tsp. Worcestershire sauce
		1	cup buttered bread crumbs

- Cook and clean shrimp.
- Mix all ingredients except bread crumbs and put in casserole.
- Sprinkle buttered bread crumbs on top.
- Grated cheese may also be added to crumb topping.
- Bake 30 minutes at 350°.

SPECIAL NOTE: THIS DISH IS FROM JR. LEAGUE OF SAVANNAH COOKBOOK.

Serves 6   *Judy Kelly*

SEAFOOD RICE SALAD

4	cups cooked, cooled rice	¼	cup olive oil
2	cups coarsely cubed cooked shrimp or crab	2	tbsp. tarragon vinegar
3	tbsp. chopped shallot	1	tsp. salt
3	tbsp. chopped parsley	¼	tsp. pepper
1	tsp. dry tarragon or 2 tbsp. fresh		

Salad greens and additional seafood for garnish

- Combine rice, shallot, cubed seafood, parsley and tarragon.
- Mix oil, vinegar, salt, pepper.
- Toss the rice mixture with dressing.
- Chill well before serving. Garnish with greens and seafood.

SPECIAL NOTE: WE LIKE A LITTLE MORE VINEGAR.

Serves 6 (or 4 hungry people)   *Virginia Petretti*

SEAFOOD QUICHE

½	cup crabmeat	½	cup Half and Half cream
½	cup shrimp pieces	½	cup sour cream
½	cup lobster pieces (if not using lobster, double the amount of shrimp)		Dash of hot sauce
			Salt (optional) to taste
			Dash of pepper
1	tbsp. butter or margarine	1	9-inch pie shell
1	tsp. paprika	1	cup shredded mozzarella cheese
2	tbsp. sherry (optional)		
2	eggs, beaten		

- Bake pie shell 5 minutes at 400°. Then let cool.
- Saute crab, shrimp and lobster in butter until hot and lightly browned.
- Add next 8 ingredients except for cheese.
- Pour into cooked pie shell.
- Top with shredded cheese.
- Bake in a 400° oven for 40 minutes or until a knife inserted in the middle comes out clean.

Serves 6-8   *Jeannie Wade*

SWORDFISH WITH BLACK OLIVE AND TOMATO TOPPING

1	tbsp. olive oil	¼	cup black olives, chopped
2	tbsp. minced onion		Dash red pepper flakes
1	tsp. minced garlic	4	swordfish steaks, 4 oz. each
2	tbsp. dry white wine	1	tbsp. lemon juice
2	medium tomatoes, peeled, seeded and chopped		

- Sauce: Put olive oil, onion and garlic in 4 cup microwavable container. Microwave on high (100% power), uncovered, 1-2 minutes to soften.
- Stir in wine, tomatoes, olives and pepper. Microwave on high, uncovered, 4-5 minutes to thicken, stirring twice. Keep sauce warm.
- Arrange swordfish on a plate with thickest part to the outside. Drizzle with lemon juice. Cover with plastic wrap, vented at one corner.
- Microwave on high 3-4 minutes until thickest portion is almost opaque.
- Let stand 5 minutes to finish cooking. Drain
- Top with olive and tomato sauce.

SPECIAL NOTE: THE SAUCE IS ALSO GOOD ON GRILLED SWORDFISH.

Serves 4   *Becky Rowell*

SEAFOOD CHOWDER

1	tsp. minced garlic	1	can Harris she-crab soup
1½	lb. shrimp peeled and deveined	1	can fancy whole baby clams, undrained
1	stick butter		White pepper to taste
2	cans Campbells chunky Manhattan clam chowder		

- Saute garlic in butter. Add shrimp and cook until pink (about 8 minutes).
- Add other ingredients.
- Can add sherry or wine to taste.
- Do not boil.

SPECIAL NOTE: SO EASY AND HEARTY!

Serves 8   *Brooke Sumerford*

THE RESURRECTION

Mary Magdalene, Mary, the mother of
Jesus, and the girl Salome arrived at the
tomb early on Easter morning bearing
coffers of sweet spices with which to
anoint the body of Jesus. The women
found the stone rolled away and a young
man, interpreted here by the artist as an
angel, seated on the right side.
They were amazed when he told them
Jesus "...has risen, he is not here."
(Mark 16: 1-8)

The window is dedicated "In memory
of Ellen Ada Phelps Dodge. Born Feb.
28, 1862. Died Nov. 29, 1883. R.I.P."

THE NATIVITY

The window shows the infant Jesus with
Mary and Joseph. Nearby, three angels
celebrate the birth with music. "Glory to
God in the Highest and on Earth
Peace." (Luke 2: 1-7)

The window is "Sacred to the memory
of Thomas Butler King, born 1800,
died 1864; and of Anna Matilda Page,
his wife. In memory of Major
William Page, born 1764, died 1827
and Hanna Timmonds, his wife,
Born 1760; died 1826."

LAMB CURRY

4½ cups cooked lamb, cubed
1 cup chopped onions
4 tbsp. butter or oil
1½ tsp.curry powder (or to taste)
1¼ cup lamb left over gravy

Salt to taste
2¼ cups chopped celery
1 tbsp. flour
½ cup hot water

- Saute onions and celery in fat in heavy fry pan. Stir in flour. Add lamb, curry, gravy, water and salt.
- Cover, simmer over low heat for 15 minutes.

Serves 8   *Nancy Krauss*

LAMB WITH GARLIC AND OLIVES

3½ lbs. lamb, cubed
1 cup pitted black olives, halved
2 garlic cloves coarsely cut or more
⅔ cup tomato puree
1 cup chopped parsley
1 large onion chopped

1 tsp. dry basil
½ cup chopped celery
½ tsp. dry oregano
½ cup fresh dill chopped or 1 tsp. dill weed dried
1 tsp. salt
½ tsp sugar

- Mix all ingredients together in heavy casserole reserving half of parsley for sprinkling over later.
- Cover casserole and bake 350° for 1 hour.
- Reduce heat to 300° continue cooking 30-45 minutes longer until meat is tender.
- Skim off any fat if necessary.

SPECIAL NOTE: THIS DISH IS VERY GOOD WITH A RICE OR LENTIL PILAF MIX. A NOTE ON THE LAMB: HAVE THE BUTCHER REMOVE THE BONE FROM THE LEG OF LAMB. USE 3½ LBS. FOR THIS RECIPE AND FREEZE THE REMAINDER FOR A LATER DISH. I CUBE THE LAMB IN ABOUT 1-INCH PIECES.

Serves 6   *Lotta M. Hunt*

BRAISED LAMB SHANKS

6 lamb shanks
flour for dredging
salt and freshly ground pepper
   to taste
½ tsp. oregano
⅓ cup salad oil
¾ cup chopped onion

¾ cup chopped celery
¾ cup chopped carrots
1 clove garlic, minced
Pinch thyme
¾ cup dry red wine
¾ cup beef bouillon

- Preheat oven to moderate temperature (350°).
- Wipe lamb shanks with damp cloth.
- Combine flour, salt, pepper and oregano and dredge shanks in mixture.
- Brown in the oil and transfer to an earthen ware casserole or Dutch oven.
- Add the vegetables, garlic and thyme to the skillet and cook 5 minutes, stirring.
- Pour the vegetables over the lamb and add the liquids.
- Cover and bake in 350° oven 1½ hours until meat is tender.
- Thicken the gravy with a little water and flour.

SPECIAL NOTE: THE SAME AMOUNT OF INGREDIENTS MAY BE USED WITH JUST 2 LAMB SHANKS. INEXPENSIVE DISH.

Serves 6   *Sally McCauley*

LAMB SHANKS

4 lamb shanks
Marinade:
1 tsp. curry powder
¼ tsp. ground ginger
1 tsp. grated lemon peel

1 tsp. salt
½ tsp. oregano
2 cloves garlic, minced
1 cup orange juice
1 cup dry white wine

- Mix together all the marinade ingredients.
- Brown shanks in 1 tbsp. olive oil (or salad oil).
- Pour marinade over shanks.
- Bake covered for at least 2 hours in 350° oven.
- Turn shanks part way through so all are well marinated.

SPECIAL NOTE: I ALWAYS COOK THE SHANKS UNTIL MEAT LITERALLY FALLS OFF THE BONE—CAN BE HELD IN LOW HEAT UNTIL READY TO SERVE.

Ruth Stewart

LAMB SHANKS AND NOODLES

6 lamb shanks
6 garlic cloves, halved
12 ozs. noodles cooked

Liberal sprinkling of
crushed rosemary
Salt and pepper to taste

- In either end of shank, place garlic next to bone.
- Sprinkle with rosemary (liberally), salt and pepper.
- Bake at 350° 1½ hours, or until meat draws up on bone.
- Take out of oven to cool.
- Make gravy using drippings from cooked meat.
- Cut bite size meat from bone—add all to cooked noodles.

Serves 8-10   *Darleen (Mrs. C.P. MacDonald, Jr.)*

LAMB STEW

2 onions coarsely chopped
3 tbsp. oil
2½- 3 lbs. boneless lamb
   shoulder, cut in 2-inch pieces
½ cup red wine
4 large tomatoes, seeded,
   peeled and chopped
2 cloves garlic
1 bay leaf
1½ tbsp. fresh rosemary
   (or 2 tsp. dried)

Zest from 1 orange
½ cup water
6 new potatoes, parboiled and
   halved
2 cups pearl onions, parboiled
   and skinned
½ cup orange liqueur
Juice of 1 orange
1 orange sliced

- In a sauté pan, cook coarsely chopped onions in oil until translucent. Transfer to a 3 qt. casserole.
- In the remaining oil, brown the lamb; do not crowd pan. Transfer the meat to the casserole.
- Deglaze the saute pan with ¼ cup red wine, then add liquid to meat.
- Add tomatoes, garlic, bay leaf, rosemary, orange zest, remaining red wine, water.
- Bake covered in a 350° oven 1-1½ hours, until lamb is tender.
- Add potatoes, pearl onions, orange liqueur and juice.
- Heat 15 minutes—be sure all vegetables are heated through.
- Garnish with orange slices.

Jeanne Wade

MOUSSAKA (GREEK)

3 medium size eggplants
1 qt. milk
3 large onions chopped
2 lbs. ground lamb or beef
3 tbsp. tomato paste
½ cup red wine
1 cup chopped parsley
1 cup fine bread crumbs
Freshly ground black pepper
   to taste

6 tbsp. flour
1 cup butter
4 eggs, beaten until frothy
Nutmeg (a dash)
2 cups ricotta cheese or cottage
   cheese
¼ tsp. cinnamon
Salt to taste
1 cup freshly grated
   Parmesan cheese

- Peel eggplant, cut in slices about ½-inch thick.
- Brown the slices in 4 tbsp. butter. Set aside.
- Heat 4 tbsp. of butter in the same skillet and brown the onions.
- Add the ground meat and cook breaking up the meat about 10 minutes.
- Combine the tomato paste with the wine, parsley, cinnamon, salt and pepper.
- Stir this mixture into the meat and simmer over low heat, stirring frequently, until all liquid has been absorbed. Remove from heat.
- Preheat oven to moderate 375°.
- Make white sauce by melting 8 tbsp. butter, blending in the flour, stirring with wire wisk.
- Bring milk to boil and add gradually to the butter-flour mixture, stirring constantly.
- When the mixture is thickened and smooth, remove it from heat.
- Cool slightly, and stir in the beaten eggs, nutmeg and ricotta cheese.
- Grease an 11-16-inch pan and sprinkle the bottom slightly with bread crumbs.
- Arrange alternate layers of eggplant slices and meat sauce in the pan. Sprinkle each layer with a little parmesan cheese.
- Pour the ricotta cheese sauce over the top.
- Bake in 375° oven 1 hour, or until golden brown. Remove from oven an cool 20 minutes. Cut into squares and serve.

SPECIAL NOTE: THE FLAVOR OF THIS DISH IMPROVES ON STANDING ONE DAY. REHEAT BEFORE SERVING. CAN BE MADE AND FROZEN BEFORE BAKING.

Serves 8-10

Jacqueline Curl

ST. MARTIN OF TOURS

St. Martin of Tours was born in
Hungary during the time of
Constantine. He was converted to
Christianity and ran away to a
monastery. But his father made him
become a soldier. One day when he was
in Amiens, France, he passed a beggar
clad in rags and suffering from the cold
weather. Martin took off his cloak and,
cutting it into two pieces with his sword,
gave half to the beggar. That night Jesus
appeared to Martin in a vision saying,
"What thou has done for that poor
man, thou has done for me."
Martin then resolved to devote his life
to Christianity. He founded
the first monastery in France and
became Bishop of Tours.
The window is dedicated "In loving
Memory of Thomas Butler King, Jr.,
Born 1829, Died 1859.

PORK

ST. GEORGE

Traditionally, St. George represents
the triumph of good over evil. Here
George of Cappadocia, depicted as a
tribune in the Roman Army, slays the
dragon of sin.

The window is dedicated "In loving
memory of Capt. Henry Lord Page
King, C.S.A., born 1831. Killed at
the Battle of Fredericksburg,
December 2, 1862."

ST. JOHN THE APOSTLE

St. John, youngest of Jesus' disciples, is
shown holding his Gospel in one hand
and a chalice in the other. The chalice
has a griffon emerging from it, representing those who persecuted the
Christians and, in this instance, a failed
attempt by Emperor Domitian to take
John's life by poisoning.

The window is dedicated "In loving
memory of Captain Mallery Page King,
C.S.A. Born March 22, 1836. Died
Brunswick, Georgia, June 20, 1899."

EASY SUPPER DISH

4	pieces of toast or waffles	4	deviled eggs
4	slices of boiled or baked ham	1	can cream of cheese soup
8	oz. can asparagus		Bread crumbs

- Depending upon the number to be fed, arrange slices of buttered toast or waffles in the bottom of a casserole dish.
- Cover with ham.
- Place drained spears of canned asparagus over ham.
- Put well seasoned deviled eggs over the asparagus.
- Beat soup until smooth and pour over the dish. Do not dilute the soup.
- Sprinkle with bread crumbs and bake at 350° for about 30 minutes.

Serves 4 *Nancy Krauss*

Ham Smothered in Tomatoes

Center cut ham slice or slices, 1-1½ lbs. about ½-inch thick

1 14½ oz. can seasoned stewed tomatoes, cajun preferably

- Trim ham steak or steaks of all fat.
- Place in an ungreased dish and pour tomatoes over.
- Place in 325° oven and bake uncovered, 1-1½ hours, basting occasionally.

SPECIAL NOTE: MOTHER ALWAYS USED FRESH TOMATOES, SLICED TO COVER THE HAM. THIS WAY IS EASY, EASY, EASY. I HAVE NEVER SEEN THIS RECIPE OR ONE LIKE IT IN ANY COOKBOOK. IT'S WONDERFUL WITH BLACKEYED PEAS!

Serves 3-4   *Davi Langston*

Pork Chop Bake

1 16 oz. jar sweet and sour red cabbage, drained
¼ tsp. caraway seeds
4 rib or loin pork chops

Salt and pepper to taste
1 large cooking apple cut in wedges

- Drain cabbage and spread in a shallow 2 qt. baking dish. Sprinkle with caraway seeds and set aside.
- Trim chops of excess fat. Melt some of the fat in a large skillet, discard fat pieces.
- Add chops and brown on both sides.
- Arrange chops on red cabbage and push down a bit.
- Sprinkle chops with salt and pepper.
- Cover and bake in a preheated 325° oven 30 minutes.
- Remove, add apple wedges, cover and return to oven for 15 minutes.
- Uncover and bake for 5-10 more minutes.

Serves 4   *Cam Caldwell*

PORK STEW

4 lbs. trimmed pork shoulder, 1-inch cubes
2 tbsp. butter
2 tbsp. vegetable oil
2 large onions, sliced
4 cloves garlic, minced
¼ cup flour
½ tsp. salt

1 14½ oz. can chicken broth
1½ cup apple juice
1 cup dark beer
2 tbsp. Dijon mustard
1 tsp. ground coriander
½ tsp. ground cinnamon
1 cup chopped dried apricots
¾ cup chopped pitted prunes

- Melt butter and oil in large pan over medium-high heat.
- Add pork and cook until brown, stirring.
- Transfer to casserole.
- Add onions and garlic to pan and cook until tender, about 10 minutes.
- Add flour and stir 3 minutes.
- Add broth, juice and beer.
- Add mustard and seasonings.
- Stir in apricots and prunes.
- Cover and bake in a 350° oven for 1 hour.
- Remove lid and continue to bake 45 minutes.

SPECIAL NOTE: IT TAKES TIME CHOPPING FRUIT AND CUTTING MEAT. DELICIOUS STEW AND WORTH THE TIME!

Serves 6-8
Jill Cunningham

PORK TENDERLOIN ANITA

1 lb. pork tenderloin, cut into 8 crosswise pieces
2 tbsp. margarine
2 tbsp. lemon juice

2 tbsp. Worcestershire sauce
2 tsp. Dijon-style mustard
Lemon pepper
2 tbsp. minced parsley

- Place each piece of tenderloin between 2 pieces of plastic wrap. Flatten gently with heel of hand.
- Sprinkle medallions with lemon pepper.
- Heat margarine in skillet; cook medallions 3-4 minutes on each side.
- Remove to serving platter and keep warm.
- Add lemon juice, Worcestershire sauce and mustard to skillet.
- Cook, stirring with pan juices until heated through.
- Pour sauce over meat and sprinkle with parsley to serve.

Anita Campbell

PREPARING VIRGINIA CURED HAM

1 whole ham (Smithfield type)
   about 16 lbs.

Glaze:
1   cup brown sugar
4   tbsp. prepared mustard
2   tbsp. flour
whole cloves

- Cover ham with cold water. Soak for 24 hours.
- Scrub ham. Rinse with fresh water and place on rack in large covered roaster.
- Add 7 cups cold water. Cover tightly. Place in preheated oven 500° and cook 15 minutes.
- Cut off oven for 3 hours (*Important—do not open oven for entire cooking time*).
- Heat again at 500° for 15 minutes. Turn off heat. Ham must remain in oven for 3 more hours and then it will be done.
- When cool enough to handle, skin ham, score in diamond pattern, insert a whole clove in each diamond and glaze.
- Bake at 350° 20-30 minutes, watching carefully that glaze does not burn.
- Prepare the day before serving. Do not refrigerate, slice very thin and serve with biscuits or rolls.

SPECIAL NOTE: NEVER BECOMES DRY WITH THIS METHOD.

Virginia Petretti

A KITCHEN PRAYER

Lord of all pots and pans and things,
Since I've not time to be a saint by doing lovely things
Or watching late with thee or dreaming in the dawn light,
Or storming heaven's gates,
Make me a saint by getting meals and
Washing up the plates.

Warm all the kitchen with thy love,
And light it with thy peace
Forgive me all my worrying and make my grumbling cease.
Thou who didst love to give men food,
In room or by the sea, accept this service that I do,
I do it unto Thee.

WOMAN, WHY WEEPEST THOU?

The risen Jesus appears before the kneel-
ing Mary Magdalene, the wounds on
His hands and feet clearly visible. When
He speaks to her, she recognizes Him,
and with reverent wonder calls Him
Master. (John 20: 11-16)

The window is dedicated "In memory
of Horace B. Gould. Many years
Vestryman and Warden of this Parish.
Born 12 August 1812. Died 7 April
1881; and in memory of Wilson
Campbell. Born July 6, 1837.
Died Dec. 6, 1868."

BEEF, VEAL

HER CHILDREN
CALL HER

ARISE UP, AND
BLESSED.

HER CHILDREN ARISE UP
AND CALL HER BLESSED

This window, attributed to Tiffany,
depicts the good wife providing
for her household and receiving the
loving praise of her family.
(Proverbs 31: 10-31)

The window is dedicated "A.M.D.G.
and in loving memory of Deborah
Abbot Gould. January 31, 1829-
September 26, 1906. From her children,
grandchildren and great grandchildren."

BEEF BURGUNDY I

4	lbs. boneless chuck (cut into bite size pieces)	1½	cups red wine
1	large pkg. fresh mushrooms	2	cans mushroom soup
2	envelopes onion soup mix	1	lb. carrots, chopped

- Mix the first 5 ingredients together. Place in Dutch oven.
- Cover and bake at 300° degrees for 3 hours.
- Add carrots.
- Bake one more hour (total cooking time 4 hours.)
- Serve over rice.

Serves 8   *Alice A. Smith*

BEEF BURGUNDY II

2	lbs. stew beef (trim fat, cut into bite sized pieces)	1	soup can of Burgundy or other red wine
1	can golden mushroom soup	1	can small onions
1	can cream of mushroom soup	1	pkg. washed mushrooms

- Mix all ingredients in a Dutch oven.
- Cover and bake in 300° oven 4 hours.
- Uncover and bake an additional hour.

SPECIAL NOTE: THIS MAKES A WONDERFUL COMPANY MEAL WITH PLAIN OLD STEW BEEF.

Serves 8-10   *Angie Burns*

Bless this food
And make us good
For Jesus' sake.
Amen

BEEF STROGANOFF

1	lb. chopped chuck roast	1	tsp. Worcestershire sauce
1	lb. ground round	¼	tsp. pepper
3	tbsp. cooking oil	½	tsp. salt
2	tbsp. flour	¾	cup chopped onions
1	cup stock or beef bouillon	2	tbsp. tomato paste or catsup
1	large can sliced mushrooms	1	cup sour cream

- Brown onions in cooking oil . Stir in flour. Gradually add stock or bouillon. Cook till smooth.
- Add tomato paste or catsup, Worcestershire sauce, salt and pepper. Simmer 10 minutes.
- Pan brown meat an add it to thickened sauce.
- Pan brown mushrooms and add to meat mixture;.
- Add 1 cup sour cream just before serving. Do not allow to boil after adding cream.
- Serve with rice.

Mary Jane Flint

BEEF TIPS AND NOODLES

4	lbs. boneless sirloin, cut into ½-inch cubes	1	large onion, chopped
½	cup all-purpose flour	½	cup chopped green pepper
½	cup vegetable oil	2	tsp. ground cumin
2	cloves garlic, minced	½	tsp. salt
1	28 oz can tomatoes, undrained and chopped	½	tsp. pepper
			Hot cooked noodles

- Dredge beef in flour, brown in hot oil in large dutch oven, stirring occasionally.
- Add remaining ingredients except noodles; cover and bring to a boil.
- Reduce heat, and simmer 1 hour or until meat is tender.
- Serve over noodles or rice

SPECIAL NOTE: MAKE A DAY IN ADVANCE EXCEPT NOODLES. REFRIGERATE AND WHEN COLD, REMOVE ALL FAT FROM TOP OF BEEF AND VEGETABLES. NEXT DAY, REHEAT, COOK NOODLES, AND SERVE.

Yield 12 servings   *Jeannie Wade*

BEEF ORIENTAL

2	onions, chopped	1	cup water
1	cup celery, chopped	¼	tsp. pepper
½	cup uncooked rice	¼	cup soy sauce
1	lb. ground beef	1	can bean sprouts
1	can mushrooms		Chinese noodles
1	can mushroom soup		

- Brown celery and onions, remove.
- Brown rice and ground beef.
- Combine soup, water, soy sauce, pepper and mushrooms. Mix with other ingredients.
- Lightly stir in bean sprouts.
- Bake covered in a 350° oven for 30 minutes.
- Uncover and bake 30 minutes more. Serve with crisp Chinese noodles.

Serves 6-8   *Kathy Palmer*

BRAZILIAN BEEF AND BLACK BEANS

1	lb. beef round steak, cut into small chunks	1	sprig parsley, chopped
½	lb. lean ground beef, broken up	2	tsp. salt
½	lb. smoked beef sausage, sliced	1	tsp. pepper
2	cups black beans	¼	tsp. garlic salt
	Water		Salsa dressing
1	red onion, chopped		Green pepper rings
1	tomato, chopped		Diced tomato
1	green pepper, chopped		Hot cooked rice

- Sort and rinse beans; soak overnight in 2 qts. water. Drain
- Place beans in Dutch oven with 4 cups water. Bring to a boil, reduce heat and simmer uncovered 30 minutes. (You may need to add water so beans do not get dry.)
- Add round steak, ground beef and sausage. Return to a boil, reduce heat and simmer 30 minutes
- Add red onions, tomato, green pepper, parsley, salt, pepper and garlic salt, stirring to combine. Continue cooking 30 minutes or until beef and beans are tender.
- Serve over rice; garnish with pepper rings and diced tomato.
- Pass salsa dressing.

Serves 6-8   *Jeannie Wade*

"THE" CASSEROLE

1½ lb. ground chuck
1 medium onion
1 clove garlic
1 2 lb. can tomatoes
1 12 oz. can tomato paste

¼ tsp. oregano
1 16 oz. pkg. shell macaroni
1 16 oz. pkg. sliced
American cheese
Salt and pepper to taste

- Brown meat together with onion, and garlic, in heavy pan. Drain any fat.
- Add tomatoes, tomato paste and seasonings (amount of salt needed will vary with brand of tomatoes).
- Simmer at least 1 hour.
- Cook macaroni as directed on package.
- In large casserole put layer of macaroni, layer of sauce, layer of cheese. Repeat ending with layer of cheese. Cover
- Bake 325° for 45 minutes. to an hour.

SPECIAL NOTE: THIS CAN SIT IN WARM OVEN IF SERVING TIME IS DELAYED. KEEPS WELL FOR COVERED DISH DINNERS AND IS GOOD COLD TOO.

Serves 6-8   *Elizabeth Wright*

CLAIRE'S ROAST BEEF

3-5 lbs. boneless chuck roast
1 No. 2 can tomatoes

1 can cream of mushroom
soup
1 pkg. dried onion soup

- Line 3 qt. Pyrex dish with 3 layers of aluminum foil that will overlap and seal edges.
- Place roast on top of foil.
- Mix tomatoes and soups and pour over roast. Seal edges well.
- Cook in preheated 250° oven for 6-8 hours.

SPECIAL NOTE: IT'S SO EASY!

Allow ⅓ TO ½ lb. per person   *Martha L. Veal*

COMPANY CASSEROLE

3 cups cooked noodles mixed
   with 1 tbsp. butter
1½ lbs. ground beef
1 16 oz. can tomato sauce
1 8 oz. pkg. cream cheese

1 8 oz. pkg. cottage cheese
¼ cup sour cream
1 green pepper, chopped
1 onion chopped

- Brown meat in a skillet, breaking up with a fork. Drain fat.
- Add tomato sauce to meat.
- In a bowl, mix cream cheese with cottage cheese and sour cream. Add chopped green pepper and onion to cheese mixture.
- Place buttered noodles in a 9- x 11-inch casserole dish .
- Cover with cheese mixture.
- Top with meat sauce.
- Bake in a 350° oven for 45 minutes.

Serves 4 or more
        Kathee Mills

CORNED BEEF

Small corned beef
½ to ¾ cup bourbon
1 clove garlic
2-3 bay leaves
A few whole cloves
A few peppercorns

Glaze:
¼ to ½ cup orange juice
¾ to 1 cup brown sugar
2-3 tbsp. of corned beef stock
1-2 tsp. mustard
⅓ to ½ cup bourbon

- Cover corned beef with water. Add ½-¾ cup of bourbon, garlic, bay leaves, cloves and peppercorns.
- Cook until tender, 2-3 hours.
- Remove from water (save water.)
- Place meat in roasting pan and pour glaze over meat. Let stand for 2 hours, turning occasionally.
- Bake at 400° for 30 minutes basting every 10 minutes.

SPECIAL NOTE: SERVE WITH CABBAGE COOKED IN CORNED BEEF STOCK.

Serves 6
        Katherine Perry

CURRIED MEATBALLS

1 lb. lean ground beef	2 tbsp. vegetable oil
⅔ cup unseasoned dry bread crumbs	1 28 oz. can undrained tomatoes
⅓ cup plain yogurt	⅛ tsp. red pepper
6 tsp. curry powder	¼ tsp. salt
¾ tsp salt	⅛ tsp. black pepper
⅛ tsp. pepper	

- In a medium bowl combine ground beef, bread crumbs, yogurt, 2½ tsp. curry powder, salt and pepper.
- Shape into 1½-inch meatballs.
- In large skillet heat oil, add meatballs and brown.
- In medium bowl crush tomatoes. Stir in red pepper, 3½ tsp. curry, salt and pepper.
- Pour tomato mixture over meatballs and simmer covered until meatballs are cooked (8-10 minutes or more.)
- Serve over spaghetti noodles or rice.

Serves 4-6

Joan Heller

EASY BEEF DISH

1 can celery soup	2 lbs. stew meat (do not brown meat)
1 can mushroom soup	¾ cup white sherry wine
1 pkg. onion soup mix	

- Mix all ingredients together. Bake in deep casserole dish for 3 hours in 300° oven. Serve over rice or noodles.

Jeannie Wade

Oh, Lord, forgive us our sins and bless these refreshments in Christ's name. Amen

18TH CENTURY GRACE, CHARLES COUNTY, MARYLAND

FILLET OF BEEF AND SAUCE MAISON

2 cloves minced garlic
1 stick butter, melted
2 tbsp. medium ground pepper
½ cup red wine
1 filet of beef

Sauce Maison:
½ cup chopped green onions
1½ cups red wine
1 stick butter
1½ tsp. salt
2 tsp. minced parsley
¼ tsp ground pepper

- Beef: Sauté garlic in butter, add pepper and wine.
- Pour mixture over beef, let stand until meat is at room temperature.
- Bake at 425° for 20-30 minutes until rare or medium rate. If not done enough, return to oven. (Remember: it will continue to cook after it is removed from the oven.)
- Sauce Maison: Boil the green onions and wine for 7 minutes until reduced in volume. When slightly cool, add the remaining ingredients.

Serves 8-10   *Melissa Barnes*

FIVE HOUR OVEN STEW

2-3 lbs. lean beef cut in 1-inch cubes
10 small onions
4 medium potatoes cut in 8 pieces
4 carrots cut in 3 pieces
2 slices white bread cut in cubes

2 cans tomato sauce
A 2-inch square of cheese, diced
1½ tsp. salt
⅛ tsp. pepper
1 beef bouillon cube
1 can tomatoes chopped
½ cup water (more if needed)

- Stir all together, place in large roaster pan.
- Cover and cook in 250° oven for 5 hours.

Mrs. Robert W. Peters

GOURMET BEEF STEW

2	lbs. lean stew meat	2	tbsp. salt
1	onion, thinly sliced	2	tbsp. sugar
1	rib celery, sliced diagonally in 1-inch pieces	2	tbsp. tapioca
		½	cup tomato juice
1	can sliced water chestnuts		Generous pinch dill
6	carrots peeled and sliced		

- Layer first five ingredients in flat casserole. (no need to brown beef.)
- Sprinkle salt, sugar, and tapioca over all.
- Add tomato juice and dill. Seal tightly with foil.
- Bake 350° oven for four hours. Do not peek.

Serves 4-6   *Mrs. Richard G. Wilkins*

GREEN PEPPER STEAK (CHINESE)

1	lb. beef chuck or round, fat trimmed	1	cup green onions, thinly sliced
¼	cup soy sauce	1	cup red or green peppers cut into 1-inch squares
1	clove garlic		
1½	tsp. grated fresh ginger or ½ tsp. ground	2	ribs celery, thinly sliced
		1	tbsp. cornstarch
¼	cup salad oil	1	cup water
		2	tomatoes, cut into wedges

- With a very sharp knife, cut beef across grain into thin strips, ⅛-inch thick.
- Combine soy sauce, garlic and ginger. Add beef. Toss and set aside while preparing vegetables.
- Heat oil in large frying pan or wok. Add beef and toss over high heat until browned. If meat is not tender cover and simmer over low heat until meat is tender.
- Turn heat up and add vegetables. Toss until vegetables are tender but crisp, about 10 minutes.
- Mix cornstarch with water. add to mixture, stir and cook until thickened.
- Add tomatoes and heat through. Serve over rice.

SPECIAL NOTE: IF SERVING 8, DOUBLE THE INGREDIENTS BUT REDUCE THE WATER TO 1⅛ CUPS. ADD ANOTHER ½ TBSP. CORNSTARCH. MAY USE SIRLOIN BEEF-CUTS COOKING TIME FOR BEEF.

Serves 4   *Jeannie Wade*

HAMBURGER CASSEROLE

1 lb. hamburger	¼ cup sour cream
2 8 oz. cans tomato sauce	⅓ cup chopped green onion
1½ cups cottage cheese	¼ cup chopped green pepper
8 oz. cream cheese	8 oz. wide noodles, cooked

- Brown hamburger, stir in tomato sauce and remove from heat.
- Combine cottage cheese, cream cheese, sour cream, onions and pepper. In a 3 qt. buttered casserole spread half the cooked noodles. cover with the cheese mixture.
- Cover with the remaining noodles.
- Spoon the hamburger mixture on top. Bake in 350° oven for 30 minutes.

Serves 8   *Jeanette Bessels*

HEARTY BEEF 'N' BREW

4 lbs. boneless beef chuck cut into 2-inch pieces	1 tsp. sugar
4 tbsp. vegetable oil, divided	½ tsp. salt
3 large onions, sliced	½ tsp. thyme leaves
3 tbsp. flour	¼ tsp. basil leaves
1 12 oz. can beer	⅛ tsp. ground pepper
¾ cup water	Hot cooked noodles
2 beef bouillon cubes	Parsley, chives, or
1 bay leaf	chopped green onions for garnish

- Heat 2 tbsp. vegetable oil in 4 qt. ovenproof saucepan or Dutch oven over medium heat.
- Cook and stir onions in oil until tender and golden.
- Remove onions with slotted spoon, reserve.
- Brown beef on all sides. Remove to onions, reserve.
- Add remaining oil to saucepan. Add flour, stirring until browned. Gradually add beer and water. Cook and stir until slightly thickened.
- Stir in bouillon, bay leaf, sugar, salt, thyme, basil and pepper.
- Add reserved beef and onions, stirring to combine.
- Cover and bake in 350° oven 2 hours or until beef is tender and gravy is thickened.
- remove bay leaf.
- Spoon beef mixture over hot noodles. Garnish.

Serves 10   *Jeannie Wade*

MARINATED FLANK STEAK

1	flank steak	1	tsp. dry mustard
¾	cup red wine	⅛	tsp. garlic, minced
¼	cup soy sauce		handful of dried onion flakes

- Mix all ingredients and marinate flank steak overnight at room temperature.
- Remove from marinade.
- Grill 5 minutes on each side.

Anita Campbell

MEAT LOAF

2	cups day old bread crumbs	1	tbsp. salt
¾	cup minced onions	1	tsp. dry mustard
¼	cup minced green pepper	¼	cup milk
2	eggs	¼	cup catsup
2	lbs. ground lean chuck	½	cup catsup
6	tsp. horseradish		

- Prepare bread crumbs. Mince onion and pepper.
- In large bowl beat eggs slightly, add ground meat and toss lightly.
- Add remaining ingredients, except last amount of catsup, and shape meat into greased loaf pan, spreading ½ cup catsup on top.
- Bake in 400° oven for 40 minutes.

SPECIAL NOTE: I DIVIDE THIS INTO THREE SMALL DISPOSABLE ALUMINUM PANS, EACH OF WHICH MAKES ENOUGH FOR TWO GOOD SERVINGS.

Mary Jane Flint

DIXIE MEAT LOAF

1½ lbs. good ground beef	1 cup crushed corn flakes or
½ lb. ground pork or	bread crumbs
ham leftovers	1 cup cold milk
2 eggs	1 tsp. salt
½ cups finely chopped celery	½ tsp. ground black pepper
1 small finely chopped onion	3 strips bacon
2 tbsp. vinegar	1 can tomatoes

- Knead meat and other ingredients together, except bacon strips.'

- Shape into a loaf and place in pan or loaf pan.

- Sprinkle top liberally with salt and place ½ a bacon strip crosswise along top of loaf, using all 3 strips in this manner.

- Bake in moderate oven 325° about 1½ hours.

- Serve with sauce made from loaf drippings combined with 1 lb.. can strained tomatoes and 2 tbsp. vinegar simmered together 10 minutes.

SPECIAL NOTE: A CHOICE RECIPE FROM EUFAULA, ALABAMA, MY GRANDMOTHER'S. SHE SAID, "...THEN RING THE DINNER BELL AND JUMP OUT OF THE WAY."

Serves 6   *Mrs. Betty Lewis McCartney*

QUICK BEEF STEW

1 tbsp. vegetable oil	2 cups cubed potatoes, cut
1 lb. ground chuck	large
1 cup chopped onion	1 cup sliced carrots
1 cup chopped celery	1 10 oz. pkg. frozen mixed
1 16 oz. can whole tomatoes,	vegetables
undrained and chopped	1 tsp. salt
2 cups water	½ tsp. coarsely ground black
	pepper

- Combine oil, ground chuck, onion and celery in large Dutch oven. Cook over high heat until beef is browned, stirring to crumble beef.

- Cover and reduce heat to low, and cook 15 minutes, stirring occasionally.

- Drain well.

- Return to Dutch oven and add remaining ingredients.

- Bring to boil, cover, reduce heat and simmer 20 minutes or until vegetables are tender.

Yield 9 cups   *Jeannie Wade*

SUPER CHUCK ROAST

4-5 lbs. chuck roast
½ cup cider vinegar
Flour
Salt
Pepper

1 cup strong coffee
6-8 potatoes
6-8 small onions
2 tbsp. vegetable oil
Fresh garlic

- Make 6-8 deep cuts in roast and insert slivers of fresh garlic in each slit.
- Place in a dish and pour the vinegar over it.
- Cover with plastic wrap and marinate overnight.
- Remove meat from vinegar, pat dry, flour then brown in a heavy roaster until very brown and crusty.
- Add salt and pepper to taste and pour strong coffee over it.
- Cover and bake 5-6 hours at 275° or 300°.
- Add potatoes and onions for the last 2 hours.

SPECIAL NOTE. THE COFFEE-FLAVORED JUICES MAKE DELICIOUS GRAVY.

Serves 8-10   *Jeanne Alaimo (Mrs. Anthony Alaimo)*

SUPER SUPPER

2 medium onions, sliced
1 cup celery pieces, cut bias
1 cup green pepper strips
2 tbsp. oil
2-3 cups cooked beef or pork
1½ cups cold water
2½ tbsp. soy sauce

3½ tbsp. cornstarch
1 tsp. sugar
½ tsp. salt
1 or 2 tomatoes in wedges
5 cups hot rice
1 tsp. powdered ginger

- Sauté the onion, pepper and celery in the oil until crisp-tender, remove.
- Add meat to hot skillet and brown or sear quickly (cook pork or beef until tender if not pre-cooked).
- Combine water, soy sauce, cornstarch, sugar, and salt, add to skillet.
- Cook and stir until thick.
- Add tomatoes and onion to mixture and heat.
- Toss the cooked rice with the ginger and serve the above over the cooked rice.

SPECIAL NOTE: GREAT DISH FOR USING LEFTOVER ROAST BEEF OR PORK.

Serves 4   *Cam Caldwell*

SWEET AND SOUR MEATBALLS

1 lb. ground beef	3 tbsp. vinegar
2 tbsp. chopped onion	½ cup sugar
Dash pepper	1 tbsp. cornstarch
2 tbsp. oil	4 slices pineapple
1 cup pineapple juice	3 large green peppers
1 tbsp. soy sauce	1 egg
6 tbsp. water	1 tsp. salt

- Mix beef egg, salt, onion and pepper. Form into small balls. Brown in oil, drain.

- To 1 tbsp. oil add pineapple juice; cook slowly for a few minutes.

- Add soy sauce, vinegar, water, cornstarch and sugar. Cook until mixture thickens.

- Add meatballs, cut up pineapple and green pepper. Heat.

Anita Campbell

VEAL APPLE CURRY

1½ lb. boned veal shoulder	1 clove garlic ,mashed
2 tbsp. flour	2 tbsp. brown sugar
2 tsp. salt	2 tbsp. raisins
2-3 tsp. curry powder	1½ tbsp. Worcestershire sauce
2 tbsp. butter	1 tbsp. flaked coconut
2 medium onion, sliced	1 cup water
2 unpared apples, sliced	2 cups cooked rice

- Trim fat from veal and cut into 1½-inch cubes.

- Combine flour, salt and curry powder, use to coat veal thickly on all sides.

- In hot butter, in large skillet brown veal and onions.

- Stir in any leftover flour mixture, apples, garlic, brown sugar, raisins, Worcestershire sauce, coconut and water.

- Simmer covered about 45 minutes or until veal is tender.

- Serve over hot rice.

Serves 6   *Jane E. Rives*

Scaloppine Marengo

12 veal scaloppine
½ cup flour
½ cup vegetable oil
8 tbsp. butter
½ tsp. chopped garlic
1 tbsp. chopped parsley
Pinch thyme and oregano
Pinch nutmeg

Salt and pepper
1 tbsp. tomato paste
1 cup chicken broth
8 fresh mushrooms, sliced
¼ cup dry red wine
2 cups canned Italian tomatoes
2 leaves fresh chopped basil (or ½ tsp. dried basil)

- Dust each veal scaloppine lightly with flour.

- Heat oil in large frying pan until very hot. Sauté scaloppine quickly on both sides in single layer. Transfer to a warm platter.

- Melt butter in a saucepan. Cook garlic 3 minutes over low heat.

- Add herbs, spices, tomato paste and ⅓ cup chicken broth. Mix well. Cook 5 minutes.

- Add mushrooms and wine. Cook 10 minutes, stirring constantly. (Add more broth if sauce becomes too thick.)

- Add tomatoes and cook 25 minutes.

- Allow sauce to cool, pour into a large baking dish; arrange the scaloppine in the sauce. Bake in preheated 350° oven 6 minutes.

- Spoon sauce over scaloppine, and serve.

SPECIAL NOTE: SERVE WITH A RED WINE, BARBARESCO OR A GOOD BARDOLINO. THIS RECIPE IS FROM OUR ONCE FAVORITE, NOW GONE, ITALIAN RESTAURANT IN NEW YORK'S GREENWICH VILLAGE. EXCELLENT WITH CAESAR SALAD AND FETTUCCINE.

Serves 6   *Judi E. Morgan*

Veal Picatta

1½ lbs. veal cut into 2 oz. medallions
½ cup drawn butter
1 cup dry white wine
Juice of 2 lemons

1½ cups chicken broth, with pinch of chicken base
flour, seasoned with white pepper and salt

- Pound veal into thin medallions. Individually flour each piece.

- Sauté in butter until lightly browned on both sides.

- Add white wine and lemon juice to hot pan and then add chicken broth

- Simmer 2 minutes, then boil down until slightly thickened.

- Replace medallions to heat, immediately remove to serving plates.

- Pour broth over medallions and serve.

Serves 4   *Cam Caldwell*

COUPER AND WYLLY

The Couper window pictures a palm
tree with the words, "Thanks be to God
who giveth us the victory."
(I Corinthians 15: 57) The Wylly
window features an Easter lily and the
quotation, "I am the resurrection and
the life." (John 11: 25) Both the palm
tree and the lily are symbolic of the
Resurrection of Our Lord.

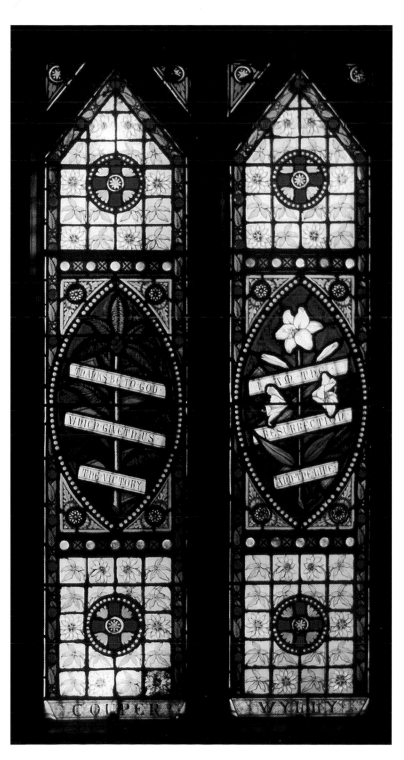

THE SERMON ON THE MOUNT

The window, installed in 1969, depicts
Jesus teaching two of his disciples,
probably Peter and John. The Biblical
quotation is from the Beatitudes,
Matthew 5: 3-12.

The window was given by Christ
Church, Frederica to the Glory of
God and in grateful memory of
Daniel E. Pomeroy.

BOMBAY CHICKEN

6 whole chicken breasts, cooked and cut into large bite-sized pieces. Save broth
1 stick butter
28 oz. can crushed or diced tomatoes
½ cup golden raisins
1 clove minced garlic
¾ tbsp. curry powder

Salt to taste
2 tbsp. chopped parsley
1 tbsp. black pepper
½ tbsp. oregano
1 large sliced onion
8 oz. chopped mushrooms
½ cup chopped yellow pepper
½ cup chopped red pepper

- Sauté onions and peppers in butter. (If using fresh mushrooms, sauté them also). Remove.

- Sauté chicken until light golden brown. Add onions and peppers and all the other ingredients plus some of the chicken broth.

- If you like things spicy, increase the seasonings (garlic, curry, pepper).

- Simmer 20 minutes.

- Serve hot over rice. May need to add more broth. It gets better if it sits overnight.

SPECIAL NOTE: IT IS THE YELLOW AND RED PEPPERS THAT GIVE THIS DISH ITS UNIQUE FLAVOR (DO NOT USE GREEN PEPPERS). THIS CAN BE MADE AHEAD AND FROZEN.

Serves 8   *Nancy Sumerford*

CHICKEN CASSEROLE

1 cup cooked chicken diced
1 pkg. noodles cooked, medium sized
1 cup English peas
1 small jar pimientos

1 small jar sliced mushrooms
2 cans celery soup plus ½ can water
½ cup sherry wine

- Cook noodles, drain.

- Butter casserole and line with noodles. Then chicken, peas, mushrooms and pimientos.

- Spoon soup mixed with water over top, then wine.

- Bake at 350° for 40 minutes (put foil over top for the last 5 minutes).

Serves 6-8   *Alice Aiken*

CHICKEN EN GELEE PRINTANIERE

4	whole chicken breasts	1	cup each cooked and chilled
2	stalks celery, 1-inch slices		peas, sliced carrots, lima
2	leeks or mild onions sliced		beans, green beans sliced or 2
1	carrot sliced		pkgs.frozen mixed vegetables
4	cups water		cooked and chilled
1	can beef consomme		Salt and pepper to taste
2	envelopes gelatin		

- Place in large pot chicken breasts, celery, onion, carrots, water, consomme and salt and pepper to taste. Bring to boil, lower heat and simmer 40 minutes until chicken is tender.
- Remove chicken and chill. Strain broth, chill and skim off fat. Save 4 cups of broth.
- Dissolve gelatin in small amount of broth, heat to dissolve and add to the remaining broth. Chill until syrupy.
- Slice chicken and arrange in bottom of 7x12 x2-inch pyrex dish.
- Arrange vegetables on top of chicken.
- Pour gelatin broth mixture to cover chicken and vegetables.
- Chill until firm overnight or can keep several days.
- Cut in squares to serve. A dressing can be used if desired.

A simple dressing:
½ cup sour cream (light)
½ cup mayonnaise
1 tsp. celery salt
- Mix, chill and put 1 tbsp. or so on top of each portion of jellied chicken.

SPECIAL NOTE: THIS IS A VERY GOOD HOT WEATHER DISH FOR LUNCHEON OR AS AN ENTRÉE.

Serves 6 to 8   *Lotta M. Hunt*

O Lord, forgive us our sins
and bless these refreshments
in Christ's name.
Amen

18TH CENTURY GRACE FROM CHARLES COUNTY, MARYLAND.

CHICKEN AND GREEN NOODLE CASSEROLE

4-6 chicken breasts
9 oz. pkg. of spinach fettuccine
1 Vidalia onion or 6 green onions chopped
4 tbsp. melted butter
1 cup mayonnaise
1 cup sour cream
1 can mushroom soup
½ cup white wine
3 tbsp. Plochman's mustard
10 oz. grated cheddar cheese
1 tbsp. chopped jalapenos peppers
Cracked black pepper to taste

- Boil breasts in salted water (bay leaf and peppercorns optional) until tender.
- When cooked cut into large bite-sized pieces.
- Cook noodles al dente. Drain.
- Saute onions in butter until clear.
- Mix drained noodles with onions and butter.
- Place noodles in bottom of large buttered casserole.
- Place chicken pieces and Jalapeño peppers over noodles.
- Mix other ingredients and pour over chicken.
- If desired, you can add a topping of bread crumbs.
- Bake in preheated 350° oven for 30 minutes.

SPECIAL NOTE: YOU WILL FIND SPINACH FETTUCCINE IN THE DAIRY CASE—DO NOT OVER-COOK IT. CAN ADD A LITTLE CHICKEN BROTH, IF DESIRED. CAN BE MADE AHEAD AND FROZEN. IF YOU CANNOT TOLERATE PEPPERS JUST LEAVE THEM OUT.

Serves 8   *Nancy Sumerford*

God be at your table.

OPHELIA'S BLESSING FROM *HAMLET*.

CHICKEN GRUYERE

½ lb. butter
3½ cups milk
2 oz. Gruyere cheese, grated
Tabasco to taste
3 whole chicken breast, boiled, boned, and diced
½ cup sour cream
Buttered bread crumbs

½ cup flour
2 oz. cheddar cheese, grated
2 cloves minced garlic (or 1 tsp. garlic powder)
½ lb. sliced fresh mushrooms, sautéed
28 oz. artichoke hearts, drained and quartered

- Melt butter and add garlic, stir in flour until smooth. Gradually add milk, stirring until thickened.
- Stir in cheese and seasonings until cheese melts.
- Add chicken, mushrooms, artichoke hearts and sour cream.
- Pour into lightly greased casserole, cover with bread crumbs.
- Bake in preheated 350° oven for 30 minutes.

Serves 6   *Marge Springhorn*

CHICKEN HOW-SO

2 cups cooked chicken
2 tbsp. butter or margarine
1 can golden mushroom soup
½ cup water
½ tsp. curry powder
1 tbsp. soy sauce
1 tbsp. worcestershire sauce
1 beef bouillon cube

1 8 oz. can bamboo shoots, drained
½ cup sliced celery
½ cup sliced onion
½ lb. mushrooms
1 small green pepper cut up
3 tbsp. white wine
½ tsp. poppy seed

- Sauté mushrooms in butter in medium skillet.
- Add soup, water, bouillon cube, soy sauce, Worcestershire sauce, curry and poppyseed, mix well, cover and simmer 15 minutes stirring occasionally.
- Add bamboo shoots, celery, onion and pepper. Cover and simmer 10 minutes or until tender.
- Add chicken and wine, simmer until thoroughly heated about 5 minutes. Serve with rice.

Cooking time 30 minutes
Serves 4-6   *Ruth D. Crichton*

CHICKEN AND RICE CASSEROLE

1½ cups raw rice
1 can cream of mushroom soup
1 can cream of chicken soup
1 can cream of celery soup

4 chicken breasts skinned, boned and cut in strips
8 oz. shredded cheddar cheese
3 cups milk
Butter or margarine

- Mix soups with 3 cups milk.
- Pour ⅓ of mixture on bottom of 9x13-inch baking dish.
- Add rice over soup mixture.
- Add ⅓ of soup mixture over rice and sprinkle with a little cheese.
- Place chicken over rice.
- Pour remaining ⅓ soup mixture over chicken. Dot with butter or margarine.
- Sprinkle remaining cheese over all. Bake uncovered in a 275° oven for 2½-3 hours.

Serves 4-6   *Sally McCauley*

CHICKEN TETRAZZINI

2 cups bite size cooked chicken
½ lb. thin spaghetti (broken into 2-inch pieces)
2 tbsp. pimiento
4 tbsp. margarine
3 tbsp. grated onion
1 4 oz. can mushroom pieces (save liquid)
½ tsp. celery salt

½ cup grated sharp cheese
¼ tsp. margarine
Dash of red pepper
½ cup slivered almonds
1 can cream chicken soup
Small can sliced water chestnuts
1 12 oz. can evaporate milk
¼ cup grated parmesan cheese

- Cook spaghetti, drain well. Mix cooked chicken and spaghetti, pimiento and mushrooms.
- In skillet melt margarine and saute onion.
- Add seasoning, mushroom liquid, soup and milk, blended together. Cook until thickened, stirring constantly.
- Mix with spaghetti mixture.
- Add sliced water chestnuts and almonds. Spread cheeses on top of casserole.
- Cover and bake at 350° for 15 minutes.
- Remove cover. Bake 15 more minutes.

SPECIAL NOTE: MAY BE MADE AHEAD AND KEPT IN REFRIGERATOR UNTIL READY TO BAKE. BRING TO ROOM TEMPERATURE BEFORE BAKING.

Ann Jarrett

CURRIED CHICKEN CASSEROLE

2-3 tsp. curry powder	1½ cup orange juice
¾ tsp. salt	1 cup rice
¼ tsp. pepper	¾ cup water
6 chicken breasts skinned or 1 fryer	1 tsp. dry mustard
	1 tbsp. brown sugar

- Combine curry powder, ½ tsp. salt and pepper. Rub seasonings into each chicken piece and set aside.

- In 10-inch skillet combine orange juice, rice, water, brown sugar, mustard and remaining ¼ tsp. salt. Mix well.

- Arrange chicken pieces over rice mixture. Bring to a boil.

- Cover and simmer 20 minutes.

- Remove from heat and let stand 5 minutes.

- Sprinkle with parsley or sunflower seeds.

Serves 6   *Alice Bradford*

"COQ AU VIN"
CHICKEN IN BURGUNDY

4 slices bacon, diced	Salt and pepper
2 (3 lb) broilers, cut up	3 cups Burgundy
1 lb. small white onions or 2 shallots	Parsley
1 lb. mushrooms	½ tsp. thyme
2 clove garlic, chopped	½ tsp. marjoram
1 small onion chopped	2 bay leaves
4 tbsp. flour	¼ cup oil
	2 tbsp. butter

- Cook bacon until crisp and remove. Add oil to pan and brown chicken pieces.

- Remove to casserole.

- Pour off all but 4 tbsp. of fat. Saute chopped garlic and small onion or shallots.

- Add flour and cook 2-3 minutes.

- Add Burgundy. Cook until thickened, season with salt and pepper.

- Add parsley, marjoram, thyme, bay leaves and bacon. Pour over chicken.

- Add butter to pan and sauté chopped onions until brown, add to casserole and sauté mushrooms. Add to casserole. Bake at 350° for 1½ hours.

SPECIAL NOTE: THIS CAN BE PREPARED EARLY IN THE DAY AND REFRIGERATED UNTIL COOKING TIME.

Serves 8   *Jill S. Cunningham*

EASY AND DELICIOUS CHICKEN

2	tbsp. oil	2	tbsp. minced onion
1	chicken cut up	2	tbsp. flour
		1½	tsp. salt
Mix together:		¼	tsp. pepper
½	tsp. thyme	1	tsp. paprika
¼	tsp. curry powder	½	tsp. garlic powder

- In a 2 qt. shallow baking dish spread, 1 tbsp. oil on bottom.
- Place chicken in dish and spread 1 tbsp. of oil over chicken.
- Sprinkle ½ of seasoning mix over chicken.
- Bake uncovered at 350° for ½ hour.
- Turn chicken and sprinkle with remaining seasoning.
- Bake ½ hour longer.

Serves 4-6   *Peggy Sullivan*

FIVE CAN CASSEROLE

1	can boned chicken	1	can water chestnuts
1	can cream of chicken soup	1	can french fried onion
1	can sliced mushrooms		

- Mix top 4 ingredients. (Optional: a little mayonnaise may be added to the soup.)
- Pour in casserole and top with onions.
- Cook at 300-325° for about 25 minutes.

SPECIAL NOTE: THIS RECIPE WAS GIVEN TO ME BY MILDRED WELLONS TYLER. SHE ALWAYS KEEPS THESE 5 CANS IN HER PANTRY IN ORDER TO BE PREPARED FOR UNEXPECTED COMPANY! FOR A LARGE CROWD I SIMPLY QUADRUPLED THE RECIPE (STEWING 8 BREASTS AND 6 THIGHS) FILLING TWO 2 QT. CASSEROLES.

Charlotte Marshall

FORTY CLOVES OF GARLIC CHICKEN

8   chicken breast halves
½   cup of olive oil
1   tbsp. of thyme
1   tbsp. oregano
1   tbsp. of savory
40 cloves of garlic (peeled)

1   bay leaf
1   top of green onion
Celery leaves from 1-2 ribs
2-3 sprigs of parsley
Salt and pepper to taste

- Put in bottom of casserole bay leaf, green onion, celery leaves and parsley sprigs.
- Add chicken breasts.
- Sprinkle 40 cloves of garlic on top of breasts. Add thyme, oregano and savory.
- Pour ½ cup olive oil over all.
- Salt and pepper to taste.
- Bake in covered casserole in 350° oven 1½ hours.

Serves 6-8   *Mrs. Richard G. Wilkins*

INDIAN SKILLET CHICKEN

½   cup long grain rice
3   boneless, skinless chicken breast halves (about 8 ozs)
2   tbsp. butter
½   cup orange juice
1   tsp. curry powder (more if desired)

Ground red pepper to taste
⅓   cup chopped onion
½   tsp. ground coriander
½   cup seedless grapes, halved
2   tbsp. apricot jam
Golden raisins (optional)

- Cook rice according to pkg. directions, adding a chicken bouillon cube.
- In a 10-inch skillet, cook breasts and onions in hot butter until brown.
- Add orange juice, curry powder, red pepper and coriander.
- Bring to a boil, reduce heat, cover and simmer for about 10 minutes.
- Stir in grapes and jam. May add golden raisins, if desired.
- Cover and keep warm until ready to serve. Serve chicken with juices over rice.

SPECIAL NOTE; WE LIKE IT SPICY, SO YOU MAY USE MORE CURRY AND RED PEPPER. CAN BE MADE AHEAD.

Serves 2-3   *Nancy Sumerford*

MARTHA'S CHICKEN PIE

2 cups cooked chicken
2 eggs, hard boiled
2 cups chicken broth
1 can cream celery soup

1 stick margarine
1 cup self-rising flour
1 cup milk

- Cut cooked chicken into bite-size pieces.
- Place in 2 qt. casserole.
- Add sliced hard boiled eggs.
- Mix chicken broth and celery soup. Pour over sliced eggs.
- Cut margarine into self-rising flour. Blend flour mixture with milk. Pour over chicken mixture.
- Bake in a 400° oven for 1 hour.

Serves 10   *Sarah B. Jones*

OVEN FRIED PARMESAN CHICKEN

1 cup of fine cracker crumbs
¼ cup grated Parmesan cheese
1 tbsp. parsley flakes (dried)
1 tsp. salt
⅛ tsp. pepper

Dash of garlic powder
1 fryer, cut up and skinned
½ cup butter or margarine, melted

- Combine first 6 ingredients and mix well.
- Dip chicken in butter.
- Dredge in cracker mixture.
- Place in 13x9x2-inch dish and bake in 350° oven for 1 hour.

Dottie O'Looney

For these and all His mercies,
God's holy Name be blessed and praised;
through Jesus Christ our Lord.

Amen

SHERRIED CHICKEN

6	chicken breasts or 1 fryer cut up	Sauce:	
¾	cup flour	6	tbsp. butter
2	tsp. salt	¾	cup sherry
10	tbsp. butter	3	tbsp. soy sauce
	Garlic powder (optional)	3	tbsp. lemon juice
		½	tsp. ginger

- Combine flour, salt and garlic powder and lightly dredge pieces of chicken. Shake off excess flour.

- Melt 10 tbsp. of butter in heavy skillet and brown chicken on all sides. Place in casserole.

- To make sauce: In a saucepan melt 6 tbsp. butter, add sherry, soy sauce, lemon juice and ginger. Bring to a boil, stirring constantly. Pour over chicken.

- Bake uncovered in 350° oven for 1 hour or until tender. Baste occasionally and turn chicken once during baking.

Serves 4-6

Mimi Rogers

STICKY CHICKEN

2	tsp. salt	¼	tsp. white pepper
1	tsp. paprika	¼	tsp. garlic powder
¾	tsp. cayenne pepper	¼	tsp. black pepper
½	tsp. onion powder	1	3 lb. chicken
½	tsp. thyme	1	cup chopped onion

- In small bowl, thoroughly combine all seasonings. Rub into chicken, inside and out, patting mixture into skin to make sure it is evenly distributed down deep into skin.

- Place in sealable plastic bag and refrigerate overnight.

- When ready to roast chicken, stuff cavity with onions.

- Roast, uncovered, at 250° about 5 hours, basting occasionally with pan juices, or until juices start to caramelize and chicken is golden brown.

SPECIAL NOTE: THE MEASUREMENTS FOR THE SEASONINGS MIX MAY BE MADE AHEAD AND STORED IN A SPICE BOTTLE. THIS IS PAUL PRUDHOMME'S MOTHERS RECIPE.

Serves 3-4

Nancy Sumerford

SUDIE'S CHICKEN

6 chicken pieces, any kind
Pancake flour to coat
1 large onion, sliced
Salt and pepper

Paprika
1 tbsp. oil
About one cup water

- Preheat frying pan with oil, coat chicken with pancake flour, salt and pepper.
- In frying pan coated with oil brown chicken pieces until light brown.
- Sprinkle with paprika. Add 1 cup of water and onion slices.
- Simmer until chicken is done and gravy is thickened.
- Serve over rice, noodles, or squares of corn bread.

SPECIAL NOTE: THIS IS GOOD MADE AHEAD FOR LARGE NUMBER OF PEOPLE. SERVE WITH TOSSED SALAD AND FRUIT DESSERT.

Serves 4   *Charlotte Parker Harris (Mrs. Walter D.)*

SWEET AND SOUR CHICKEN

4 lbs. chicken cut up or your favorite pieces
1 12 ozs bottle Heinz Chili Sauce

1 cup apple jelly or red plum jam
3 chicken bouillon cubes
2 tsp. instant minced onion
2 tsp. Dijon mustard

- Combine all sauce ingredients. Mix well in a medium sauce pan. Simmer 20 minutes.
- Meanwhile arrange chicken parts on grill. Grill 20 minutes, baste with sauce and turn.
- Continue to baste, turning every 10 minutes until chicken is done, about 45 minutes.

SPECIAL NOTE: SO, SO GOOD! MEN LOVE IT.

Serves 6-8   *Mrs. Robert Allen*

DUCK ORANGE

4 lb. duckling
1 ¾ oz pkg. brown gravy mix
¼ cup flour
2 tsp. salt
⅛ tsp. pepper

2 tbsp. sugar
1 cup hot water
2 tbsp. orange marmalade
1 6 oz. can frozen orange juice, thawed

- Combine all ingredients except duckling and pour into brown-n-bag. Place bag in pan, turning to moisten all sided.
- follow brown-n-Bag cooking instructions.
- Add duck to bag, turning to miosten all sides.
- Bake in 375° oven for 1½ or 2 hours or until tested tender.
- Pour sauce to serve with duck into bowl and skim off excess fat.

Serves 2-4   *Gerda B. Brown*

ROASTED WILD DUCK
IN OVEN BAG

1 oven bag
1 medium to large duck
Salt
1 apple, quartered and cored
1 tbsp. butter

¼ cup honey
¼ cup orange juice
1 tsp. orange peel
¼ tsp. ginger
¼ tsp. basil leaves

- Preheat oven to 375°.
- Wash duck well and dry with paper towels. Salt body cavity and outside of duck and stuff cavity with pieces of apple.
- In saucepan, heat the next 6 ingredients until the butter melts.
- Place duck in oven bag.
- Place ½ of the liquid mixture into duck cavity and the rest over duck.
- Tie the bag and make 6 (½-inch) slits in the top of the bag.
- Cook for 1 hour and 45 minutes or until tender.
- Pour sauce into a bowl and skim off excess fat.
- Remove and discard apple. Serve sauce with duck.

Rosalynn Carter (Mrs. Jimmy Carter)

GINNY'S ROAST DUCK

Cleaned, wild ducks, 3 mallards
or 5-6 teal or wood ducks
1   slice bacon per duck
2-3 tbsp. vinegar per duck
1   tsp. baking soda per duck

2-3 apples, sectioned
2-3 onions, sectioned
3   oranges
Salt and pepper to taste

- Soak cleaned ducks overnight in salty water to which vinegar and baking soda have been added.

- Pour water off and dry ducks well.

- Preheat oven to 350°.

- Stuff cavity of each duck with ½ onion, sectioned, and ½ apple, sectioned. Salt and pepper inside and out, and place a strip of bacon over each duck.

- Put ducks on rack in a roaster, adding water to the level of the roaster rack. Cook with roaster covered and vent closed for 1-1½ hours for wood ducks or teal, or 2½-3 hours for mallards, basting with the juice of one orange every 45-60 minutes.

- Serve with cornbread dressing and giblet gravy from the following recipes.

Cornbread Dressing

Combine for cornbread:
1   cup meal
2   tsp. baking powder

1   tsp. salt
1   tsp. sugar

- Mix the above four ingredients together. Add ¾ cup milk. Bake at 375° in greased pan for 25-30 minutes.

Combine for dressing:
Cornbread
Old biscuits, stale bread
3   ribs celery, chopped
1   onion, chopped
1   tsp. poultry seasoning

Salt and freshly ground
    pepper to taste
2   eggs
2   chicken bouillon cubes
Liquid from ducks
Butter

- Prepare the night before.

- Mix 3 parts cornbread to 1 part bread. Add all the other ingredients, adding enough liquid to yield a thick soupy consistency.

- Next day put slices of butter on top of mixture before baking in a preheated oven at 350° for 45-60 minutes.

- Test for doneness. When dressing springs back to touch, remove from oven.

(Giblet Gravy recipe to accompany 'Ginny's Roast Duck' on top of next page)

Giblet Gravy to Serve Over Dressing

Duck livers, gizzards, and
    hearts (giblets)
Salt and pepper to taste
2   eggs, boiled

1½ tbsp. flour
Chicken bouillon cubes
3   cups water

- Bring water to boil, add bouillon cubes, salt and pepper. Cook livers, gizzards and hearts in broth on slow heat until done.
- Remove giblets and dice.
- Add diced giblets and diced boiled eggs to broth.
- Dissolve flour in ½ cup hot water and add to broth. Cook until thickens.

SPECIAL NOTE: RECIPE OF MRS. W.L. SHIPMAN, DYERSBURG, TENNESSEE.

Serves 6

Susan Shipman

QUAIL ON TOAST

8-10 quail breasts
1   stick butter
Thin sliced whole wheat bread

1   large or 2 small lemons
Lemon pepper
¼   cup water

- (Note: wild birds should be well washed, removing shot and pin feathers.)
- Melt ¼ stick of butter in iron skillet (if possible). Brown birds in butter. Sprinkle with lemon pepper.
- Squeeze juice of one lemon over browned birds. Add water. Cover.
- Simmer for 45 minutes. Turn several times during cooking. Add more water if needed.
- Cut bread slices in triangles. Butter lightly and toast in oven until crisp.
- Arrange on platter, one triangle for each breast. When birds are fork tender, place on toast.
- Add remaining ¾ stick of butter to drippings and juice of 1 lemon. Stir and cook for 3-4 minutes. Pour over birds and toast.

SPECIAL NOTE: THIS IS AN OLD FAMILY RECIPE AND THE BEST WAY TO COOK QUAIL I HAVE FOUND. COMMERCIAL BIRDS DO NOT HAVE THE FLAVOR WILD BIRDS DO.

Serve 2 birds per person

Angie Burns

THE CONFESSION OF ST. PETER

This window shows Jesus at Caesarea
Philippi with Peter, John and James.
Jesus asked the disciples who they said
that He was. Peter's reply was, "Thou art
the Christ, the Son of the living God."
(Matthew 16: 16) This was a profound
act of faith on Peter's part; for, at
the Baptism of Jesus, the pronunciation
was for Him alone, and the
Transfiguration had not yet occurred.
Peter's words appear in Greek at the bottom of the window.

The window was executed in 1899 by
Mayer & Company, Munich, Germany.
It is dedicated "To the memory of the
Rev. Anson Green Phelps Dodge, Jr.,
STB. Born June 30, 1860.
Died August 20, 1898."

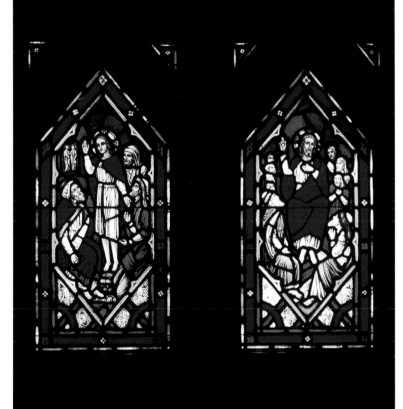

BAPTISTRY WINDOWS

The window on the left depicts Jesus as a boy of twelve in the temple with the elders. Mary and Joseph are shown entering a door in the background.

The window on the right shows Jesus seated, teaching. He is surrounded by nine figures, all assuming an attitude of reverence.

The windows are dedicated "To the Glory of God and in loving memory of two who made the supreme sacrifice: 2nd Lt. Edward Burson Tucker, Born Sept. 22, 1919. Died October 13, 1943. Lost in the South Pacific. T/Sgt. James Postell Shadman. Born Sept. 18, 1921. Died Sept. 12, 1944. Lost in European Theatre."

ASPARAGUS CASSEROLE

1 can small green peas, drained
1 can asparagus (cut or whole), drained

1 can cream of mushroom soup

- Place drained peas in the bottom of a 1 qt. casserole dish.
- Spread half can of mushroom soup over them.
- Add drained asparagus as the next layer and top with rest of mushroom soup.
- Bread crumbs may be added.
- Cook at 350° for 35 minutes.

Jane Fann Sanders

BROCCOLI CASSEROLE I

2 pkgs. frozen broccoli
1 can seasoned green beans
1 box cheese crackers, crushed

Mix together for sauce:
1 cup mayonnaise

1 chopped onion
½ tsp. pepper
1 tsp. salt
1 cup sharp cheddar cheese
2 beaten eggs
1 can mushroom soup

- Cook and drain broccoli and arrange half of it in buttered casserole.
- Cover with layer of half of the beans, drained.
- Top with half of the mixed sauce, repeat and cover with cracker crumbs.
- Bake at 325° for 45 minutes.

Evelyn French

BROCCOLI CASSEROLE II

2 pkgs. frozen chopped broccoli, cook and drain
1 can mushroom soup
1 cup mayonnaise

2 beaten eggs
1 small onion, chopped
1 cup cheese Ritz-type crackers
1 cup grated mild cheese

- Mix first 5 ingredients.
- Add half the cracker crumbs and the cheese which have been combined.
- Turn into a casserole dish and top with remaining cheese-cracker mixture.
- Bake in preheated oven at 350° for 25 minutes or until bubbly.

SPECIAL NOTE: THIS DISH CAN BE MADE AHEAD AND REHEATED. IT ALSO TRAVELS. TO MAKE A LOWER FAT AND CHOLESTEROL VERSION USE REDUCED FAT MAYONNAISE AND EGG SUBSTITUTE (SUCH AS EGGBEATERS.)

Serves 8

Brenda Hartsell

BROCCOLI CASSEROLE III

1 pkg. 10 oz. frozen chopped broccoli	2 eggs
1 can cream of mushroom soup	1½ cups grated cheese
	1 cup mayonnaise
	Crushed potato chips

- Cook broccoli as directed on package, drain.
- Combine soup, eggs, mayonnaise and cheese, mix well, add broccoli.
- Pour into casserole and bake in oven, 350° until set, approximately 15 minutes.
- Remove from oven, cover with chips and bake until light brown.

SPECIAL NOTE: THIS CASSEROLE HAS MADE BROCCOLI A FAVORITE VEGETABLE FOR OUR CHILDREN AND GRANDCHILDREN.

Serves 4   *Alice Bradford*

CATHEDRAL DOMAIN BROCCOLI

2 pkg. chopped broccoli	½ stick margarine, divided
½ lb. Velveeta Cheese, cut into small squares	¼ of small box of Ritz crackers

- Cook broccoli 2 minutes. Drain in fine sieve.
- Put half of broccoli into buttered baking dish. Over the top put cheese and quarter stick oleo.
- Put in remaining broccoli.
- mix quarter of small box of Ritz crackers, crumbled, and quarter stick oleo, melted. Spread on broccoli. Cook 15-20 minutes at 350°.

SPECIAL NOTES: CATHEDRAL DOMAIN IS KENTUCKY'S EPISCOPAL CHURCH CAMP. THIS BROCCOLI WAS ALWAYS A BIG HIT WITH CAMPERS AND MY CHILDREN LOVED IT.

Serves 6-8   *Annabelle Salter*

BRAISED RED CABBAGE

2	to 2½ lb. cabbage	⅓	cup water
4	tbsp. butter	⅓	cup white vinegar
1	tbsp. sugar	¼	cup red currant jelly
1	tbsp. salt	1	tbsp. grated apple

- Thoroughly wash cabbage, cut fine. There should be approximately 9 cups of shredded cabbage when you finish.
- Preheat oven to 325°.
- Combine butter, sugar, salt, water and vinegar in a heavy stainless or enameled 4-5 qt. casserole. Heat.
- When it comes to a boil and the butter has melted, add the shredded cabbage and toss thoroughly with wooden spoons.
- Bring to a boil again, cover tightly and place in the center of oven to braise for 2 hours.

SPECIAL NOTES: THERE IS LITTLE DANGER THAT THE CABBAGE WILL DRY OUT DURING COOKING, BUT DO CHECK ON THE LIQUID. ADD A LITTLE WATER, IF NECESSARY.

Serves 6   *Gerda B. Brown*

CARROTS AND WHITE GRAPES

1	13½ oz. can small Belgian carrots	4	tbsp. butter
30	seedless white grapes (in can)	4	tbsp. cointreau

- Drain carrots and grapes well.
- In a skillet melt butter—add cointreau—mix.
- Add carrots and grapes—cook over low heat 4-5 minutes. Stir and serve.

Serves 4-6   *Virginia Leveau*

LEMON GLAZED CARROTS

2 lbs. carrots, scraped and diagonally sliced
¼ cup butter or margarine
¼ cup firmly packed brown sugar
¼ cup lemon juice
½ tsp. salt

- Cook carrots in a small amount of boiling water 12-15 minutes or until crisp-tender, drain.
- Melt butter in a small saucepan, add remaining ingredients. Bring mixture to a boil, stirring constantly.
- Pour over carrots, and toss gently.

SPECIAL NOTES: THIS IS MY MOTHER, STACEY WILSON'S RECIPE THAT WAS PUBLISHED IN "SOUTHERN LIVING" MAGAZINE.

Serves 8   *Brenda Hartsell*

SPECIAL CARROTS

4 cups cooked, mashed carrots
1 stick melted margarine
2 eggs, beaten
3 tbsp. flour
1 tsp. baking powder
⅔ cup sugar
Pinch cinnamon

- Blend above ingredients
- Place in buttered one and a half quart casserole.
- Bake in 400° oven for 15 minutes, then 350° oven for 45 minutes more.

Wynelle Ruehle

CHILE RELLENOS CASSEROLE

2 4 oz. cans Olde el Paso mild chopped green chiles, drained
1 lb. jack cheese, grated
6 eggs, separated
⅔ cup evaporated milk
Generous dash of Tabasco
½ tsp. salt
2 tbsp. flour
3 ripe tomatoes, sliced

- Toss chiles and cheese and place in greased 9x13-inch casserole dish.
- Beat egg whites stiff.
- Beat egg yolks and add milk, flour and seasonings. Fold in whites.
- Pour over cheese and chiles, lifting mixture with fork to gently ooze into chiles and cheese mixture.
- Bake uncovered in a preheated 350° oven for 30 minutes. Remove from oven, top with tomatoes and bake for 10 more minutes. Serve hot.

Serves 8   *Marge Springhorn*

CORN PUDDING I

4 cups (1 qt.) milk	4 eggs well beaten
½ cup plus 2 tbsp. yellow corn meal	½ stick melted butter
¼ cup sugar	1 tsp. vanilla
½ tsp. salt	1 tsp. baking powder
32 ozs. yellow corn or 12 medium ears cut off cob	

- Grease 3 qts. baking dish.
- Scald milk in large saucepan, remove from heat, stir in corn meal, sugar and salt.
- Place over medium heat bring to a boil, reduce heat to medium-low and simmer, stirring constantly for 5 minutes.
- Remove from heat, add corn, stirring.
- Gradually add eggs stirring vigorously.
- Add butter, vanilla and baking powder, blend well.
- Pour into dish. Bake at 350° for 45-50 minutes or until set.

SPECIAL NOTE: THE BEST CORN PUDDING I HAVE EVER TASTED.

Serves 8   *Anna Belle McCaskill Friedman*

CORN PUDDING II

4 ears fresh corn	1 tbsp. sugar
2 cups half and half cream	1 tsp. salt
2 tbsp. cornstarch, sifted	4 tbsp. butter, melted
3 eggs, well beaten	

- Split corn kernels and cut from cob. With back of knife scrape cob to remove as much liquid as possible.
- Beat eggs, add half and half, sugar, salt, cornstarch, melted butter and the corn and liquid. Stir well.
- Pour into a buttered shallow (1½ to 2-inch deep) 2 qt. baking dish.
- Bake at 350° for 60 minutes.

Serves 6   *Virginia Petretti*

CORN SOUFFLE

1	can kernel corn and liquid	1	box Jiffy corn muffin mix
1	can cream corn	2	eggs, beaten
1	cup sour cream		

- Mix all together.
- Pour into buttered 9 x 12-inch pan.
- Bake 45 minutes in 350° oven.

Serves 8-10

Catherine C. Keith

*Give us grateful hearts, our Father
for all thy mercies, and make us mindful
of the needs of others; through Jesus Christ our Lord.
Amen.*

THE BOOK OF COMMON PRAYER

GREEN BEANS ELISE

5	cups green beans or 3 pkgs. frozen	1	tsp. salt
2	tbsp. flour	¼	tsp. pepper
2	tbsp. butter	½	cup grated cheddar cheese
¼	cup chopped onion	½	tsp. grated lemon rind
1	tbsp. minced parsley	1	cup sour cream
			Bread crumbs

- Boil beans, saute onion and parsley in butter.
- Mix in flour, add salt, pepper, lemon rind. Add to drained beans. Mix in sour cream.
- Put in baking dish, top with cheese, sprinkle with bread crumbs. Dot with butter.
- Bake in 350° oven for 30 minutes.

Serves 6-8

Lucile G. Walker

SWEET PEPPERS OVER RICE

½ stick butter	½ red pepper, chopped
1 tsp. garlic	½ yellow pepper, chopped
2 tsp. curry	½ green pepper, chopped
1-2 tbsp. lemon juice	1 rib celery, chopped
Golden raisins	1 onion, chopped
Rice	1 chicken bouillon cube

- Sauté vegetables in garlic butter. Add lemon juice, curry, pepper and salt, raisins.
- Serve over rice cooked with chicken bouillon cube.
- Great with chicken, pork, or fish.

Serves 2-4   *Nancy Sumerford*

CLASSIC POTATOES

8-10 medium potatoes (6 cups shredded)	½ tsp. white pepper
	½ stick butter
1 cup shredded provolone cheese	1 cup half and half
	1 tsp. seasoned salt
1 tbsp. grated onion	

- Boil potatoes until nearly tender.
- Drain and cool. Peel and shred. Combine shredded potatoes with cheese and onion.
- Layer half of potato mixture in buttered 9x9-inch baking dish.
- Sprinkle with a third of the seasoned salt and pepper.
- Dot with a third of butter.
- Repeat layers twice more.
- May be covered and refrigerated at this point. When ready to bake, pour half and half over and bake at 375° for about 1 hour or until browned and crispy.

Serves 4-6   *Mary Allen*

CREAMED POTATOES

4	baking potatoes (Idaho)	Salt and pepper
1	pint heavy cream	

- Boil potatoes until they can just be pierced with a fork.
- Cool a few minutes, then peel.
- Shred potatoes in food processor or with hand grater.
- Layer in baking pan (8x11-inch) or larger depending on amount) and salt and pepper between layers.
- Pour cream over all.
- Refrigerate 24 hours or overnight.
- 30 minutes before baking remove from refrigerator. Bake for 1 hour at 300°.

SPECIAL NOTE: EXCELLENT BUFFET DISH WITH RED MEAT. TASTES LIKE POTATOES AU GRATIN WITHOUT THE CHEESE.

Serves 4-6   *Susan Baumgardner*

A neighbor asked a small boy if his family said prayers
before meals. "No," he replied. "We don't have to.
My mother is a good cook."

HASH BROWN POTATOES

2	lbs. bag of frozen hash browns (thawed)	2	cups grated cheese
½	cup softened butter	16	oz. sour cream
½	cup onion (chopped)	1	tsp. salt
1	can cream of chicken soup	¼	tsp. pepper

- Mix above ingredients.
- Place in 13- x 8-inch casserole.
- Bake 45 minutes (uncovered) at 350°.

Kay Palmer

POTATO-SNOW PEA STIR-FRY

2 tbsp. butter or margarine	1 small onion, sliced and
4 small new potatoes,	separated into rings
quartered	½ tsp. salt
1 lb. fresh snow peas	

- Melt butter in a wok or heavy skillet.

- Add potatoes. Stir fry on medium heat 10 minutes or until potatoes are golden and crisp-tender.

- Add snow peas, onion and salt. Stir fry 5-7 minutes or until peas are crisp-tender.

- Serve immediately.

Main dish variation:

- Saute 1 cup strips of chicken in margarine for the last 5 minutes while cooking potatoes, before adding snow peas.

- Sprinkle 1 tsp. dried basil over all last 5 minutes.

SPECIAL NOTE: THIS RECIPE OF MY MOTHER, STACEY WILSON, WAS PUBLISHED IN SOUTHERN LIVING MAGAZINE.

Serves 6   *Brenda Hartsell*

MAGIC CASSEROLE:
POTATO 'N BROCCOLI SUPREME

3 cups hot mashed potatoes (5-6 medium)	1 can (2.8 oz.) Durkee french fried onion rings
1 pkg. (3 oz.) cream cheese, softened	2 pkg. (10 oz.) frozen broccoli spears, cooked and drained
¼ cup milk	1 cup (4 oz.) shredded
1 egg	American cheese
2 tbsp. margarine	

- Whip together first 5 ingredients until smooth. Season to taste with salt and pepper.

- Fold in half a can french fried onion.

- Spread potato mixture over bottom and up sides of a buttered 8- x 12-inch baking dish to form a shell.

- Bake at 350° for 25-30 minutes.

- Arrange hot broccoli spears in potato shell, sprinkle with cheese and remaining onions.

- Bake uncovered 5 minutes longer.

Serves 8   *Elizabeth Wright*

NEW POTATOES GRATINEE

6 tbsp. butter or margarine, divided
1 lb. mushrooms
12 medium red skinned potatoes, thinly sliced
1 medium onion, finely chopped
½ cup finely chopped parsley
1¼ cups gruyere or Swiss cheese (6 oz.)
2 cloves of garlic, finely chopped
1 tsp. salt
½ tsp. freshly ground pepper
2 cups heavy cream and ½ cup water mixed

- Preheat oven to 325°. Generously butter 13- x 9-inch baking dish. Trim mushrooms and thinly slice.

- In a large bowl, gently toss potatoes with mushrooms, onion, parsley, 1 cup of cheese, the garlic, salt, pepper and 2 tbsp. butter, melted. Place in prepared dish.

- Pour cream over potato mixture. Sprinkle with the remaining cheese, and dot with butter.

- Bake 1½ hours, covering with a loose tent of foil after the cheese has browned. Remove from oven, cover securely to help keep the potatoes warm until serving.

Serves 8-10   *Cam Caldwell*

"CALDERO" RICE WITH SEAFOOD

2 tbsp. olive oil
1 green pepper, chopped
1 onion, chopped
2 cloves garlic, minced
2 cups raw long grain rice
1 28 oz. can tomatoes
3 cups chicken broth
1 tsp. salt
⅛ tsp. pepper
¼ tsp. Tabasco (more if you are Spanish)
¼ tsp. basil
¼ tsp. thyme
Small pinch of saffron dissolved in 1 tbsp. hot water (optional)
1 lb. shrimp, shelled and deveined and/or other fish as well

- In Dutch oven, saute onion, green pepper and garlic in hot olive oil until tender—about 3 minutes.

- Add rice and cook until slightly brown.

- Add tomatoes, broth and other seasonings and bring to a boil. Reduce heat and cover.

- Simmer 15 minutes and stir in shrimp. Cover and cook 5 more minutes.

- Serve with hot rolls or bread.

SPECIAL NOTE: CONTRIBUTED BY THE COOK ABOARD THE REPLICA OF THE SANTA MARIA SHIP WHILE ANCHORED IN THE BRUNSWICK RIVER.

Serves 10-12

ROYAL CASSEROLE

2 10 oz. pkg. of frozen
   spinach, defrost and drain
2 cups (cans) mushroom stems
   and pieces
6 tbsp. butter, divided
1 tbsp. flour

½ cup milk
2 cans artichoke hearts cut in
   half—quarters if large
½ cup mayonnaise
2 tbsp. lemon juice

- Saute mushrooms in butter and set aside. Mix flour in remaining butter and milk (white sauce). Add spinach and mushrooms and heat thoroughly.

- Butter casserole 8x11½ x 2-inch (2 qt).

- Line bottom with artichokes. Pour spinach mixture over artichokes. Combine mayonnaise with lemon juice and spread over top.

- Bake at 350° for 30 minutes.

Jane Brady/Agnes Famous

KRISTEN'S SAUERKRAUT

1 16 oz. can sauerkraut,
   drained
1 medium onion, chopped
1 medium apple, chopped

3 strips bacon
Caraway seeds
Fresh ground pepper
1 tbsp. brown sugar

- Fry bacon until crisp, remove from skillet and set aside.

- In bacon drippings cook apple and onions until soft. Add sauerkraut, caraway, seeds, ground pepper and brown sugar.

- Adjust seasonings to taste.

- Heat on top of stove or in greased casserole in 350° oven for 30 minutes.

- Garnish with crumbled bacon.

- Good with turkey, duck or pork.

Serves 4   *Carolyn V. Krider*

Spinach for Company

1 small onion, chopped	2 pkg. frozen chopped spinach
3 tbsp. butter	½ cup cracker or bread crumbs
1 16 oz. can creamed corn	parmesan cheese

- Brown onions lightly in butter and set aside.
- Cook spinach as directed. Place in colander. Press with spoon to drain.
- Mix onions, corn and drained spinach.
- Pour into a 9x13-inch greased baking dish.
- Sprinkle crumbs and cheese on top.
- Bake covered at 300° for 40 minutes.

SPECIAL NOTE: EASY TO MAKE—MEN LIKE IT.

Serves 6-8   *Lucrece Truax*

Nut-Glazed Acorn Squash

2 Acorn Squash	½ cup chopped pecans or
4 tbsp. butter or margarine	walnuts
2 tbsp. brown sugar	Salt

- Rinse squash, cut in half lengthwise and remove seeds.
- Sprinkle each half lightly with salt, and fill each with 1 tbsp. butter, ½ tbsp. brown sugar, and 2 tbsp. pecans.
- Place squash in a baking dish; add half inch of water to dish.
- Cover and bake at 325° for 1 hour and 15 minutes or until squash is tender.

SPECIAL NOTE: COOK THESE AND REALLY FEEL FALL IS IN THE AIR—BUT GOOD AT ANYTIME THE SQUASH ARE IN THE MARKET.

Serves 4   *Jane Ledbetter*

SQUASH CASSEROLE I

1½ lb. yellow squash
1 small jar pimiento, chopped
2 small onions grated
1 pkg. Pepperidge Farm seasoned stuffing, divided

1 cup sour cream
2 medium carrots, grated
1 can cream of chicken soup
¼ lb. melted margarine

- Cook squash in salted boiling water until soft. Drain.

- Press in a sieve—pour off excess water.

- Add remaining ingredients, holding back half of stuffing and butter.

- Mix remaining stuffing with a quarter lb. melted margarine. Line casserole (reserve a little topping).

- Fill with squash mixture—put stuffing lightly over top.

- Bake in 350° oven for 30 minutes.

SPECIAL NOTE: BETTER IF MADE THE DAY BEFORE—THEN COOKED.

Serves 8-10   *Virginia Leveau*

SQUASH CASSEROLE II

3 lbs. yellow squash, chopped into quartered slices
1 to 1½ large onions, chopped
1 pint sour cream

1 stick (melted) margarine
1 can mushroom soup
1½ cups Pepperidge Farm dressing

- Mix all of the above ingredients well.

- Pour into an 8"x8" greased dish. Bake in 350° oven 35 minutes.

SPECIAL NOTE: MY MOTHER'S RECIPE.

Serves 6   *Susan Shipman*

SQUASH SOUFFLE

1 cup grated sharp cheese
1½ cups mashed boiled squash
1 cup cracker crumbs
2 tbsp. parsley
1 tbsp. onion juice
3 tbsp. butter

1 cup scalded milk
2 eggs, beaten
½ green pepper, chopped
½ tsp. salt
¼ tsp. pepper
Dash cayenne pepper

- Mix all ingredients, adding scalded milk last. (Be sure that the milk is hot.)

- Bake in greased casserole at 350° about 45 minutes.

- (Pimiento may be substituted for green pepper; parsley may be omitted.)

Serves 6   *Charlotte Marshall*

FRIED GREEN TOMATOES
"THE SOUTHERN WAY"

2	firm medium sized green tomatoes	½	tsp. pepper
½	tsp. salt	½	cup white corn meal
		½	cup bacon drippings

- Cut tomatoes into ½-inch slices, sprinkle with salt and pepper.
- Dredge in corn meal.
- Heat bacon drippings in a heavy skillet.
- Add tomatoes, and cook over medium heat until browned, turning once.

Yield 2-3 servings   *Betty Lewis McCartney*

VEGALL CASSEROLE

1	16 oz. can Vegall	1	cup sharp cheddar cheese, grated
1	can sliced water chestnuts		
1	cup chopped celery	1	cup mayonnaise
1	cup chopped onion	20	Ritz crackers, crushed
		1	stick butter

- Mix together first six ingredients and place in an oblong pyrex casserole.
- Top with 20 crushed Ritz crackers and 1 stick of butter cut in small pieces.
- Bake in 350° oven for 1 hour.

Serves 10-12   *Eileen B. Hutcheson*

*To eat or drink without regard for God is to
deny the honor due the host; and to eat or drink
without concern for the other guests is to deny
the host's right to choose the guests.*

JOHN E. BURKHART

VEGETABLE CASSEROLE I

1	box frozen mixed vegetables	½ cup sour cream
1	box frozen peas	¼ cup mayonnaise
1	box frozen baby limas	Salt and pepper to taste
1	onion, chopped	½ tsp. dried basil
1	tbsp. butter or margarine	Buttered, crushed Cheez-its
1	tbsp. flour	crackers

- Cook the frozen vegetables briefly. Strain. Put in large bowl.

- Saute the onion in butter or margarine.

- Sprinkle the flour over the onion. Add to bowl.

- Add sour cream, mayonnaise, salt, pepper and dried basil.

- Mix all together and put in buttered casserole.

- Top with buttered crushed cheez-Its.

- Bake at 350° about 20 minutes until bubbly.

FRESH VEGETABLES MAY BE SUBSTITUTED.

Serves 8-10   *Jeanne Alaimo (Mrs. Anthony)*

VEGETABLE CASSEROLE II

1	can shoepeg corn, drained	½ box crushed cheese crackers
1	can French cut beans, drained	½ cup chopped onions
1	can cream of celery soup	½ cup chopped celery
¼	cup chopped green peppers or 1 small jar pimiento	¼ pt. sour cream
		½ cup sliced almonds
	Salt and pepper to taste	¼ cup margarine, melted

- Combine corn, beans, soup, green pepper, onions, celery, sour cream, salt and pepper in greased dish.

- Sprinkle with crackers.

- Top with melted margarine and almonds.

- Bake at 350° for 40 minutes.

Barbara Appleby

LAST MINUTE VEGETABLES
FOR COMPANY DINNER

2	onions sliced paper thin	1	tsp. salt
1	green pepper sliced paper thin	½	lb. fresh mushrooms sliced paper thin
1	tbsp. vegetable oil	2	tbsp. soy sauce
1	tbsp. sugar	2	pkgs. frozen broccoli (or
½	tsp. red hot pepper		spinach) thawed and drained

- In large pan, cook green pepper and onions in vegetable oil.
- Push to one side and cook mushrooms.
- Blend vegetables and add sugar, salt, hot pepper and soy sauce.
- Arrange broccoli over vegetables pushing stems only down in pan to steam for 10-12 minutes.
- Carefully toss while cooking for 3-4 minutes longer being careful not to break vegetables.
- Add a spoon or two of water if necessary.
- Vegetables should be slightly crisp.

SPECIAL NOTE: MARVELOUS WITH ROAST BEEF.

Serves 6   *Laura R. Brown*

LIKKER PUDDIN'

2½	cups milk	¼	stick butter
3	medium yams	¼	cup blanched slivered almonds (optional)
2	cups sugar	½	cup rum or whiskey
2	tsp. cinnamon		
3	eggs		

- Put milk in 2 qt. casserole. Grate yams, adding to milk as you grate to prevent potatoes from turning dark.
- Beat eggs well and add sugar gradually. Add cinnamon (and almonds) and mix well with potatoes.
- Dot generously with butter and bake in a 325° oven until firm, about 1¼ hours.
- Just before serving pour half cup rum or whiskey over the pudding.

SPECIAL NOTE: DELICIOUS WITH TURKEY. MAY BE USED WITHOUT "LIKKER," (BUT NOT AS GOOD!).

Serves 6   *Nancy Krauss*

APSE WINDOWS

Located on either side of the altar, the
bosses in the outer windows are the
symbols of the four evangelists.
St. Matthew is represented as the winged
man, St. Mark as the lion, St. Luke as
the winged ox and St. John as the eagle.

The windows are dedicated "In memory
of The Revd. Edmund Matthews, some-
time Rector of this Parish, who entered
into rest Decr. 1, 1827."

EGGS, CHEESE, PASTA, RICE, GRAIN

APSE WINDOWS

Located on either side of the altar, the bosses in the outer windows are the symbols of the four evangelists.
St. Matthew is represented as the winged man, St. Mark as the lion, St. Luke as the winged ox and St. John as the eagle.

The windows are dedicated "In memory of The Revd. Edmund Matthews, some-time Rector of this Parish, who entered into rest Decr. 1, 1827."

Brunch O'Billy

Canadian bacon
Tomatoes, sliced
Onions, chopped
Swiss cheese, sliced

Cheddar cheese, sliced
Eggs
Butter
Salt and pepper

- In individual casseroles layer first five ingredients in order, dotting with butter, salt, pepper. I use Jane's Krazy Mixed Up Salt.
- Put in 350° oven until bubbly.
- Remove from oven and break eggs over top. Sprinkle additional salt and pepper if desired.
- Bake until eggs are set to your liking.
- Per individual, use 2 slices Canadian bacon, ½ tomato, 2 eggs, onion and cheese to your taste preference. The more cheese, the more filling.

SPECIAL NOTE: DELICIOUS SERVED WITH ROLLS OR TOAST, AND FRESH FRUIT.

Nancy Sumerford

Mock Omelet

8   slices white bread, crusts
    removed
¾   lb. sharp cheese, grated
4   eggs

2   cups milk
1   tsp. salt
1   tsp. dry mustard

- Butter the bread, tear into pieces. Butter 2 qt. casserole. Put bread on bottom of casserole.
- Put grated cheese on top of bread.
- Mix other ingredients and pour over cheese and bread.
- Refrigerate overnight.
- Place casserole in pan of water. Bake at 325° for 1 hour.

Ann Jarrett

CHEESE SOUFFLÉ WITH DILL

8	slices white bread trimmed and cubed (about 12 cubes per slice)	4	eggs beaten with fork
1	stick butter, melted	1	pint of Half and Half
12	oz. sharp cheddar cheese in bite-sized cubes	4	drops Tabasco
		½	cup chopped onion
		¾	tsp. dill weed
			Salt and pepper to taste

- Toss cubed bread in melted butter until butter is absorbed.
- Lightly mix all ingredients and pour into sprayed casserole.
- Place in refrigerator overnight or for at least 3 hours.
- Remove and bake about 1¼ hours at 350°. Bacon crumbled on top optional.

Jeannette S. MacPherson

CONTINENTAL CHEESE BAKE

1	cup sliced onion	¾	cup milk
1	tbsp. butter or margarine	1	tsp. prepared mustard
8	hard-cooked eggs, sliced	½	tsp seasoned salt
2	cups shredded process Swiss cheese	¼	tsp. dill weed
1	can condensed cream of mushroom soup	¼	tsp. pepper
		6	slices rye bread, buttered and cut into triangles

- Heat oven to 350°.
- Cook and stir onion in butter until onion is tender. Spread mixture into oblong baking dish.
- Top with egg slices; sprinkle with cheese.
- Beat remaining ingredients (except bread) in bowl.
- Pour soup mixture over cheese; overlap bread slices on top of casserole. Bake 30 to 35 minutes or until heated through.
- Set oven to broil or 550°. Place casserole 5-inches from source of heat; broil 1 minute until bread is toasted.

SPECIAL NOTE: TO PREPARE AHEAD; PREPARE CASSEROLE AS DIRECTED EXCEPT DO NOT TOP WITH BREAD OR BAKE. REFRIGERATE SEVERAL HOURS OR OVERNIGHT. AT BAKING TIME PLACE BREAD SLICES ON TOP AND BAKE 40- TO 45 MINUTES.

Serves 6   *Sally McCauley*

BOURSIN CHEESE

3 8 oz. pkgs. cream cheese, softened
1½ sticks butter, softened
1 8 oz. bottle of Green Goddess dressing

1 tsp. garlic powder
1 tsp. ground black pepper
1 tsp. dried parsley

- Blend together cream cheese and butter with mixer.
- Add the next four ingredients to mixture and blend well.

SPECIAL NOTE: YOU WILL HAVE A LOVELY BOURSIN AT A FRACTION OF THE USUAL COST. THIS FREEZES VERY WELL.

Mrs. Robert W. Peters

PIMIENTO CHEESE CASSEROLE

8 slices loaf bread
1 cup milk
1 small jar chopped pimiento
2 eggs

2 tbsp. oleo, melted
¾ lb. sharp cheese
1 tsp. salt
1 tsp. pepper

- Break up bread, soften with milk.
- Add beaten eggs, grated cheese, pimiento, oleo, salt and pepper. Mix well
- Pour into greased casserole. Bake in 350° oven 30 to 45 minutes until golden brown.
- More milk may be added for a more moist texture.

SPECIAL NOTE: THIS CAN BE MADE AHEAD OF TIME AND KEPT IN THE REFRIGERATOR UNTIL READY TO BAKE. A PLUS FOR THIS DISH IS THAT IT GETS BETTER WARMED OVER.

Ann Jarrett

Lord Jesus, be our holy Guest,
Our morning Joy, our evening Rest,
And with or daily bread impart
Thy love and peace to every heart.Amen

THE BOOK OF COMMON WORSHIP.

BROCCOLI-MUSHROOM LASAGNA

9 lasagna noodles
¼ cup margarine or butter
¼ cup flour
1 tbsp. instant minced onion
2 tsp. instant chicken bouillon
1 tsp. garlic salt
½ tsp. thyme leaves
¼ tsp. pepper
2½ cups milk

12 oz. carton (1½ cups cottage cheese)
20 oz (6 cups) frozen cut broccoli, thawed and drained
2 2H oz. jars sliced mushrooms, drained
12 oz. (3 cups) shredded Swiss cheese
⅓ cup grated Parmesan cheese

- Cook lasagna noodles following package directions.
- Preheat oven to 350°.
- Melt margarine in Dutch oven or 4 qt. saucepan.
- Stir in fllour, instant minced onions, bouillon, garlic salt, thyme and pepper. Cook until mixture is smooth and bubbly.
- Gradually add milk, stir constantly until mixture boils and thickens. Blend in cottage cheese, broccoli and mushrooms.
- In 13- x 9-inch baking dish, layer ⅓ of noodles, ⅓ of sauce (about 2 cups) and ⅓ of Swiss cheese; repeat layers twice more.
- Bake at 350° 25-30 minutes or until thoroughly heated. Sprinkle parmesan over top. Let stand 10 minutes before serving.

SPECIAL NOTE: CAN BE PREPARED A DAY AHEAD AND REFRIGERATED. BAKE NEXT DAY.

Serves 12 *Jeannie Wade*

FOUR CHEESE LASAGNA

8 oz. lasagna, cooked and drained
4 oz. ricotta cheese

4 oz. mozzarella cheese, shredded
8 oz. cheddar cheese, shredded
2 oz. parmesan cheese, grated
30 oz. jar spaghetti sauce

- Heat sauce while noodles are cooking. Mix all cheeses in a bowl.
- In a large rectangular baking pan spoon a thin layer of sauce. Then place a layer of noodles across the bottom. Spoon another layer of sauce, then generously sprinkle a layer of cheese to cover.
- Repeat the process (noodles, sauce, cheeses). This will give you 3 to 4 layers depending upon the size of the pan.
- Bake in 350° oven for 45 minutes or until bubbly.
- Cool 15 minutes before cutting.

SPECIAL NOTE: GROUND BEEF CAN BE ADDED TO SAUCE IF DESIRED. USE ANY BRAND OF SAUCE YOU LIKE (I USUALLY DOCTOR UP THE STORE BRAND).

Serves 8-10 *Ruth Marie Gould*

SHORTCUT LASAGNA

3	lbs. ground lean beef	2	tsp. oregano
2	qts. spaghetti sauce with mushrooms	1	tbsp. chili powder
		1	pkg. lasagna noodles
2	onions chopped	1	24 oz. carton cottage cheese
1	bell pepper chopped	2	8 oz. pkgs. mozzarella cheese
1	tsp. garlic powder	1	cup parmesan

- Saute meat until crumbly.
- Sauté onion and peppers.
- Add spaghetti sauce and seasonings. Bring to boil and simmer 20-30 minutes.
- Cover bottom of 9 x 13 -inch pan with thin layer of meat sauce.
- Add a layer of uncooked noodles, cottage cheese, mozzarella and parmesan. Repeat until all ingredients are used.
- Bake at 350° for 1 hour.
- Can be frozen before cooking.

SPECIAL NOTE: SPAGHETTI SAUCE CAN BE MADE AHEAD AND FROZEN UNTIL USED.

Serves 8-10   *Mary C. Freeman*

CHEESE GRITS

4	cups water	2	cups shredded cheddar cheese (8 oz.)
½	tsp. salt		
1	cup quick cooking grits	½	cup butter or margarine
		½	cup milk
		2	eggs, beaten

- Bring water and salt to boil. Stir in grits. Follow package directions. Stir to remove lumps.
- Remove from heat; add shredded cheese and butter, stir until melted. Stir in milk
- Add a small amount of hot grits to beaten eggs stirring well. Stir egg mixture into remaining grits. Pour grits into lightly greased 2 qt. casserole. Bake at 350° for 30-40 minutes or until set (will be golden brown).

SPECIAL NOTE: EXCELLENT WITH FISH OR ANY FRIED SEAFOOD. ALSO EXCELLENT FOR BREAKFAST.

Serves 6-8   *Jeannie Wade*

CHEESE GRITS CASSEROLE

1 tsp. salt	2 cloves garlic, crushed
4½ cups water	2 eggs
1 cup quick grits	⅔ cup milk
½ cup (1 stick) plus 2 tbsp. butter or margarine	Dash hot pepper sauce
½ lb. grated sharp cheddar cheese	2 cups cornflake crumbs
	Dash paprika

- Add salt to water; bring to boil.
- Slowly add grits and continue boiling 3 to 5 minutes. Remove from heat and add ½ cup butter, cheese and garlic. Stir until butter melts.
- Beat eggs; stir in milk. Add to grits mixture. Add pepper sauce. Mix well.
- Pour into greased 2½ qt. casserole.
- Dot top with remaining 2 tbsp. butter. Sprinkle with cornflakes crumbs and paprika.
- Bake in preheated 350° oven about 1 hour.

Serves 6-8

Mary Jane Flint

GEORGIA CHEESE GRITS

4 cups water	2 6 oz. pkgs. processed cheese with garlic
1¼ cup quick grits (not instant)	
½ cup (1 stick) butter or margarine cut in pieces	2 large eggs, lightly beaten
	1 tsp. seasoned salt

- Preheat oven to 325°. In a large saucepan bring salted water to boiling. Stir in grits, cook as the package directs.
- Remove from heat. Add butter and cheese; stir until both are melted, then stir in eggs and seasoned salt.
- Lightly butter a 2 qt. shallow casserole. Spread mixture into casserole evenly. Bake uncovered 1 hour.

Serves 6-8

RICE CASSEROLE

½ cup chopped onion, green or vidalia
1 clove garlic, minced
2 cans chicken broth
¼ cup chopped walnuts or pecans

2 tbsp. Liptons Onion Soup Mix
1½ cups uncooked regular rice
1 8 oz. can mushrooms, stems and pieces
2-3 tbsp. margarine
Salt and pepper to taste

- Sauté onion in margarine until soft.
- Add rice and garlic and sauté briefly. Remove to bowl.
- In same skillet sauté mushrooms, add to bowl.
- Add broth, walnut pecans, salt, pepper and onion soup mix.
- Bake at 350° 1¼ hours in buttered casserole, cover with lid or foil.

SPECIAL NOTE: THIS IS GOOD MADE WITH BROWN RICE, IN WHICH CASE ADD A LITTLE MORE LIQUID. YOU COULD USE THE LIQUID FROM THE MUSHROOMS, OR WATER, AND BAKE 1½ HOURS.

Serves 10-12   *Jeanne Alaimo (Mrs. Anthony Alaimo)*

BAKED RICE

2 cups long grain rice
4 tbsp. butter

4 cups beef consommé (or water)

- Heat consommé/water to boiling point.
- Warm a large casserole in oven before starting rice.
- In skillet on top of stove, melt butter. When good and hot, add rice and stir constantly until well coated and slightly browned.
- Transfer to hot casserole and add the boiling stock or water.
- Bake in a 375° oven 1 hour or until dry and fluffy.

SPECIAL NOTE: IF THERE IS ANY LEFT OVER IT IS JUST AS GOOD THE NEXT DAY, JUST STIR WITH A FORK AND REHEAT.

Serves 8   *Helen D. Moore*

HERB RICE

1 cup uncooked rice
2 beef bouillon cubes
½ tsp. each salt, rosemary, marjoram, thyme

1 tsp. dried onion flakes
2 cups water
1 tbsp. butter or margarine

- On high heat in a heavy saucepan, combine dry ingredients with water and margarine.
- Bring to a boil, reduce heat to medium low. Stir once with a fork.
- Cover tightly and cook until all liquid is absorbed. (15 minutes.)

SPECIAL NOTE: THIS IS A GOOD DISH TO SERVE WITH CHICKEN.

Serves 4-6   *Brenda Hartsell*

RICE RISOTTO

1	tbsp. butter	1	10¾ oz. can beef consommé
1¼	cup long grain rice, uncooked	1	4 oz. can sliced mushrooms, undrained
1	10¾ oz. can Campbells French Onion Soup	½	cup grated parmesan cheese

- Lightly grease a 1½ qt. covered casserole.
- Pour soup and consommé over rice, add mushrooms and butter.
- Cover and bake at 325° for 1 hour.
- Sprinkle cheese on top and return to oven until cheese is melted.

Serves 4   *Becky Rowell*

WILD RICE CASSEROLE

1	cup wild rice, soaked overnight	1½	cup finely chopped celery
1	10¾ oz. can consommé	6-8	green onions, sliced
4	tbsp. butter	1	6 oz. can water chestnuts, drained and sliced
¾	lb. fresh mushrooms, sliced	½	cup dry vermouth

- Wash and drain soaked rice and combine with consommé in large saucepan.
- Simmer, covered for about 30 minutes or until liquid is absorbed.
- Melt butter in a skillet and sauté mushrooms, onions and celery until limp.
- Mix with water chestnuts and rice and put in a buttered 2 qt. casserole.
- Refrigerate until ready to use.
- When ready to reheat add vermouth and dot top with butter.
- Bake at 350° for 30 to 40 minutes.

SPECIAL NOTE: I HAVE USED COMBINATION OF WILD AND BROWN RICE OR BROWN RICE, ALONE, ADJUSTING LIQUID TO AMOUNT GIVEN ON RICE PKG.

Serves 8   *Melissa Barnes*

APSE WINDOWS

Next to the altar on the Gospel side is
the Agnus Dei, or Lamb of God, shown
with the Easter banner.

The windows are dedicated "In memory
of The Revd. Edmund Matthews, some-
time Rector of this Parish, who entered
into rest Decr. 1, 1827."

SOMETIME RECTOR

DESSERTS, CAKES, PIES, COOKIES

APSE WINDOWS

Next to the Epistle side of the altar is the descending dove, representing the Holy Spirit.

The windows are dedicated "In memory of The Revd. Edmund Matthews, sometime Rector of this Parish, who entered into rest Decr. 1, 1827."

BROWNIES

1	square unsweetened Baker's chocolate	1	cup sugar
1	square semi-sweet Baker's chocolate	2	eggs
		⅛	tsp. salt
¼	cup butter	½	cup flour
		1	tsp. vanilla

- Melt chocolate over hot water in a saucepan large enough to use as a mixing bowl.
- Remove from heat. Add butter and stir until melted.
- Add sugar while stirring.
- Carefully add slightly beaten eggs, salt, flour and vanilla.
- If you like, you may add walnut or pecan pieces.
- Spread evenly in a buttered 8-inch square pan.
- Bake at 300° for 40-50 minutes. Cut into squares.

SPECIAL NOTE: BAKE AT 350° FOR 25 MINUTES FOR CAKE-LIKE BROWNIES.

Louise Shipps

CHOCOLATE BROWNIE PIE

2	sticks margarine	1	can (2 cups) Angel Flake coconut
1	cup chocolate chips		
4	eggs	1	cup chopped nuts
2	cups sugar	3	unbaked pie shells

- Melt margarine with chocolate chips over low heat.
- Beat eggs thoroughly (not with electric beater) and add sugar, mixing well.
- Mix egg mixture and chocolate chip mixture.
- Add coconut and nuts. Mix well.
- Pour into 3 unbaked pie shells.
- Bake at 350° for 45 minutes. If you like a softer pie, cook at 300°.

Ann Jarrett

CRÈME DE MENTHE BROWNIES

½ cup butter (soft)
1 cup sugar
4 eggs
1 cup flour
½ tsp. salt
1 16 oz chocolate syrup
1 tsp. vanilla

¼ cup butter
2 cups sifted powdered sugar
2 tbsp. crème de menthe
¼ cup butter
1 6 oz. package semi-sweet chocolate chips

- Cream butter and sugar. Beat until fluffy.
- Add eggs, beat after each addition.
- Combine flour and salt. Add to egg mixture alternately with chocolate syrup. Begin and end with flour mix.
- Stir in vanilla.
- Pour into 13- x 9-inch greased and floured pan.
- Bake at 350° for 25-28 minutes. Cool completely.
- Cream ¼ cup butter. Add powdered sugar and crème de menthe. Mix well and spread over brownies. Chill 1 hour.
- Combine chocolate chips and remaining butter in double boiler. Melt and stir. Spread over chilled brownies. Chill 1 additional hour. Cut into squares.

Yield 3½ dozen

Weezie Campbell

CRISPIES (BROWNIES)

½ cup oleo
1 cup sugar
2 eggs
1 cup self rising flour

3-4 tbsp. cocoa
1 tsp. vanilla
chopped nuts

- Cream oleo and sugar. Add beaten eggs.
- Add flour, cocoa and vanilla.
- Spread in 9- x 12 inch pan. Sprinkle nuts on top.
- Bake in a 350° oven for 15-20 minutes, until brown.
- Cool and cut into squares.

Mary C. Freeman

SOUTHERN BROWNIES

2	cups sugar	Icing:	
2	eggs	1	stick butter or margarine
½	cup sour cream	6	tbsp. milk
2	cups flour (self rising)	4	tbsp. cocoa
1	tsp. baking soda	1 box confectioners sugar	
2	sticks margarine or butter		(10 - XXXX)
1	cup water	1 tsp. vanilla	
4	tbsp. cocoa	1 cup pecans (chopped)	
1	tsp. vanilla		

- Cream sugar and eggs.
- Add sour cream and beat 'til fluffy.
- Add flour and soda and blend.
- Melt butter in saucepan. Add water and cocoa. Boil 1 minute. Add vanilla.
- Add cocoa mixture to first mixture and mix well.
- Pour into 2½ qt baking pan (14- x 10- x 2-inch is a good size).
- Bake 30 minutes at 350°.
- Icing should be made last 5 minutes before cake is done.
- Icing: Melt butter in saucepan. Add milk and cocoa. Boil 1 minute.
- Add confectioners sugar, vanilla, and chopped pecans. Blend together.
- Pour over baked brownie cake while both are hot.

Yields 36   *Jeannie Wade*

White Chocolate Brownies

½ cup unsalted butter
8 oz white chocolate chips or coarsely chopped white chocolate, divided.
2 large eggs
½ cup sugar

½ tsp. vanilla
½ tsp. salt
1 cup all - purpose flour
8 oz semi - sweet chocolate chips

- Preheat oven to 350°.
- Lightly butter 8-inch square pan. Line bottom with foil or parchment. Lightly butter foil.
- Melt butter in small saucepan over low heat. Remove pan from heat.
- Add half of white chocolate; do not stir.
- Using electric mixer, beat eggs with pinch of salt until frothy. Gradually add sugar and beat until pale yellow and slowly dissolving ribbons form when beaters are lifted.
- Add butter/white chocolate mixture, vanilla, ½ tsp. salt, and flour. Mix until just combined.
- Stir in semi-sweet chips and remaining white chocolate chips. Spoon mixture into prepared pan; smooth top with spatula.
- Bake until tester inserted in center comes out almost clean, covering top with foil if browning too quickly (about 30 minutes).
- Cool brownies in pan on rack. Cut into 16 squares.
- Can be prepared 1 day ahead. Store in airtight container.

Becky Rowell

Back Home Tea Cakes

½ cup shortening
1 cup sugar
1 egg
2 tsp. vanilla

2 cups all - purpose flour
1 tbsp. baking powder
¼ cup milk

- Cream shortening.
- Gradually add sugar. Mix well on medium speed.
- Add eggs and vanilla. Beat well
- Combine flour and baking powder. Add to mixture alternating with milk. Mix well.
- Cover. Chill two hours. Roll out ½ of dough on floured surface.
- Cut with cookie cutters. Bake on cookie sheet in 375° oven for 6-8 minutes.

Makes 3 dozen

Harriette Miller

BRICKLE BARS

Batter:
1   stick butter
½   cup oleo
1   cup dark brown sugar
1   egg yolk beaten
1½ cup flour
1   tsp. vanilla

Topping:
6   Hershey bars, broken
1   bag Brickell Bits, grind finely
½   cup nuts, grind finely

- Mix first 6 ingredients.
- Spread batter on cookie sheet with raised edges.
- Bake at 350° for 15 minutes.
- Put broken Hershey pieces over batter while hot.
- When chocolate melts, spread evenly.
- Sprinkle Brickell Bits and nuts over top of chocolate.
- Cool then slice in small pieces.

Mary Lou Hull

CAN'T STOPS

1   stick of butter
1   stick of margarine
1   cup sugar
1½ cup flour
½   tsp. baking soda

½   tsp. baking powder
2   cups Rice Krispies
½   cup chopped nuts
1   tsp. vanilla

- Cream butter, margarine, and sugar.
- Sift flour with baking soda and baking powder. Add to sugar mixture slowly.
- Fold in Rice Krispies and nuts. Add vanilla.
- Drop by teaspoon on sprayed cookie sheet.
- Bake in 350° oven until lightly brown on edges, 8 - 10 minutes. Let cool slightly before removing from sheet.

Lauretta K. Baumgardner

CONGO SQUARES

2¾ cups sifted flour
1½ sticks butter, melted
2 cups light brown sugar
3 eggs
2½ tsp. baking powder

¾ tsp. salt
1 tsp. vanilla
1 package Nestles semi - sweet chocolate morsels
½ cup chopped nuts

- Grease and flour 9- x 12- inch pan.
- Sift together flour, baking powder and salt.
- Cream together butter (melted first) and sugar. Add eggs.
- Fold in chocolate bits and pecans. Pour into prepared pan.
- Bake at 350° for 25 - 30 minutes.

Selma F. Shelander

CRISP COOKIES

2 sticks butter
1 cup sugar
1 tsp. vanilla

2 cups all purpose flour
½ cup chopped nuts
1 egg, separated

- Cream butter, sugar and vanilla. Add egg yolk and blend well.
- Add flour and blend well.
- Butter 12- x 18-inch cookie sheet.
- Press dough on cookie sheet as flat as possible.
- Brush top with slightly beaten egg white.
- Sprinkle chopped nuts on top. Press in slightly.
- Bake in a 225° oven for 2 hours.
- Cut while hot. Cool in pan. Store in tight containers.

Yields about 80 cookies   *Billie - Jo Edwards*

CRUNCH BAR

1	column saltines from 4 pack package	1	cup light brown sugar
2	sticks butter	1	12 oz. package chocolate morsels

- Pre-heat oven to 400°.
- Layer saltines on foil-lined 15- x 10-inch pan.
- Boil butter and sugar for 3 minutes. Pour or spoon butter / sugar mixture over saltines.
- Bake at 400° for 7 minutes. Watch carefully.
- Remove from oven and spread chocolate morsels over the top of the cooked saltines. (Using the back of a spoon helps.)
- Do not let it cool at all before spreading the chocolate. I do it right on the oven door so that the syrup is still hot.
- Cool in the refrigerator, break into pieces. This freezes well.

SPECIAL NOTE: NO ONE WOULD GUESS THAT SALTINES ARE AT THE BOTTOM OF IT!

Mrs. Robert W Peters

DATE BARS

½	cup margarine	½	tsp. baking powder
1	cup sugar	⅓	tsp. salt
2	eggs	1	cup chopped dates
1	tsp. vanilla	¾	cup chopped walnuts
1	cup cake flour		

- Cream margarine and sugar.
- Add 2 well beaten eggs and 1 tsp. vanilla.
- Sift together cake flour, baking powder and salt.
- Add to margarine, sugar and egg mixture.
- Add chopped walnuts and dates.
- Spread on a 9- x 12-inch or 9- x 9-inch lightly greased pan.
- Bake at 375° for 25 minutes.
- When cool, sprinkle top with confectioners sugar.

SPECIAL NOTE: THE COOKIES CAN BE CUT ½ THE SIZE EASILY. CAN BE FROZEN. THIS IS A TRIED AND TRUE RECIPE GIVEN TO ME MANY YEARS AGO.

Yield: Approximately 2 dozen 1 X 2 - inch cookies   *Lotta M Hunt*

DIXIE BARS

2	sticks butter, melted	½	tsp. salt
2	cups dark brown sugar	1	cup chopped pecans
2	eggs	1	tsp. vanilla
2	cups flour		

- Melt butter. Add sugar and eggs. Beat until creamy.

- Sift flour and gradually add to the sugar, eggs and butter.

- Add salt, vanilla and chopped nuts. Pour into greased pan, 8- x 12-inch.

- Bake at 350° for 25-30 minutes.

Selma F. Shelander

DREAM BARS

1	stick butter	½	tsp. baking powder
½	cup brown sugar	1	tsp. vanilla
1	cup flour	1	cup coconut
2	eggs	1	tbsp. butter
1	cup granulated sugar	2	tbsp. lemon juice
2	tbsp. flour	1	cup 10-X sugar
¼	tsp. salt		

- Combine butter, brown sugar and flour. Press mixture into 9- x 12-inch Pyrex dish.

- Bake at 350° for 15 minutes.

- Combine next 7 ingredients.

- Spread mixture over crust.

- Bake 30 minutes more. Cool slightly and top with mixture of remaining butter, lemon juice and sugar.

- Cut into squares.

Mrs. W.S. Ledbetter, Jr. (Jane)

FORGOTTEN COOKIES

2 egg whites
⅔ cup sugar
1 pinch salt
1 tsp. vanilla

1 6 oz. package semi - sweet chocolate chips
1½ cups of combined Rice Krispies and pecans

- Beat whites very stiff.
- Add sugar gradually while beating.
- Add salt and vanilla.
- Fold in rice Krispies and pecans. Mix with a spoon. Add chocolate chips and stir.
- Put foil on two large cookie sheets. Drop by tsp. on foil.
- Place in oven heated to 350°. Immediately turn oven off and leave cookies in oven at least 4 hours.
- Cool and store in airtight container.

Yields 2 - 3 dozen Harriette Miller (submitted by her daughter, Ellen Otte)

GEORGIA GEMS

½ cup soft butter
½ cup light brown sugar, packed
½ tsp. extract of vanilla
1 egg
½ tsp. baking soda

¼ tsp. salt
1½ cups all-purpose flour
½ cup chopped unsalted peanuts
½ cup crunchy peanut butter

- Cream butter with sugar and peanut butter.
- Add vanilla and egg, beat until fluffy.
- Stir in baking soda and salt.
- Blend in flour. Mix until a stiff dough forms.
- Add chopped unsalted nuts.
- Shape into walnut size balls.
- Place on lightly greased cookie sheet, press with fork crisscross to flatten.
- Bake at 375° for 10 minutes or until lightly browned.

SPECIAL NOTE: THIS IS WHY GEORGIA IS THE PEANUT STATE. DELICIOUS!

Yields 2½ dozen   *Mrs. Robert Allen*

LIZZIE'S SUMMERTIME COOKIES

2 cups sugar
½ cup milk
1 stick butter
3 tbsp. cocoa
¼ tsp. salt

1 tsp. vanilla
1 tsp. white Karo syrup
½ cup creamy peanut butter
3 cups quick cooking oatmeal

- Combine sugar, milk, butter, cocoa and Karo syrup.
- Bring to a full boil for ONE minute, no more.
- Add salt and vanilla.
- Blend in peanut butter and oatmeal, mix well.
- Drop by teaspoon onto wax paper.
- Let stand 15 minutes until solid.

Yields about 4½ dozen

Mrs. Robert W. Peters

MACADAMIA NUT COOKIES

2¼ cups all purpose flour
1 tsp. baking soda
1 tsp. salt
1 cup softened butter
½ cup granulated sugar
½ cup brown sugar, packed

2 eggs
1¼ cup macadamia nuts, chopped
½ cup flaked coconut
9 oz. butterscotch chips
1 tsp. extract of vanilla

- Sift together dry ingredients and set aside.
- Cream butter with sugars until light and fluffy.
- To butter mixture add vanilla and eggs, beat well.
- Stir in dry ingredients until thoroughly blended.
- Mix in butterscotch chips, nuts, and coconut.
- Drop by rounded tbsp. onto ungreased cookie sheet.
- Bake at 350° for 12 minutes or until lightly browned.
- Remove from baking sheet and cool on rack.
- Store in airtight tin.

SPECIAL NOTE: UTTERLY DELICIOUS!

Yields 40 cookies

Mrs Robert Allen

MARTHA COOKIES

1½ sticks margarine, room
     temperature
1   box light brown sugar
1   tsp. vanilla

2   eggs, beaten
1   tsp. baking powder
1½ full cups of flour
¾   cup chopped pecans

- Cream margarine and brown sugar. Add vanilla, eggs, baking powder and flour. Blend in pecans.
- Pour into greased 9- x 12-inch pan.
- Bake at 350° for 25 munutes. Do not overcook as they are best when chewy and fresh.
- Sprinkle with powdered sugar after they are cool.

SPECIAL NOTE: THIS RECIPE WAS FOUND IN THE NEWSPAPER BY MY HUSBAND'S GRANDMOTHER. IT WAS ATTRACTIVE TO HER BECAUSE THERE WERE SO MANY MARTHA'S IN THE FAMILY. I WISH I KNEW HOW MANY TIMES I'VE MADE THESE COOKIES!

Serves 12 - 14

Martha Fitzgerald

MOLASSES SPICE COOKIES

2   cups flour
2   tsp. soda
2   tsp. cloves, ground
2   tsp. ginger
2   tsp. cinnamon

Pinch salt
¾   cup butter
1   cup sugar
1   egg
4   tbsp. molasses

- Combine flour, soda and spices.
- Cream butter, add sugar then egg.
- Combine butter and flour mixtures.
- Add molasses and chill.
- Dip walnut size balls in sugar. Place on cookie sheet.
- Bake in 350° oven about 10 minutes.

Ruth Stewart

OLD FASHIONED GINGER SNAPS

¾	cup shortening	2	tsp. soda	
1	cup sugar	1	heaping tsp. ground ginger	
¼	cup molasses	1	heaping tsp. ground cloves	
1	egg	1	heaping tsp. ground	
2	cups flour		cinnamon	
¼	tsp. salt			

- Mix ingredients, cover and chill. Form into small balls and roll in granulated sugar.
- Place on greased cookie sheet, not too close, and press down in middle to flatten.
- Bake at 375° for 9 to 12 minutes.
- Watch carefully after 9 minutes so they won't get too brown—ovens vary. If you like them chewy, cook less time.

SPECIAL NOTE: HAVE MADE THESE FOR YEARS FOR MY CHILDREN. THERE HAVE BEEN TIMES WHEN I HAVE MIXED THE DOUGH AND PLACED IN THE REFRIGERATOR TO CHILL AND "LITTLE PEOPLE" WOULD EAT THE UNCOOKED DOUGH LIKE CANDY BEFORE I COULD COOK THE COOKIES!

Martha Fitzgerald

PECAN WAFERS

2	eggs	¼	tsp. salt	
1	cup brown sugar, firmly packed	¼	tsp. baking powder	
⅔	cup sifted all purpose flour	1	tsp. vanilla	
		1	cup chopped nuts	

- Beat eggs until thickened.
- Gradually add brown sugar, while continuing to beat.
- Sift flour, salt and baking powder together.
- Carefully fold into egg and sugar mixture.
- Add vanilla and nuts.
- Drop by teaspoonfuls 2 inches apart on greased cookie sheets.
- Bake at 400° for 6 to 7 minutes.
- Remove at once to cool on a wire rack.

SPECIAL NOTE: GIVEN TO ME 40 YEARS AGO BY MY GRANDMOTHER. AS GOOD TODAY IS IT WAS THEN.

Yields 5 dozen

Lotta M. Hunt

SWEDISH ALMOND COOKIES

½ cup shortening
½ cup butter or margarine
1 cup sifted powdered sugar
½ tsp. salt
2 cups all purpose flour

1 tbsp. water
1 tbsp. vanilla
1¼ cups finely chopped almonds
Additional powdered sugar

- Cream shortening and butter until light and fluffy.
- Add 1 cup powdered sugar and salt. Mix well.
- Add next 4 ingredients, stirring well.
- Shape dough into 1-inch balls. Place on an ungreased cookie sheet. Slightly flatten each cookie. Bake at 350° 15 to 17 minutes.
- Remove from cookie sheet, placing on wire racks with paper towels under racks and sift powdered sugar over the cookies.

SPECIAL NOTE: IF YOU WISH, YOU CAN USE SOME CARDAMOM IN PLACE OF SOME OF THE VANILLA OR ALMOND EXTRACT.

Yields 5 dozen   *Cam Caldwell*

ANNIE'S MOCHA CAKE

5 eggs, separated
1 cup granulated sugar
1½ tbsp. instant coffee dissolved
  in ¼ cup water
1 cup sifted flour
1 tsp. baking powder

Filling:
½ pint heavy cream, whipped
2 tsp. sugar

2 tsp. instant coffee in a
  little water

Icing:
¾ Package confectioner's sugar
¾ tbsp. melted butter
2 tsp. instant coffee
  in ¼ cup water
Milk as needed to
spreading consistency

- Beat egg yolks until lemon-colored.
- Add coffee and sugar gradually.
- Beat egg whites separately until they peak.
- Add yolk mixture and flour to whites, alternately and fold in.
- Grease bottom only of two 9-inch pans.
- Preheat oven to 350° and bake for 20 to 25 minutes, until cake springs back to touch. Cool on rack.
- Filling: Mix whipped cream, sugar and coffee to spread.
- Icing: Blend sugar, butter and coffee. Add only as much milk as needed for spreading consistency.

Serves 8   *Jane E. Rives*

APPLE DAPPLE CAKE

2 cups sugar
3 eggs
1⅓ cups cooking oil
3 cups flour
1 tsp. soda
1 tsp. salt
3 cups apples, chopped

1 cup nuts (I use pecans), chopped

Topping:
1 cup light brown sugar
1 stick margarine
¼ cup evaporated milk

- Mix sugar, eggs and oil thoroughly.

- Fold in flour, soda, salt, apples, and nuts.

- Bake at 350° for 45 minutes in pan approximately 10- x 18-inches, greased and dusted with flour. Cool.

- Cut in squares and serve with ice cream, whipped cream, a wedge of sharp cheese or Apple Dapple topping.

- Topping: Make topping just as the cake finishes baking.

- Combine ingredients and bring to boil. Boil 2½ minutes.

- Pour over top of cake while cake is hot.

SPECIAL NOTE: WE LIKE THE CAKE BETTER WITHOUT THE TOPPING AND WITH WHIPPED CREAM, CHEESE, ICE CREAM OR NOTHING.

Mary Jane Flint

APPLE RAISIN CAKE

2 sticks margarine, melted
¼ cup water
2 eggs
2 cups sugar
3 cups all - purpose flour
1 tsp. salt
1 tsp. cinnamon
1 tsp. baking soda

3 cups diced peeled apples
1 cup raisins
1 tsp. vanilla

Topping:
1 cup light brown sugar
4 tbsp. margarine
4 tbsp. milk

- Combine vanilla, margarine, eggs, water, and sugar. Mix well.

- In a separate bowl, combine flour, cinnamon, salt and soda.

- Set aside 1 cup of flour mixture. Dredge apples and raisins in it.

- Add the remaining flour mixture to sugar mixture, blend well.

- Add apples and raisins. Batter will be thick.

- Spoon batter into greased and floured 9- x 13-inch pan.

- Bake at 350° for 40 to 45 minutes, or until done.

- Cool 30 minutes. Cake can be removed or left in pan.

- Topping: Combine ingredients. Boil 2 to 3 minutes over medium heat. Spread on warm cake.

Mary C. Freeman

APPLESAUCE CAKE

1	package 2 layer yellow cake mix	¼	cup oil
1	package (4 serving size) Jello instant pudding & pie filling	4	eggs
		½	tsp. ground cinnamon
1	cup applesauce	½	tsp. ground nutmeg
½	cup water	¼	tsp. ground allspice
		½	cup raisins, finely chopped

- Combine all ingredients in large mixing bowl.
- Blend well, then beat at medium speed for 4 minutes.
- Pour into two greased and floured 8- x 4-inch pans.
- Bake at 350° for 50 to 55 minutes or until cake tester in center comes out clean and cake begins to pull away from sides of pan. Do not underbake.
- Cool in pan 15 minutes.
- Remove from pan to finish cooling.

Ruth Hughes

ANN'S LEMON CHEESECAKE

1	cup butter	**Filling:**
2	cups sugar	½ cup butter
1	tbsp. baking powder	1 cup sugar
3	cups sifted cake flour	6 egg yolks
¾	cup milk	Grated rind and juice of
6	egg whites, stiffly beaten	2 lemons

- Cream butter and sugar with mixer, beating until light and fluffy.
- Add sifted dry ingredients alternately with milk.
- Fold in egg whites.
- Pour into 3 greased and floured 8-inch cake pans.
- Bake in 350° oven for 25-30 minutes, or until cake springs back when lightly touched.
- Cool on racks.
- Filling: Combine butter, sugar, and egg yolks in top of a double boiler. Cook over hot water, stirring constantly until thick. Cool.
- Place between layers and on top of cake.
- White seven minute icing may be used to frost sides of cake.
- Sprinkle cake with coconut, if desired.

Jane Ledbetter

BING CHERRY
CHEESE CAKE

Crust:
16 graham crackers, crumbled
3 tbsp. sugar
¼ cup butter

Filling:
2 8 oz. packages of cream
   cheese, softened
½ cup sugar
2 eggs
1 tsp. vanilla
1 tsp. almond extract

Sour cream mixture:
1 cup sour cream
3 tbsp. sugar

Topping:
1 No. 2 can bing cherries, dark,
   pitted, drained (save juice)
1 cup juice
2 tbsp. cornstarch
2 tbsp. sugar
½ tsp. almond extract
½ tsp. vanilla

- Crust: Press mixture on the bottom and up the sides of a spring form pan. Bake at 375° for 8 minutes. Cool.
- Filling: Add ingredients in order listed and blend thoroughly.
- Spoon into cooked graham cracker crust.
- Bake at 350° for 20 minutes. Cool.
- Sour cream mixture: Combine sour cream and sugar. Spread over filling. Bake at 400° for 10 minutes. Cool.
- Topping: Combine ingredients and cook until clear. Cool. Spread over cake for topping.

SPECIAL NOTE: TRULY ELEGANT DESSERT, VERY RICH!

Sally McCauley

BUTTER-PECAN CHEESECAKE

Crust:
⅓ cup melted margarine
1½ cup graham cracker crumbs
⅓ cup sugar
½ cup chopped pecans

Garnish: 1 cup pecan halves

Cake:
3   8 oz. packages cream cheese
1½ cups sugar
3   eggs
2   cups sour cream
1   tsp. vanilla
1   cup chopped nuts

- Preheat oven to 475°. Mix crust ingredients and press into bottom and slightly up sides of 9-inch spring form pan.

- Beat cream cheese and sugar with electric mixer.

- Add eggs, one at a time, beating well after each.

- Add sour cream. Add vanilla. Stir in pecans.

- Pour into pan. Bake at 475° for 10 minutes.

- Reduce temperature to 300° and bake 50 minutes longer.

- Turn oven off. Open door slightly and let cake sit in oven 1 hour.

- Remove from oven. Garnish with pecan halves around edge.

- Chill and eat when cold. Cake will crack on top, this is normal.

Serves 10 - 12   *Linda Allen*

NEW YORK CHEESECAKE

1   cup graham cracker crumbs
¾   cup sugar
¼   cup plus 2 tbsp. melted butter
1½ cup sour cream

2   eggs
2   tsp. vanilla
16 oz. cream cheese broken
     into small pieces

- Melt ¼ cup butter and mix with ¼ cup sugar and cracker crumbs.

- Press into bottom of 8 or 9-inch springform pan.

- In blender, blend sour cream, ½ cup sugar, eggs & vanilla 1 minute.

- Add cream cheese. Blend until smooth.

- Add 2 tbsp. melted butter and blend. Pour into pan.

- Bake in lower third of oven at 325° for 45 minutes. Remove from oven.

- Broil cheesecake in oven until top begins to bubble and turn brown.

- Refrigerate overnight before cutting and serving.

SPECIAL NOTE: WE SERVE THIS WITH A TART SAUCE OF PURÉED STRAWBERRIES AND LEMON JUICE AT THE MEETINGS OF OUR COASTAL GEORGIA CHAPTER OF THE EPISCOPAL SYNOD OF AMERICA AND PRAYER BOOK SOCIETY.

Serves 12   *Peg Morrissey & Betsy Enney*

CHOCOLATE-ANGEL FOOD CAKE

1   small angel food cake, diced (about 3 cups)
2   6 oz. packages semi - sweet chocolate chips

4   eggs, separated
1   pint whipping cream
½   cup pecans, broken pieces are better

- Dice cake in bite-sized cubes.
- Melt chocolate chips in boiler on very low heat. Important: Don't allow chocolate to get too hot. Set aside to cool.
- While chocolate softens, beat egg yolks until fluffy.
- Beat egg whites until they form peaks
- Whip the cream until peaks form.
- Add egg yolks to melted chocolate, stirring constantly.
- Fold in whipped cream with chocolate mixture.
- Fold in egg whites and nuts, then the diced cake.
- Pour into a pretty bowl and refrigerate overnight.
- Dollops of whipped cream may be added when served.

SPECIAL NOTE: THIS DESSERT IS POPULAR WITH JUST ABOUT EVERYONE. CAN BE MADE SEVERAL DAYS AHEAD.

Serves 10 - 12   *Hazel Dean*

CHOCOLATE CHIP CAKE

1   box chocolate cake mix
1   box chocolate instant pudding
4   eggs

½   cup liquid oil
1   cup water
1   cup sour cream
1   12 oz. bag chocolate chips

- Blend all ingredients, except chocolate chips.
- Blend 3 minutes on medium speed.
- Fold in chocolate chips, low speed.
- Bake in well greased bundt pan at 350° for 75-85 minutes.
- Let cool 25 minutes before removing from pan.

Serves 8 - 12   *Darleen MacDonald (Mrs. C.P.)*

CHOCOLATE FUDGE SHEET CAKE

1 cup water	1 tsp. soda
½ cup oil	1 tsp. vanilla
1 stick margarine	Icing:
1 tbsp. cocoa	1 stick margarine
2 cups sugar	3 tbsp. cocoa
2 cups flour	6 tbsp. milk
½ tsp. salt	1 tsp. vanilla
2 eggs	2 cups chopped pecans
½ cup buttermilk	1 pound confectioners sugar

- Bring water, oil, margarine and cocoa to a boil.
- Pour over mixture of sugar, flour and salt. Mix well.
- Add eggs, buttermilk, soda and vanilla. Mix well.
- Bake in greased sheet cake pan (11½- x 17½-inches) at 350° for 20 to 25 minutes.
- Icing : While cake is baking prepare icing. Combine margarine, cocoa and milk. Heat until margarine melts. Beat in remaining ingredients, adding nuts last.
- Spread on cake as soon as it comes out of oven.

SPECIAL NOTE: BEST WHEN MADE A DAY IN ADVANCE. IT KEEPS AND FREEZES WELL. MAY BE CUT AS FINGER FOOD OR SERVED AS A DESSERT WITH ICE CREAM.

Serves 20   *Lila Hoven*

Bless us, O Lord, and these Thy gifts, which we are about to receive from Thy bounty, through Christ Our Lord. Amen

A CATHOLIC GRACE

MARTHA'S CHOCOLATE ECLAIR CAKE

2 packages Instant French Vanilla Pudding
3 cups milk
8 oz. container Cool Whip, defrosted
Graham crackers

Topping:
2 oz. Baker's unsweetened chocolate
3 tbsp. butter, softened
2 tbsp. light Karo syrup
3 tbsp. milk
1½ cup confectioner's sugar (sift if it's lumpy)
1 tsp. vanilla

- Mix pudding and milk and let set.
- After this has thickened, fold in Cool Whip.
- Spray Pam in 9- x 13 inch Pyrex dish.
- Line bottom of dish with graham crackers.
- Spread ⅓ of pudding mixture over crackers.
- Make two more layers of crackers and pudding mixture, ending with crackers.
- Chocolate Topping: Melt chocolate in double boiler over water. Mix in butter and other ingredients. Beat until smooth and of pouring consistency. Add a little more milk if needed
- Pour evenly over crackers and spread to cover.
- Cover tightly with plastic wrap and place in referigerator for 3 days before serving.

SPECIAL NOTE: REMEMBER TO MAKE 3 DAYS AHEAD. FIND A GOOD SPOT IN THE REFRIGERATOR TO HIDE FROM CHILDREN. TRY TO FORGET IT IS THERE. NO SNITCHING.

Serves 12   *Martha Fitzgerald*

CHOCOLATE TURTLE CAKE

1	package chocolate cake mix	Frosting:
14	oz. package caramels	1 stick butter
1	can Eagle Brand condensed milk	1 cup chopped nuts
		1 lb. powdered sugar
1	stick butter	Dash salt
1	cup chocolate chips	3½ tbsp. cocoa
1	cup chopped nuts	⅓ cup milk

- Prepare cake mix according to directions.
- Pour ½ batter into greased 9- x 13-inch pan.
- Bake at 350° for 15 minutes.
- Remove from oven.
- Melt caramels, Eagle Brand and butter in double boiler.
- Cool some, then spread over cake.
- Sprinkle chips and nuts over caramel.
- Pour rest of batter over caramel and bake 30 minutes more.
- Frosting: Bring butter, cocoa and milk to a boil over medium heat.
- Add sugar and nuts.
- Pour over cake while both are hot.

SPECIAL NOTE: SINFULLY DELICIOUS!

Anita Campbell

QUINCY'S GERMAN CHOCOLATE CAKE

1	cup chopped pecans	½ cup margarine
1	cup coconut	8 oz. cream cheese
1	pkg. German chocolate cake mix	1 box powdered sugar

- Put nuts and coconut on bottom of 9- x 13-inch pan. Do not grease or flour.
- Mix cake according to directions on box and spread on top of nuts and coconut.
- Melt together margarine and cream cheese.
- Mix in a whole box of powdered sugar. Spread on cake.
- Bake at 350° for about 40 minutes. Cool and cut in squares.

SPECIAL NOTE: THE FROSTING ALL ENDS UP ON THE BOTTOM OF THE CAKE, SO SERVE UPSIDE DOWN. IT IS SO EASY AND SO GOOD!

Jane Fann Sanders

COCA COLA CAKE

2 cups unsifted flour
2 sticks margarine
½ cup buttermilk
¼ tsp. salt
1 tsp. vanilla
2 cups sugar
2 tbsp. cocoa
2 eggs
1 tsp. baking soda

1 cup Coca Cola or Pepsi Cola
Icing:
1 stick margarine
2 tbsp. cocoa
6 tbsp. Coca Cola
1 box 4X sugar
1 tsp. vanilla
1 cup chopped nuts (optional)

- Sift flour and sugar together into large mixing bowl.
- In pan, heat margarine, cocoa and Coca Cola to boiling.
- Pour over flour and sugar mixture, stir. Add milk, soda, eggs and vanilla. Batter will be thin.
- Bake in oblong pan which has been greased well and floured.
- Bake at 350° for 30 to 35 minutes.
- Ice cake while hot.
- Frosting: Heat margarine, cocoa and Coca Cola to boiling point.
- Pour this mixture over sugar. Add vanilla and nuts.
- Pour over cake while hot.
- The cake will keep for three weeks.

Mary Freeman

"DIET" CAKE

1 box Duncan Hines devil's food cake mix
1½ cups water

½ cup cooking oil
1 can cherry pie filling
3 eggs

- Mix all ingredients and bake according to package directions in a 9- x 13-inch pan.
- Bake at 350° for 35 minutes.
- Frost according to personal preference.

Anita Campbell

Fruit Cake

Put together in large bowl (do not use electric mixer):
1   qt. uncut shelled pecans
½   lb. uncut crystallized red cherries

1   package (½ lb.) whole pitted dates
5   slices crystallized pineapple (each slice cut in 8 pieces)

- Mix and sift following ingredients over ingredients listed above.

1   cup plain flour
1   rounded tsp. baking powder
⅛   tsp. salt

- In second bowl put the following ingredients.

4   eggs
1   cup sugar
1   tsp. or less vanilla

- Beat with slit spoon until sugar is stirred well.
- Pour egg mixture over dry mixture and stir well.
- Grease pan generously; then line bottom with heavy brown well-greased paper; then flour.
- Pour mixture into pan and bake about 2 hours, first 15 minutes at 300° and then at 250°. Don't let pan touch each other or walls of oven.
- About the last 15 minutes, place a pan of water under cake pan to prevent top from becoming too dry.

Aunt Annie

HAWAIIAN CAKE

1   box white cake mix
1   3 oz. package orange
    pineapple gelatin
1   cup cooking oil
6   eggs
1   cup crushed pineapple
3   bananas, chopped
1   cup coconut
1   cup pecans, chopped
½   cup milk

Frosting:
8   oz. package cream cheese,
    softened
1   stick margarine
1   lb. confectioner's sugar
1   tsp. vanilla
½   cup crushed pineapple,
    drained
½   cup chopped pecans
½   cup coconut

- Combine cake ingredients in large bowl, stir with spoon, *not electric mixer*, until dry ingredients are moist.
- Bake in 3 well greased and floured 9 -inch cake pans at 350° for 25 to 30 minutes.
- Cool in pans 10 minutes.
- Remove and cool completely before frosting.
- Frosting: Cream margarine and cream cheese.
- Add sugar and other ingredients.
- Spread on cake.

Serves 12   *Jane Roebuck*

LAMINGTONS

½   cup butter
1   cup sugar
3   eggs
4   tbsp. milk
1   cup flour
1   tsp. baking powder

Mocha Icing:
1½ tbsp. butter
1½ cups confectioner's sugar
1½ tbsp. cocoa
3   tbsp. strong coffee
Pinch salt
Vanilla
Coconut

- Sift flour and baking powder. Cream butter and sugar. Add eggs.
- Add milk and flour alternately. Pour into greased 8-inch square pan. Bake at 350° for 25 to 30 minutes.
- Cool cake, cut in 2-inch squares. Frost with icing, dip each side in fine coconut.
- Mocha Icing: Cream butter, add confectioner's sugar and cocoa.
- Beat until light and fluffy. Add coffee and vanilla.

Jill Cunningham

MISSISSIPPI MUD CAKE

1 cup oil
⅓ cup cocoa
4 eggs
1¾ cup sugar
1½ cup self - rising flour
3 tsp. vanilla
1 cup chopped nuts
1 small package miniature
marshmallows

Topping:
⅓ cup cocoa
½ cup evaporated milk
1½ sticks melted margarine
1 box powdered sugar
1 tbsp. vanilla

- Mix cake ingredients together.
- Put in a greased and floured 13- x 9- x 2-inch pan.
- Bake at 300° for 45 minutes or until done.
- Remove from oven. Cover with marshmallows while cake is hot.
- Run under broiler enough to soften marshmallows.
- Topping: Mix ingredients and pour over hot cake and marshmallows. Do not cook.

Serves 12 to 15

Catherine (Kay) Keith

OATMEAL CHOCOLATE CHIP CAKE

1¾ cup boiling water
1 cup quick oats
1 cup lightly packed brown
sugar
1 cup sugar
1 stick melted margarine
2 large eggs

1¾ cups unsifted flour
1 tsp. soda
½ tsp. salt
1 tbsp. cocoa
1 large package chocolate chips
¾ cup nuts

- Mix water and oats. Let stand 10 minutes.
- Add brown sugar, sugar and margarine. Stir well
- Mix in eggs.
- Sift flour, soda, salt and cocoa. Add to mixture.
- Thoroughly mix in ½ package chocolate chips.
- Pour into 9- x 13-inch greased and floured pan.
- Sprinkle remaining chips and nuts over top.
- Bake in 350° oven for 35 minutes.

SPECIAL NOTE: STAYS VERY MOIST.

Serves 12

Nancy Butler

APRICOT BRANDY POUND CAKE

1	cup butter - no substitutes	1	cup sour cream
3	cups sugar	½	tsp. rum flavoring
6	eggs	1	tsp. orange flavoring
3	cups flour, measured after sifting	¼	tsp. almond extract
		½	tsp. lemon extract
¼	tsp. soda	1	tsp. vanilla
½	tsp. salt	½	cup apricot brandy

- Grease and flour large tube or bundt pan.
- Cream butter and sugar.
- Add eggs one at a time, beating well after each addition.
- Sift together flour, soda and salt 3 times.
- Combine sour cream, flavorings and brandy. Add dry ingredients alternately with cream mixture, ending with dry.
- Bake at 325° for 1 hour and 10 minutes. Note: Freezes well.

Serves 15   *Evelyn French*

BROWN SUGAR POUND CAKE

1	cup Crisco	1	tsp. vanilla flavoring
1	stick margarine	1	cup nuts (pecans or walnuts), chopped
1	lb. box light brown sugar		
½	cup sugar		
5	eggs		Glaze:
3	cups all - purpose flour	1	stick margarine
½	tsp. salt	1	cup dark brown sugar
½	tsp. baking powder	¼	cup milk
1	cup milk	½	tsp. maple flavoring
1	tsp. maple flavoring	¾	box confectioner's sugar

- Cream Crisco and margarine.
- Add sugars, mix well.
- Add eggs one at a time, beating well after each addition.
- Sift together dry ingredients and add alternately with milk to sugar/egg mixture. Mix thoroughly with each addition.
- Add flavoring and nuts.
- Bake at 325°in greased, floured tube pan 1¼ hour. Cool cake.
- Glaze: Cream brown sugar and margarine. Add milk. Bring to a boil and add confectioner's sugar. Add flavoring last.
- Spread on cake.

Miriam McKern

ONE STEP POUND CAKE

2½ cups plain flour
½ tsp. baking soda
1 tsp. grated lemon peel
1 cup butter or margarine
2 cups sugar
½ tsp. salt
1 tsp. vanilla

1 cup pineapple yogurt or sour cream
3 eggs, beaten
Glaze:
2 tbsp. lemon juice or rum
1 cup of confectioner's sugar

- Place cake ingredients in a bowl. Blend at low speed.
- Pour into a greased bundt pan.
- Bake at 325° for 60 to 65 minutes.
- Remove from pan.
- Glaze: Gradually pour liquid over confectioner's sugar. Stir.
- Pour glaze over warm cake.

Julia M. Powell

POUND CAKE

9 eggs
1½ cups Crisco oil
3 cups plain flour

3 cups sugar
2 tbsp. vanilla

- Sift flour.
- Mix eggs with sugar.
- Add oil, flour and vanilla.
- Beat mixture for 11 minutes.
- Pour into lightly greased pound cake pan.
- Bake at 300° in 1½ hours.

Kathy Sams

PRUNE CAKE

2	cups self - rising flour	1	cup oil
2	cups sugar	3	eggs, beaten
1	tsp. nutmeg	½	cup chopped nuts (walnuts
1	tsp. cinnamon		or pecans)
1	tsp. allspice	1	6 oz. jar baby food prunes

- Use two bowls.
- Stir together flour, sugar, nutmeg, cinnamon, and allspice in one large bowl.
- In a second bowl, stir together oil, eggs, nuts and prunes.
- Pour second mixture (wet) into first mixture (dry). Fold together until all is moistened.
- Pour mixture into a 10-inch tube pan.
- Bake in a 300° oven until straw inserted into the cake comes out clean; approximately 1 hour.

SPECIAL NOTE: WHEN I CAN'T FIND PRUNES, I SUBSTITUTE BABY FOOD PLUMS.

Serves 10 - 12   *Brenda Hartsell*

For these and all His mercies,
God's holy Name be blessed and praised;
through Jesus Christ our Lord.
Amen

Scripture Cake

3½ cups sifted all-purpose flour
(*I Kings 4:22*)
1 tbsp. baking powder
(*Galatians 5:9*)
¼ tsp. salt (*Leviticus 2:13*)
1½ tsp. ground cinnamon
½ tsp. ground nutmeg
½ tsp. ground cloves
1 tsp. ground allspice
(*I Kings 10:2*)
1 cup (2 sticks) butter,
softened (*Judges 5:25*)

2 cups firmly packed brown
sugar (*Jeremiah 6:20*)
2 tbsp. honey (*Exodus 16:31*)
6 eggs (*Luke 11:12*)
1 package (8 oz.) pitted dates,
chopped (*Deuteronomy 34:3*)
2 cups raisins (*I Samuel 30:12*)
1 cup walnuts, chopped
(*Solomon 6:11*)
1 cup milk (*Judges 5:25*)

- Grease and flour an angel cake tube pan.
- Preheat oven to 325°.
- Sift flour, baking powder, salt, cinnamon, nutmeg, cloves and allspice on wax paper.
- Beat the butter, sugar, honey, and eggs in a large bowl with an electric beater until they are light and fluffy, about 3 minutes.
- Sprinkle ¼ of the flour mixture over the fruits and nuts.
- Add remaining flour mixture alternately with the milk to the fluffy butter mixture, beating until smooth.
- Stir in fruits and nuts.
- Spoon into prepared pan.
- Bake in preheated oven for 1 hour and 20 minutes until top springs back when lightly touched. Cool 20 minutes.

SPECIAL NOTE: TAKEN FROM "CHRISMONS AND CHRISTMAS COOKERY," ST. ANDREWS EPISCOPAL CHURCH, PANAMA CITY, FLORIDA.

Gladys G. Fendig (Mrs. Albert, Sr.)

SOUR CREAM ORANGE CAKE

¾ cup butter
1½ cups sugar
2 whole eggs, beaten
1 cup sour cream
¾ cup raisins
2 cups flour
½ tsp. Salt

1 tsp. baking soda
1 tsp. vanilla
¾ cup chopped nuts
1½ tsp. orange zest
Icing:
½ cup orange juice
½ cup confectioner's sugar

- Cream butter, add sugar, and beat until fluffy.
- Add beaten eggs then sour cream.
- Remove enough flour to coat raisins and nuts.
- Sift remaining flour with soda and salt. Stir into creamed mixture.
- Add the grated orange rind and floured raisins and nuts.
- Turn into a greased and floured 9-inch tube pan.
- Bake in a 350° oven for 45-50 minutes. Use pick to test.
- Remove from oven. Let stand 10 minutes.
- Slowly pour icing over cake. Let stand for 15 minutes.
- Remove from pan and cool on rack.

Virginia Petretti

SOUTHERN CHRISTENING CAKE

7 eggs
¾ lb. butter
3 tsp. nutmeg
1 cup chopped nuts
2 heaping tsp. baking powder

4 cups flour
4 cups sugar
1 cup sherry
1½ lbs. raisins or currants

- Cream butter and sugar until well blended.
- Separate eggs.
- Beat yolks until light and lemon colored.
- Add to butter and sugar mixture.
- Sift flour, baking powder and nutmeg together. Add alternately with the sherry.
- Add raisins and pecans.
- Fold in the stiffly beaten egg whites and bake in well buttered cake pan in 300°oven for 4 hours.
- Frost with favorite white icing.

Martha Russell

WINE CAKE

1	3 oz. package vanilla instant pudding mix	½	cup chopped nuts (walnuts or pecans)
1	box Duncan Hines golden butter cake mix		Glaze:
4	eggs	1	stick butter or margarine
½	cup Crisco oil	1	cup sugar
½	cup water	¼	cup water
½	cup white wine	¼	cup white wine

- Spray 10-inch tube pan with Pam or Baker's Joy or lightly grease.
- Scatter nuts in bottom of pan.
- Combine pudding mix, cake mix, eggs, oil, water and wine.
- Pour batter over nuts.
- Bake at 350° for 45 minutes. Test with a straw.
- Glaze: Combine butter, sugar and water.
- Boil 3 minutes.
- Remove from heat, add wine, stir well.
- Use broomstraw or skewer to poke holes in warm cake.
- Pour half of glaze over. Cool.
- Turn cake out, make more "pricks" and pour remaining glaze over, slowly.

SPECIAL NOTE: I SERVED THIS CAKE AT A PARTY ONE NIGHT AND WHEN I REMOVED THE DISH IT LOOKED AS IF IT HAD BEEN LICKED CLEAN!

Serves 10 - 12   *Brenda Hartsell*

APPLE CRUMB PIE

4	tart apples	dash of nutmeg
¾	cup flour	⅓ cup margarine
1	cup sugar	Deep dish pie crust
½	tsp. ginger	
1	tsp. cinnamon	

- Peel and slice apples.
- Mix flour, sugar and spices. Cut in margarine.
- In a large bowl, mix apples with other ingredients and put into pie crust. If using a prepared one, be sure it is the "deep dish" kind.
- Bake at 450° for 10 minutes. Reduce heat to 350° and bake 40 more minutes.

Legene Mullis

SOUR CREAM VELVET FROSTING

1   6 oz. package semi - sweet
    chocolate chips
¼   cup margarine
½   cup sour cream

1   tsp. vanilla
¼   tsp. salt
2½ cups confectioner's sugar

- Melt chocolate chips and margarine, remove from heat.
- Add sour cream, vanilla, salt.
- Beat in sugar until of spreading consistency

Frosts 2 layer cakes or 1 tube cake   *Julia M. Powell*

NORWEGIAN APPLE PIE

1   egg
¾   cup sugar
1   tsp. vanilla
1   tsp. baking powder
¼   tsp. salt
1   tsp. cinnamon

½   cup flour
½   cup chopped walnuts or
    pecans.
2   small tart apples, diced
    (about 1 cup)

- Generously butter 9-inch pie pan, set aside.
- Preheat oven to 350°.
- In large bowl combine all ingredients and stir until blended.
- Mixture will be stiff. Spoon into pan.
- Bake 30 minutes or until brown and slightly puffed.
- Top with whipped cream or ice cream if you desire.

SPECIAL NOTE: I USE GRANNY SMITH APPLES.

Serves 6 - 8   *Cornelia C. Ferguson*

Banana Cream Pie

2 large bananas
¾ cup sugar
2 tbsp. flour
2 tbsp. butter
Pinch salt
3 eggs separated

2 cups rich milk (1 can of evaporated and the rest whole milk)
Pinch of salt
2 tsp. vanilla
6 tbsp. sugar
1 9-inch pie shell, baked

- In double boiler stir together ¾ cup sugar and flour.
- Add butter, salt, egg yolks, and milk.
- Cook until thick.
- Remove from heat and add 1 tsp. vanilla.
- Slice bananas, put into a baked crust.
- Pour filling over bananas.
- Make meringue: Beat egg whites until stiff, gradually adding remaining sugar, salt and 1 tsp. vanilla.
- It is best to spread the meringue on the filling while filling is still hot.
- Bake at 350° until meringue is lightly browned, 12-15 minutes.

SPECIAL NOTE: USING CANNED MILK MAKES THIS A VERY RICH PIE. THE FILLING ALSO MAKES A GOOD BANANA PUDDING.

Serves 8					*Jeanne Alaimo*

Blueberry-Raspberry Pie

1 9- inch pie shell, baked
1 pint blueberries, (2 cups)
1 pint raspberries (or 1 10 oz. package, frozen)

⅔ cup sugar
3 tbsp. cornstarch liquified in 2 tbsp. water

- Purée raspberries in blender.
- Line a strainer with 2 layers of cheesecloth (this will prevent the small seeds from going through) and strain the purée into a sauce pan.
- Add 1 cup blueberries, the sugar, and liquified cornstarch.
- Cook until thick, stirring constantly.
- When thickened, add 1 cup blueberries and heat 2 minutes.
- Put in shell and chill. Serve with whipped cream.

Serves 6					*Virginia Petretti*

BRANDY ALEXANDER PIE

1   envelope plain gelatin
3   eggs, separated
⅔   cup sugar, divided
⅛   tsp. salt
¼   cup brandy

¼   cup crème de cacao
1   cup heavy cream
Baked pie shell or 9- inch
     graham cracker crust

- Dissolve gelatin in ½ cup water.

- Separate 3 eggs.

- Put ⅓ cup sugar, egg yolks and gelatin mix in top of double boiler.

- Blend over heat, stirring constantly, until thickened. DO NOT BOIL.

- Stir in salt, brandy and crème de cacao.

- Chill until mixture mounds slightly.

- Beat egg whites stiff. Fold ⅓ cup sugar into beaten egg whites. Fold in 1 cup heavy cream, whipped.

- Pour into pie shell. Chill several hours.

- Garnish with whipped cream.

Serves 6 - 8   *Nancy Krauss*

CHESS PIE

1   pie shell, baked
1   stick margarine, melted
1½   cups sugar
2   tsp. vanilla

1   tbsp. white vinegar
1   tbsp. cornmeal
3   eggs lightly beaten

- Mix all other ingredients, blending well.

- Pour into baked pie shell. Bake at 325° for 50-60 minutes or until set.

- Serve at room temperature.

SPECIAL NOTE: UNUSUAL INGREDIENTS, BUT A GREAT TASTE. THIS IS AN OLD LOUISIANA RECIPE.

Serves 8   *Becky Rowell*

CHOCOLATE AMARETTO PIE

¼   cup (½ stick) butter
½   cup unsweetened cocoa
     powder
1   cup (2 sticks) unsalted
     butter, room temperature
1½ cups superfine sugar

¼   cup Amaretto liqueur
4   eggs, room temperature
1   9- inch baked pie crust (I use
     Pate Brisee)

- Melt ¼ cup butter in a heavy small saucepan. Remove from heat.
- Stir in cocoa powder.
- Cream 1 cup butter with sugar and Amaretto in a large bowl of electric mixer.
- Add eggs, one at a time, beating 3 minutes after each addition. Continue beating until sugar is dissolved.
- Add cocoa and butter mixture.
- Pour into baked crust.
- Cover and referigerate until firm, at least 4 hours.

Serves 6-8   *Cam Caldwell*

COCONUT CREAM PIE

¾   cup sugar
⅓   cup flour
2   cups milk
2   eggs separated

1   cup coconut
1½ tsp. vanilla
1   baked pie shell

- Combine and mix well the flour and ½ cup sugar. Add milk to beaten egg yolks. Add to flour and sugar in top of a double boiler.
- Place over boiling water, stirring until mixture begins to thicken, then cover and cook until well thickened.
- Add 1 cup coconut and 1 tsp. vanilla.
- Pour into baked pie shell.
- Beat egg whites gradually adding 4 tbsp. sugar until stiff, glossy peaks form. Fold in ½ tsp. vanilla.
- Spread on pie and bake until brown in 350° oven.

Serves 6 - 8   *Mary Evelyn Cook*

COCONUT PIE

1¼ cups coconut
½ cup milk
¼ cup butter
1 cup sugar

3 eggs
1 tsp. vanilla
1 9- inch unbaked pie shell

• Soak coconut in milk and set aside.
• Bake pie shell in 350° oven for 10 minutes.
• Cream butter and sugar; add eggs and beat.
• Add vanilla and coconut and milk mixture.
• Pour into cooked pie shell and bake at 350° for 20 minutes.

SPECIAL NOTE: A DOUBLE RECIPE MAKES 3 PIES.

Frances Burns (Mrs. Allen, Sr.)

COTTAGE CHEESE DELIGHT

1 graham cracker pie crust
1 small can chunk pineapple, drained
1 16 oz. container cottage cheese

1 3 oz. package strawberry, raspberry or orange Jello
1 8 oz. container Cool Whip
½ cup chopped nuts or coconut

• Drain pineapple, mix with cottage cheese and jello as it comes from package.
• Add Cool Whip and mix thoroughly.
• Pour into graham cracker pie crust.
• Chill at least 20 minutes.
• When ready to serve, top with additional Cool Whip.
• Sprinkle with chopped nuts or coconut.

Serves 6 easily

Virginia Laveau

EASY MUD PIE

26 chocolate chip cookies
5 tbsp. melted butter or margarine
1 12 oz. package semi - sweet chocolate chips
2 cups mini marshmallows
½ cup confectioner's sugar
1 tsp. vanilla extract
2 pints chocolate ice cream (or frozen yogurt)
1 pint coffee ice cream (or frozen yogurt), softened
2 cups sweetened whipped cream
1 package of Heath Bits 'o Brickle
¾ cup water

- Finely chop the cookies in a food processor.

- With the motor running, add the melted butter. Process until moistened.

- Spoon mixture into a 10-inch pie plate. Press down evenly with a measuring cup or spoon to line the bottom and sides. Freeze until firm.

- Make chocolate / marshmallow sauce: In a 2 quart saucepan, combine chocolate, marshmallows, ¾ cup water and the confectioner's sugar.

- Stir constantly over medium heat until melted and blended. Boil 2 minutes and remove from heat.

- Stir in vanilla. Cool.

- When sauce is room temperature, assemble pie.

- Spread 1 pint of chocolate ice cream in crust. Spread ½ cup sauce evenly over ice cream. Sprinkle ½ cup of the bits 'o brickle. Freeze until firm, at least 1 hour

- Repeat layering using coffee ice cream and freezing, then layer with chocolate again. Save some brickle for the top.

- Spread the sweetened whipped cream on the last frozen layer, drizzle with chocolate sauce and brickle. You can keep in the freezer and remove 20 minutes before serving.

SPECIAL NOTE: GREAT BIRTHDAY FAVORITE!

Serves 8   *Cam Caldwell*

FRENCH MINT PIE

Filling:
1 stick butter
1½ cups sifted confectioner's sugar
2 squares melted bitter chocolate
2 eggs, beaten
½ tsp. vanilla

5 drops oil of peppermint (obtained at drug store)

Topping: whipped cream

Crust:
⅓ cup melted butter
1¼ cup vanilla wafer crumbs

- Crust: Mix vanilla wafer crumbs and butter. Shape in 8-inch pie pan.
- Bake in preheated 350° oven for 10 minutes.
- Filling: Cream butter and sugar. Add melted chocolate.
- Add beaten eggs, vanilla and peppermint oil. Continue beating until light in color.
- Pour in cooked crumb crust and chill overnight.
- Top with sweetened whipped cream when ready to serve.

SPECIAL NOTE: ALWAY'S A WINNER!

Melissa Barnes

FRENCH SILK PIE

1 stick butter
¾ cup sugar
1 square melted dark chocolate
1 tsp. vanilla

2 eggs
1 baked pie shell or Keebler butter crust shell

- Beat butter until fluffy. Beat in melted chocolate and vanilla. Beat well.
- Add one egg at a time and beat 3 minutes after each addition.
- Pour into pie shell and chill.
- Top with whipped cream (not Cool Whip).

Mrs. Robert W. Peters

PECAN PIE

1 cup white corn syrup
1 cup dark brown sugar
⅓ cup melted butter
3 whole eggs (beaten)

Dash vanilla
Pinch salt
1 heaping cup shelled pecans
1 unbaked 9 - inch pie shell

- Mix first seven ingredients well.
- Pour into an unbaked 9-inch pie shell.
- Bake at 350° for 45 or 50 minutes until set. Cool.
- Top with whipped cream if desired.

Mary Jane Flint

SOUTHERN PECAN PIE

1 9-inch pastry shell
1 cup pecans
3 eggs
1 cup corn syrup

⅓ cup sugar
⅛ tsp. salt
¼ cup melted butter

- Line the pastry shell with pecans.
- Beat eggs well and add the corn syrup, sugar, salt and butter.
- Turn into the crust.
- Bake at 325° for 50 minutes.

SPECIAL NOTE: PECAN PIE IS AS TYPICALLY SOUTHERN AS SPANISH MOSS OR CAMELLIAS. THIS RECIPE CAME FROM THE HISTORIC EXCHANGE HOTEL, MONTGOMERY, ALABAMA. IT WAS A FAVORITE OF JEFFERSON DAVIS WHO RESIDED IN THE HOTEL AND VISITED EUFAULA, ALABAMA, IN THE EARLY DAYS OF THE CONFEDERACY.

Elizabeth Rhodes McCartney

PEACH COBBLER

6-8 large ripe peaches peeled
   and sliced
2½ tbsp. cornstarch
¾ to 1 cup sugar
Crust:
1 cup all purpose flour

2 egg yolks
¼ cup butter or margarine,
   melted
1 tsp. baking powder
1 cup sugar
2 egg whites, stiffly beaten

- Combine peaches, cornstarch and sugar.
- Pour into a greased 13- x 9- x 2-inch baking pan.
- For crust, combine all ingredients except egg whites in a mixing bowl.
- Gently fold stiffly beaten egg whites into batter.
- Spread over peaches.
- Bake at 375° for about 45 minutes or until the fruit is bubbling around the edges and top is golden.

Yields 12 servings

Katherine K. Perry

PEACH COBBLER

3-4 cups sliced unpeeled peaches
1½ cup sugar (divided)
1 stick butter
¾ cup flour

2 tsp. baking powder
Pinch salt
¾ cup milk
Fresh ground nutmeg to taste

- Wash and slice peaches.
- Mix fruit with 1 cup of the sugar; set aside.
- Preheat oven to 350°.
- Put butter in a deep 2 quart baking dish and set in oven to melt butter.
- Make a batter of ½ cup sugar, flour, baking powder, salt, milk and nutmeg. Pour this over melted butter-do not stir.
- Put sugared fruit on top of batter-do not stir.
- Bake about one hour. The batter will rise to the top and get crisp and brown.
- Serve while hot topped with ice cream.

SPECIAL NOTE: I SOMETIMES USE PEACHES AND BLUEBERRIES TOGETHER. I PUT THE COBBLER IN THE OVEN RIGHT BEFORE SERVING DINNER. IT'S READY JUST AS WE'RE FINISHING UP CLEARING THE TABLE.

Serves 6-8   *Annabelle Salter*

NO STIR PEACH COBBLER

Batter:
1 cup sugar
¾ cup flour
2 tsp. baking powder
Salt
¾ cup milk

¾ stick butter
Filling:
2 cups cut fresh peaches
½ cup sugar
2 tbsp. brown sugar
Cinnamon and nutmeg

- Batter: In a round, deep Pyrex casserole dish, melt ¾ stick of butter. Mix batter well. Pour batter into middle of melted butter. Do not stir.
- Filling: Combine filling ingredients and pour into middle of batter. Do not stir.
- Bake at least 30 to 40 minutes at 350°, until brown. (may take longer)
- Turn oven off and let it sit in warm oven a while to set. Best served with ice cream or cream.

Serves 4-6   *Nancy Sumerford*

PEACH BLUEBERRY PIE

1   unbaked pie crust
¾   to 1 stick of light margarine
¼   cup flour
1   beaten egg

1   cup sugar
4   large ripe peaches
1   cup fresh blueberries

- Slice peaches. Arrange in crust.
- Pour blueberries over peaches.
- Melt butter. Add flour, sugar and egg.
- Mix with wire whip or fork. Spread over fruit.
- Bake at 350° for 50 minutes or until brown.
- Cool to room temperature to serve.
- Store in refrigerator, but take out 30 minutes before serving

Serves 6   *Angie Burns*

PEANUT BUTTER PIE

8   oz. cream cheese, softened
1   8 oz. container frozen
    whipped topping, thawed
1   12 oz. jar peanut butter
2   cups powdered sugar

2   tbsp. vanilla
2   Graham cracker crusts
Whipped topping
Few chopped peanuts

- Cream together cream cheese, whipped topping, peanut butter, sugar and vanilla. Pour into crusts.
- Top with whipped topping, sprinkle with nuts and freeze.
- Thaw in refrigerator several hours before serving.
- Keep refrigerated. Makes 2 pies.

SPECIAL NOTE: FOR WHEN YOU NEED A SOUTHERN DESSERT

Serves 12-16   *Alva Lines*

PUMPKIN CHIFFON PIE

Ginger cookie crust:
¼ cup butter or margarine, melted
1¼ cup fine ginger-snap crumbs

Meringue:
3 egg whites
¼ tsp. cream of tarter
6 tbsp. sugar

Filling:
1 tbsp. gelatin
¼ cup cold water
¾ cup brown sugar
1⅓ cup pumpkin
3 large egg yolks
½ cup milk
½ tsp. salt
2 tsp. cinnamon
½ tsp. ginger
½ tsp. allspice

- Crust: Mix butter and crumbs. Press into pie pan. Bake at 350° for 10 minutes. Cool.
- Meringue: Mix beaten egg whites, cream of tarter and sugar. Set aside.
- Filling: Blend gelatin and cold water.
- Mix remaining ingredients in a saucepan. Cook over low heat until the mixture boils, stirring. Boil 1 minute.
- Stir in gelatin.
- Fold in meringue.
- Pile into crust. Chill.

Serves 8 or more

Sally McCauley

PUMPKIN PIE

¾ cup sugar
2 eggs, seperated
2 tbsp. butter
1 No. 2 can pumpkin

½ cup cream
Pinch salt
1 tsp. nutmeg
1 tsp. cinnamon

- Cream butter and sugar.
- Add egg yolks, one at a time and beat well.
- Add rest of ingredients except for egg whites and mix thoroughly.
- Fold in beaten egg whites.
- Put in unbaked pie shell and bake at 400° for 5 to 10 minutes. Turn oven down to 350° and bake for 30 minutes more.

SPECIAL NOTE: THIS RECIPE CAME FROM MY MOTHER AND I HAVE BEEN USING IT FOR 38 YEARS.

Serves 6-8

Janet S. Daniel

Sweet Potato-Pecan Pie

⅛	tsp. ginger	1	cup chopped pecans
¼	tsp. cinnamon	1	unbaked 9-inch pie shell
4	eggs	¼	tsp. maple flavoring
½	cup brown sugar	2 cups cooked, mashed, sweet	
¼	tsp. salt		potatoes
½	cup granulated sugar		

- Preheat oven to 375°.
- In large mixing bowl, thoroughly combine potatoes, sugars, salt, spices and flavoring. Add beaten eggs.
- Beat vigorously until combined.
- Stir in pecans.
- Pour into pie shell.
- Bake in preheated 375° oven for 45 minutes.
- Reduce heat to 325° and bake for an additional 10 minutes.

Yields 8 small or 6 large servings   *Jeannie Wade*

Thank you for the world so sweet
Thank you for the food we eat
Thank you for the birds that sing
Thank you God for everything.

AN OLD SCOTCH TABLE GRACE

Aunt Jennie's
Chocolate Dessert

1	pint whipping cream	6	tbsp. cocoa
1	cup sugar	1	angel food cake

- Stir cream, sugar and cocoa together.
- Let sit in refrigerator for several hours or overnight.
- Slice cake into two layers.
- Whip cream and spread between layers and ice cake.

SPECIAL NOTE: VERY QUICK AND EASY.

Serves 12

Martha L. Veal

Blueberry Dessert

½ cup butter	Cinnamon
1¼ cup sugar	1 can blueberries
16 Graham crackers, crushed	1 Lemon, juice
2 eggs, beaten	2 tbsp. cornstarch
½ lb. cream cheese	Whipped cream
½ tsp. vanilla	

- Mix together butter, ½ cup sugar and graham crackers. Press into 12- x 9-inch pan.
- Cream together eggs, ½ cup sugar, cream cheese, and vanilla.
- Pour over crumbs, and sprinkle with cinnamon.
- Bake at 375° for 15 minutes.
- Drain 1 can blueberries (save blueberries).
- To juice of blueberries add ¼ cup sugar, juice of lemon and cornstarch.
- Cook until thick. Remove from stove.
- Add berries. Cool to lukewarm.
- Pour over crust and let set.
- Chill and serve with whipped cream.

SPECIAL NOTE: YOU MAY USE A CAN OF INSTANT BLUEBERRY PIE MIX. EASY—MEN LOVE IT!

Serves 10-12

Lucrece Truax

BRANDY ALEXANDER SOUFFLE

2	envelopes of unflavored gelatin	3	tbsp. Creme de Cacao
2	cups water	3	tbsp. brandy
4	eggs, separated	¼	cup sugar
¾	cup sugar	1	cup cream, whipped
1	8 oz. package cream cheese, softened		

- Make a collar of aluminum foil around the neck of a 1½ qt. souffle dish. Oil the side against the dish and attach with tape, allowing the collar to extend 3-inch above the neck of the dish.

- Combine the gelatin and 1 cup of water in top of a double boiler; bring water in the bottom of the boiler to a boil. Cook, stirring constantly, until gelatin dissolves.

- Stir in remaining 1 cup of water.

- In an electric mixer, beat egg yolks until thick and light.

- Gradually add ¾ cup of sugar, beating well.

- Stir into gelatin mixture. Cook over low heat 20-25 minutes until thickened, stirring constantly.

- Beat cream cheese until smooth; gradually add egg yolk mixture, beating well.

- Stir in Creme de Cacao and brandy.

- Chill until slightly thickened.

- Beat egg whites (room temperature) until foamy; gradually add ¼ cup sugar, beating until stiff peaks form.

- Gently fold whipped cream and beaten egg whites into cream cheese mixture.

- Spoon into prepared souffle dish, and chill until firm. Remove collar when ready to serve.

SPECIAL NOTE: WONDERFUL COMPANY DISH BECAUSE IT CAN BE PREPARED WELL AHEAD.

Serves 8   *Cam Caldwell*

BUCKEYES

1	lb. butter	2	12 oz. packages semi-sweet
2	lbs. smooth peanut butter		chocolate bits
3	lbs. powdered sugar	1	stick paraffin

- Soften butter, thoroughly blend peanut butter and butter.
- Add sifted powdered sugar, 1 lb. at a time.
- Shape into walnut sized balls and place on waxed paper-lined cookie sheets and chill.
- In top of double boiler over simmering water melt together the paraffin and chocolate.
- With tooth pick, dip peanut butter balls into chocolate mixture, do not cover entire ball.
- Chill again until chocolate is firm.

SPECIAL NOTE: FREEZES WELL.

Yields 250 pieces   *Mrs. Robert W. Peters*

CHOCOLATE NUT FUDGE LOG

1⅓	cups sugar	1	tbsp. light karo syrup
¼	tsp. salt	2	tbsp. butter
2	tbsp. cocoa	1	tsp. vanilla
¾	cup milk	½	cup finely chopped nuts

- Combine sugar and salt in heavy saucepan. Mix well. Gradually stir in milk and syrup.
- Cook over medium heat, stirring occasionally, until soft ball stage of 236°.
- Remove from heat, stir in butter and vanilla.
- Pour into a buttered 15- x 10-inch jellyroll pan. Let cool for 10 minutes.
- With a spoon, stir candy in pan until it can be picked up and kneaded.
- Shape into roll, roll in chopped nuts.
- Wrap in plastic wrap, let stand at room temperature for 1 hour until completely cooled, cut into ½ inch slices.

Mrs. Robert W. Peters

COUPE GRAND-MARNIER

2   large scoops vanilla ice cream
1   large scoop orange sherbet
4   oz. Grand Marnier

4   chilled champagne or parfait
    glasses
Whipped cream
4   maraschino cherries

- Place ice cream and sherbet in large mixing bowl.
- Using a large spoon, blend together until slightly softened.
- Add the Grand Marnier and mix well. Fill chilled glasses to top.
- Add whipped cream and cherry. May also be made ahead, placed in freezer and served when needed.

SPECIAL NOTE: VERY REFRESHING AND TASTY. SIMPLE TO MAKE.

Serves 4   *Mrs. Robert Allen*

CHOCOLATE FONDUE DROPS

2   boxes confectioners
sugar
½   cup margarine, melted
1   can condensed milk
2   cans Angel Flake
coconut

2   cups pecans, finely
chopped
½   block paraffin wax
8   oz. Nestle chocolate
chips (or semi - sweet
chocolate blocks)

- Mix first 5 ingredients together. Roll in balls, freeze for 2 hours or leave in refrigerator overnight.
- In a double boiler melt ½ block of paraffin wax and Nestle chocolate chips.
- While still warm dip balls in melted wax and chocolate, and drop on waxed paper.

SPECIAL NOTE: COCONUT CAN BE OMITTED AND MORE NUTS ADDED OR ADD CHOPPED CHERRIES TO MIXTURE.

Beegie Searcy

FRUIT

2   green apples
2   red apples
3   kiwi
2   cups red grapes
3-4 bananas

1   16 oz can chunk pineapple,
drained
1   large pkg. instant vanilla
pudding mix
2   tbsp. Tang

- Mix juice from pineapple with pudding mix.
- Add 2 tbsp. of Tang. Pour over fruit.

SPECIAL NOTE: I HAVE USED OTHER FRUIT IN THIS RECIPE AND ALSO HALVED THE PORTIONS. GOOD FRUIT SUBSTITUTES ARE CANTALOUPE, CHERRIES AND PEACHES.

Mary Freeman

GRANDMOTHER'S CHRISTMAS PUDDING

1 lb. suet, ground	4 eggs, well beaten
1 lb. stale bread, cubed	½ tsp. nutmeg
1 lb. seedless raisins, whole	1 tsp. cinnamon
1 cup white sugar	½ tsp. cloves
1 cup molasses	¼ tsp. salt
1 cup milk	¼ lb. chopped citron
1 cup wine or ½ cup brandy	½ cup plum jelly
1 cup white flour	Hard sauce or foamy sauce
2 tsp. baking powder	(recipes below)

- Beat eggs and add sugar.
- Blend in flour, baking powder and salt, alternating with molasses and milk.
- Add remaining ingredients. Mix and beat well.
- Pour into a well-buttered mold.
- Cover top with wax paper. Steam 5 or 6 hours.
- Remove wax paper after steaming. Cool, and keep in a cool place until one hour before serving.
- To serve hot, re-steam or place in microwave.
- Serve with sauce. Makes 4 lbs. of pudding.

Hard Sauce:
½ lb. butter
2 cups powdered sugar
½ cup hot white wine

- Beat butter to cream. Add sugar slowly.
- When very light, add hot wine a little at a time.
- Sauce should be smooth and foamy.
- Cool to serve.

Foamy Sauce:
2 egg whites
1 cup powdered sugar
½ cup hot milk
1 tsp. brandy

- Beat eggs until stiff. Add sugar a little at a time.
- Continue beating gradually adding milk and brandy.
- Serve over hot pudding.

SPECIAL NOTE: GOOD ENOUGH TO BE WORTH THE EFFORT!

Serves 12-14   *Louise Rodormer*

GREEN GRAPES

1-1½	lbs. green seedless grapes	1½	tsp. lemon juice
1	cup brandy	3	tbsp. powdered sugar
1	cup honey	1	cup sour cream

- Wash, stem and dry grapes. Put into deep bowl.
- Mix brandy, honey, lemon juice and sugar. Pour over grapes.
- Chill for at least 5 hours.
- Serve in small bowls (juice and all) with dollop of sour cream on top.

SPECIAL NOTE: THIS IS VERY GOOD SERVED AFTER A DUCK, WILD GAME OR VERY FILLING MEAL.

Serves 8   *Nancy Krauss*

IRISH TRIFLE

8	oz. sponge cake or lady fingers	½	cup sherry
1	pint fresh sliced strawberries	2	tbsp. brandy
1	large can sliced pears, drained	½	jar raspberry jam
		1	pint whipped cream
1	pint soft custard or vanilla pudding mix		Maraschino cherries
			Slivered almonds

- Spread raspberry jam on sliced sponge cake or lady fingers.
- Line the bottom of a glass bowl with the slices.
- Layer with strawberries and pears.
- Mix sherry and brandy together and moisten above ingredients.
- Cover with custard that is thin enough to pour.
- Repeat this layering procedure until the bowl is filled. There are usually three layers.
- Keep in refrigerator until ready to serve.
- Before serving, cover with whipped cream and garnish with cherries and slivered almonds.

Serves 8   *Sally McCauley*

COTTAGE CHEESE DELIGHT

1 small can chunk pineapple	1 medium container Cool Whip
1 medium container small curd cottage cheese	1 graham cracker pie crust
1 small package strawberry jello	Chopped nuts
	Coconut

- Drain the pineapple.
- Mix with medium container of small curd cottage cheese and the package of jello.
- Add the Cool Whip, mix thoroughly.
- Pour into graham cracker crust.
- Top with additional Cool Whip, sprinkle chopped nuts and coconut on top.

SPECIAL NOTE: THIS PIE MAY ALSO BE MADE WITH RASPBERRY OR ORANGE JELLO.

Serves 6   *Virginia Leveau*

ITALIAN BANANA SPLITS

1 quart amaretto ice cream	12 stemmed maraschino cherries
3 medium partially ripe bananas	1 cup chopped walnuts or whole salted peanuts
1¼ cups butterscotch sauce	

- Place 2 scoops ice cream in each of 6 dessert dishes.
- Split bananas lengthwise and arrange 1 half in each dish.
- Pour sauce over each serving.
- Sprinkle with nuts and garnish with cherries.

SPECIAL NOTE: SATISFY THE SWEETEST TOOTH.

Serves 6   *Mrs. Robert Allen*

POTATO CANDY

¾ cup mashed potatoes	4 cups coconut
4 cups confectioner's sugar	

- Mix all together; form into balls and dip in melted chocolate.

Anita Campbell

KAHLUA DESSERT

1 6 oz. package semi - sweet chocolate morsels
2 eggs
2 tbsp. Kahlua or other flavored coffee liqueur, divided
½ tsp. instant coffee granules
½ cup sugar
½ cup water
1 cup whipping cream, whipped
1 3 oz. package of lady-fingers split and halved crosswise.
1 1⅛ oz. package of English toffee candy bar, crushed.
Sweetened whipped cream

- Put chocolate morsels in a 2 - cup glass measure; microwave at HIGH for 1½ to 2 minutes, stirring once. Stir morsels until smooth and melted. Let chocolate cool.
- Combine chocolate, eggs, 1 tbsp. Kahlua, and coffee granules in a mixing bowl; set aside.
- Combine sugar and water in a 2 - cup glass measure. Microwave on HIGH for 2½ to 3 minutes, stirring once, until mixture boils and sugar dissolves.
- Beat the chocolate mixture at medium speed of an electric mixer, and gradually add hot sugar syrup in a thin stream. Continue beating until well blended. Chill several hours or until mixture is thickened. Fold in whipped cream.
- Divide lady-fingers halves evenly among 8 six oz. dessert dishes, cut side facing center of dish. Spoon chocolate mixture into prepared dishes. Cover and chill at least one hour. Garnish with whipped cream and crushed candy before serving.

Serves 8

LIME MOUSSE

⅓ cup lime juice (2-3 limes)
1 tsp. flour
3 eggs
1½ cups sugar
¼ tsp. salt
1 cup boiling water
1 tsp. grated lime rind
1 egg white, beaten
1 cup heavy cream, whipped
Tiny mint sprigs

- Combine lime juice and flour.
- In a large saucepan, whisk 3 eggs, sugar, and salt until light colored.
- Add lime juice mixture, then boiling water, continuing to beat briskly with a whisk.
- Place over medium heat and continue to stir until slightly thickened and first beginning to boil. Remove from heat.
- Chill in refrigerator, stirring periodically, or set over a bowl of ice and whisk until cold.
- Fold in grated lime rind, beaten egg white, and whipped cream, blending° gently, but firmly. Chill until serving time.

SPECIAL NOTE: SERVE IN STEMMED GLASSES WITH TINY SPRIGS OF MINT OR IN SHALLOW GLASS BOWLS WITH SUGARED FRESH RASPBERRIES.

Mrs. H Ellis Jones

MYSTERY TORTE

16   ritz crackers
⅔   cup chopped nuts (pecans or
        walnuts)
3   egg whites

½   tsp. baking powder
1   cup sugar
1   tsp. vanilla

- Finely chop crackers and nuts together (or whirl in blender).

- Sift together baking powder and sugar.

- Beat egg whites until stiff gradually adding the baking powder/sugar mixture. Add vanilla.

- Pour into lightly greased 8- inch pie plate. Bake in 350° oven for 30 minutes. Cool.

- Decoration Preparation: Whip ½ pint whipping cream and sweeten to taste.

- Spread over entire *cooled* torte.

- Garnish with bittersweet or bitter chocolate curlicues, or more chopped nuts. Refrigerate for at least 3 hours before serving. Can refrigerate all day if necessary.

SPECIAL NOTE: CAN BE FILLED WITH ICE CREAM OR THE WHIPPED CREAM.

Ann Howard

NEVA'S FLAN

1   can condensed milk
1   can evaporated milk
8   oz. plain milk
4   tbsp. sugar

5   eggs, separated
1   tsp. vanilla
Dash salt

- Preheat oven to 350°.

- Liberally sprinkle baking pan with granulated sugar.

- Brown it over burner, stirring rapidly to prevent burning. Set flan pan aside.

- Beat egg whites until fluffy. Add slightly beaten egg yolks and salt.

- Beat constantly as you add rest of ingredients.

- Pour into flan pan. put flan pan into another pan with water halfway up the sides.

- Cook in 350° oven about 1 hour or until set.

- Cook the day before serving so sugar will melt for sauce when turned out.

Martha Russell

PEANUT OR PECAN BRITTLE

1	cup sugar	1	tbsp. oleo
⅓	cup white Karo	1	tbsp. vanilla
½	tsp. salt	1	tbsp. baking soda
1	cup nuts		

- Put sugar and Karo in 4 cup microwave container. Cook on high for 2 minutes.

- Stir and cook 2 minutes more.

- Add salt and nuts. Cook on high for 4 minutes. When mix is light brown, cut this time short and remove.

- Add vanilla and oleo. Cook 1 minute.

- Add soda and stir rapidly, then pour quickly onto greased jelly - roll pan. (Sweep across pan as rapidly as possible for thinnest layer.)

SPECIAL NOTE: I USE "JUMBO" RAW PEANUTS (12 OZ.) SPLIT IN HALVES.

Peggy Manley

TIPSY SQUIRE

2	1 lb. pound cakes	Custard sauce:	
½	cup sherry	3	eggs
1¾	cups toasted slivered almonds	¼	cup sugar
		⅛	tsp. salt
1	cup whipped cream	2	cups milk
¼	tsp. almond extract	1	tsp. vanilla
Candied cherries			

- Cake: Slice pound cake into 12 pieces; sprinkle sherry generously over all slices and cover for 3 hours.

- Custard Sauce: Put mixed ingredients in top of double boiler. Cook slowly over boiling water; stir until thickened.

- Pour 1½ cups of custard over cake layer.

- Sprinkle with almonds.

- Continue in layers and top with whipped cream flavored with almond extract.

- Top with cherries.

SPECIAL NOTE: MY AUNT CONSTANCE LIVES IN YORK, ENGLAND, AND THIS IS ONE OF HER FAVORITE DESSERTS TO SERVE AT TEA.

Martha Russell

VIENNESE COFFEE VELVET

Vanilla or coffee ice cream　　　**Whipping cream**
Hot double strength coffee　　　**Nutmeg**

- Place a scoop of ice cream in tall glass. Pour enough hot coffee to fill glass ⅔ full.
- Top with second scoop of ice cream then fill glass with hot coffee.
- Garnish with whipped cream and a dash of nutmeg.

Jeanette Bessels

ORANGE BAVARIAN CREAM

2 to 3 oranges	¾ cup strained orange juice
2 tbsp. cornstarch	1½ cups hot milk
7 egg yolks	2 tbsp. orange liqueur
5 egg whites	1 cup sugar
1 envelope gelatin	1 tsp. vanilla
Pinch of salt	

- Grate the rind of 2 oranges. Place in mixing bowl with 1 tbsp. sugar. Mix together well.
- Squeeze oranges and strain juice to get ¾ cup. Pour over gelatin and set aside.
- Add the egg yolks to the orange - sugar mix and beat until eggs are a light color, gradually adding sugar. Beat 2 - 3 minutes.
- Add cornstarch.
- Add heated milk slowly to egg mixture until it coats a wooden spoon.
- Remove from heat and add orange juice and gelatin.
- Beat egg whites until soft peaks form, then slowly add sugar and beat until stiff.
- Fold into hot custard, then set in refrigerator to cool.
- Stir occasionally to prevent separation. Whip cream until it doubles in volume.
- When custard is cold and begins to set, add vanilla and orange liqueur. Fold in whipped cream. Pour in 1 quart mold. Cover with waxed paper and place in refrigerator until time to serve.
- Unmold on chilled serving plate and garnish with rosettes of whipped cream flavored with 1 tbsp. orange liqueur and shaved semi - sweet chocolate.

SPECIAL NOTE: SERVED BY LADY BIRD JOHNSON AT THE WHITE HOUSE.

Serves 8

APSE WINDOWS

Located on either side of the altar, the
bosses in the outer windows are the
symbols of the four evangelists.
St. Matthew is represented as the winged
man, St. Mark as the lion, St. Luke as
the winged ox and St. John as the eagle.

The windows are dedicated "In memory
of The Revd. Edmund Matthews, some-
time Rector of this Parish, who entered
into rest Decr. 1, 1827."

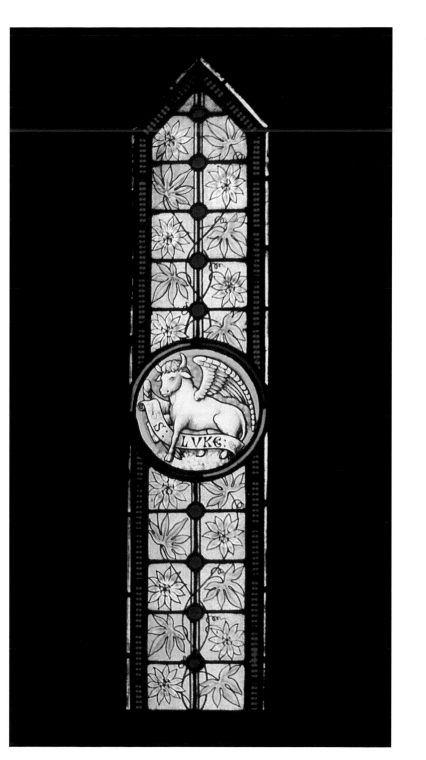

Sauces, Marinades, Accompaniments

APSE WINDOWS

Located on either side of the altar, the
bosses in the outer windows are the
symbols of the four evangelists.
St. Matthew is represented as the winged
man, St. Mark as the lion, St. Luke as
the winged ox and St. John as the eagle.

The windows are dedicated "In memory
of The Revd. Edmund Matthews, some-
time Rector of this Parish, who entered
into rest Decr. 1, 1827."

BENJAMIN'S BARBEQUE SAUCE

¼	cup mustard	1	tsp. lemon juice
1	cup ketchup	½	tsp. vinegar
4	tbsp. brown sugar	1	tsp. Louisiana hot sauce
4	tbsp. honey	1	tsp. liquid smoke

- Mix all ingredients in sauce pan and simmer about 5 minutes. Refrigerate until used.

Benjamin Allen

CHOCOLATE PRALINE SAUCE

1⅔	cup chopped pecans	¼	cup cocoa
¼	cup butter or margarine	3	tbsp. all-purpose flour
1½	cups firmly packed brown sugar	¾	cup light corn syrup
		1	(5 oz.) can evaporated milk

- Spread pecans on a large glass pie plate.

- Microwave on high for 5-6 minutes until lightly toasted, stirring every 2 minutes. Set aside.

- Put butter in a 1 qt. glass bowl. Microwave on high for 50 seconds or until melted.

- Combine sugar, cocoa, and flour. Add to butter, stirring well.

- Stir in corn syrup and milk.

- Microwave on high for 5 minutes or until mixture is hot, stirring every two minutes.

- Stir in pecans.

- Serve over ice cream, pound cake, or angel food cake.

- Store in the refrigerator.

Yield: 3½ cup

EGGPLANT SPAGHETTI SAUCE

1	eggplant, cut into cubes (peeled or unpeeled)	1	green pepper, sliced
3	tbsp. oil	1	cup plum tomatoes
1	onion, sliced	1	cup tomato juice
1	garlic clove, minced	1	tsp. oregano
		2	tsp. basil

- Sauté eggplant in oil about 7 minutes.
- Add onion, garlic and pepper, and sauté 3 additional minutes, or until tender.
- Combine tomatoes, tomato juice and herbs. Add to the eggplant mixture.
- Cover and simmer for ½ hour. Serve over spaghetti.

Rosalynn Carter

MUSHROOM SAUCE FOR STEAK

1	stick butter or oleo	1	tbsp. lemon juice
2	tsp. dry mustard	1	tbsp. Worcestershire sauce
¾	lb. fresh mushrooms, trimmed and sliced	1	tsp. salt
1½	cup sliced green onions	¼	cup chopped parsley

- Melt butter in saucepan. Stir in mustard, mushrooms and onions.
- Sauté 10 minutes or until onions are soft.
- Stir in lemon juice, Worcestershire sauce, salt and parsley. Remove from heat.

SPECIAL NOTE: THIS SAUCE REALLY DRESSES UP HAMBURGERS TOO! A REAL FAVORITE.

Davi Langston

CRANBERRY-ORANGE RELISH

1	lb. washed cranberries	2	oranges, quartered and seeded
2	cups sugar		

- Put cranberries and oranges through food chopper.
- Add sugar. Refrigerate.

Margaret McCormick

PESTO

2 cups basil leaves
4 good sized garlic cloves, chopped
1 cup walnuts
1 cup olive oil

1 cup parmesan cheese
½ cup romano cheese
Salt
Freshly ground pepper

- In a food processor, chop the basil, garlic.
- Add walnuts, process.
- Add olive oil and cheeses. Process.
- Add seasonings to taste.

SPECIAL NOTES: KEEPS WELL IN REFRIGERATOR COVERED WITH A LAYER OF OLIVE OIL. FOR LONG TERM STORAGE, POUR INTO AN ICE CUBE TRAY. FREEZE AND POP SQUARES OUT AND STORE IN FREEZER CONTAINER IN FREEZER. AN EXCELLENT ADDITION TO PASTA SALAD. MAY ALSO BE LAYERED WITH A ½ CREAM CHEESE, ½ BUTTER MIX TO MAKE A TORTA HORS D'OEUVRE.

Davi Langston

PESTO (BASIL)

¼ cup olive oil
½ cup chopped pine nuts or walnuts
2 cups snipped fresh basil

½ cup freshly grated parmesan cheese
3 cloves of garlic, minced
Pepper to taste

- Process the oil, chopped nuts, basil, parmesan cheese and garlic in blender or food processor until smooth. Add pepper to taste.

SPECIAL NOTES: KEEP IN THE REFRIGERATOR IN A CLOSED GLASS JAR. IF NECESSARY, WILL KEEP ABOUT 10 DAYS.

Yield: 1 cup

Cam Caldwell

Fr. Tom's whimsical blessing at an ECW luncheon:
Heavenly Father, bless this bunch as they munch their lunch.
Amen

QUICK 'N EASY HOLLANDAISE SAUCE

3   egg yolks
2   tbsp. lemon juice
Dash salt

Dash cayenne pepper
½   cup butter, melted

- Beat egg yolk in blender until light and fluffy.
- Add lemon juice and seasoning.
- Heat butter until melted and hot.
- Remove feeder cap and add hot melted butter gradually.
- Process until thick.

SPECIAL NOTE: CAN EASILY BE DOUBLED.

Martha Fitzgerald

SPAGHETTI SAUCE

2   cups chopped onion
3   cloves garlic, chopped
2   tbsp. olive oil
3½ cups canned Italian-style
    plum tomatoes, undrained
2   6 oz. cans tomato paste

6   beef bouillon cubes dissolved
    in 2 cups boiling water
1   bay leaf
½   tsp. salt
¼   tsp. black pepper
¼   tsp. oregano
¼   tsp. basil

- Sauté onion and garlic in olive oil until brown, stirring often.
- Add tomatoes, tomato paste, bouillon, bay leaf, salt and pepper. Simmer uncovered, stirring occasionally about 2 hours.
- Add the oregano and basil and continue cooking about fifteen minutes.
- Remove the bay leaf.
- Serve over cooked spaghetti or use as an ingredient in other dishes.
- Also good with two 4 oz. cans sliced mushrooms added with the tomatoes. Freezes well.

SPECIAL NOTES: A GREAT WAY TO SERVE A CROWD INEXPENSIVELY. WITH THE BEEF BOUILLON, NO ONE REALIZES THIS IS A MEATLESS DISH.

Serves 6

Becky Rowell

SPICED APRICOTS

1   can (1 lb. 13 oz.) whole   ½   tsp. pumpkin pie spice
    apricots   1   tbsp. white wine vinegar
2   tbsp. brown sugar

- Drain syrup from apricots.

- Measure 1 cup of syrup and add brown sugar, pumpkin pie spice
  and vinegar in a saucepan.

- Add apricots and simmer for 15 or 20 minutes.

SPECIAL NOTE: SERVE HOT OR COLD WITH CHICKEN, HAM OR ROAST MEATS.

Serves 6-8   *Kay Keith*

CRANBERRY FRAPPE

1   lb. cranberries   1   orange
2   cups water   2   cups sugar

- Cook cranberries in water until soft. Sieve.

- Add grated rind and juice of one orange.

- Add sugar and dissolve over heat.

- Freeze, beat, then refreeze.

SPECIAL NOTE: THIS REFRESHING AND BEAUTIFUL FRAPPE COULD BE CALLED A
SORBET AND SERVED BETWEEN COURSES. WHEN I WAS A CHILD, THOUGH, IT
WAS AN ACCOMPANIMENT TO HAM OR TURKEY AT THANKSGIVING AND
CHRISTMAS. THESE DAYS, IT IS WISE TO BUY SEVERAL PACKAGES OF
CRANBERRIES AS SOON AS THEY ARE AVAILABLE—FOR GROCERS ARE OFTEN
UNABLE TO SUPPLY MORE BY CHRISTMAS TIME.

Serves 24   *Carolyn Mattingly*

*Give us grateful hearts, our Father, for all Thy mercies,
and make us mindful of the needs of others; through
Jesus Christ our Lord. Amen*

BOOK OF COMMON PRAYER, 1976

240

CRANBERRY SHERBET

1	cup water	½	cup orange juice
4	cups cranberries	2	egg whites
2	cups sugar	Dash of salt	

- Boil cranberries and water in a covered pan for 10 minutes or until berries pop.
- Add sugar, salt and orange juice.
- Run through ricer.
- Let begin to set in refrigerator.
- Freeze, beat egg whites.
- Add berry mixture and re-freeze.

SPECIAL NOTE: WE ALWAYS HAVE THIS FOR THANKSGIVING AND CHRISTMAS. EXCELLENT WITH A TURKEY DINNER.

Serves 8   *Janet Daniel*

GREESON'S GREEN GODDESS DRESSING

3	cups mayonnaise	2	tbsp. tarragon leaves
8-10	filet anchovies, chopped	1	tbsp. chives, minced
2	sprigs parsley (fresh), chopped	½	cup tarragon vinegar
2	green onion, sliced	1	clove garlic, minced

- Blend all ingredients together.
- It takes a few hours for the ingredients to "marry" so best to make a day ahead.

SPECIAL NOTE: THIS RECIPE IS ORIGINALLY FROM A SAN FRANCISCO RESTAURANT.

Nancy Sumerford

MARTHAS HOT MUSTARD

4   oz. Coleman (only) dry   1   cup white sugar
    mustard   1   tsp. salt
1   cup white vinegar   2   eggs

- Place dry mustard into small glass bowl.
- Gradually add vinegar, stirring to get a smooth paste.
- Cover and let stand overnight.
- Next day, put mustard mixture in double boiler and add sugar, salt and well beaten eggs.
- Cook over hot water (do not boil rapidly) until it thickens, stirring constantly with a wooden spoon.
- Cool, put in jars and refrigerate.

Martha Fitzgerald

NACHO CHIP DIP

1   lb. ground beef   1   can Nacho cheese soup
1   16 oz. box Velveeta cheese   1   8 oz. jar taco sauce

- Brown meat, drain.
- Add cheese, soup and taco sauce.
- Heat on stove top until well blended.
- Put in casserole.
- Serve warm with nacho chips.

Kathryn Tison

A BIT OF PARAPHRASING BY FR. TOM:

Give us grateful hearts, our Father, for all Thy mercies,
and make us needful of the minds of others; through
Jesus Christ our Lord. Amen

OYSTER DRESSING

1	small pkg. Pepperidge Farm dressing mix	8	eggs, beaten
1	small pkg. Pepperidge Farm corn bread dressing mix	¼	lb. margarine
		1	large onion, diced
1	12 oz. can evaporated milk	4	stalks celery,diced
2	14 ½ oz. cans chicken broth	1	pt. oysters, drained, reserve
2	cups buttermilk		juice

- Mix evaporated milk, chicken broth, buttermilk, beaten eggs, oyster juice, margarine all together and cook until hot.
- While hot, pour over dressing mix.
- Add the pt. of drained oysters (chopped if large oysters) and onion and celery. Mix in well.
- Pour into large greased baking casserole. Bake at 350° for 1-1¼ hour, or until golden brown. When dressing springs back to touch, remove from over.

Serves 12   *Susan Shipman*

PEAR CHUTNEY

4	qts cut up pears	1	tsp. allspice
4	cups brown sugar	1	clove garlic
2	cups cider vinegar	3	sweet (bell) peppers
1	medium onion, sliced	1	tbsp. salt
2	small hot peppers	2	tbsp. mustard seeds
1	box dark seedless raisins	1	tbsp. ground ginger
1	small box candied ginger (2-3 oz.)	1	large lemon, chopped

- Cook pears, sugar, vinegar, garlic, onion, peppers and lemon until soft.
- Add spices, raisins, ginger, and simmer 30 minutes.
- Let stand overnight.
- Next day bring to a boil.
- Put in sterilized jars. For a sure seal, boil jars in deep water five minutes.

SPECIAL NOTE: THIS RECIPE IS BEST MADE WITH THOSE HARD, DIFFICULT TO PEAL AND CHOP SAND PEARS.

Yields: 12 (12 oz) jars   *Barbara Morgan*

POOZIES DILL-SWEETS

1	gal. dill pickles (regular)	4	tbsp. pickling spice
8	cups sugar	2	tbsp. whole cloves
4	tbsp. whole allspice	1	cup pickle juice

- Cut large dills into chunks.
- Put into a large glass or plastic bowl.
- Add remaining ingredients. Stir often for 3 days.
- Return to empty jar. Keep refrigerated.

Sarah B. Jones

GREEN TOMATO PICKLE

25	lbs. (½ bushel) green tomatoes		1 heaping tbsp. each of:
8	lbs. white onion		Powdered mace
12	large green bell peppers		Cinnamon
6	lbs. white cabbage		Turmeric
5	lbs. sugar		Black pepper
3	qts vinegar		Celery seed
1	lb. salt	2	tbsp. mustard seed (heaping)

- Chop or shred vegetables.
- Mix and layer in large stainless or enamel container, sprinkling 1 lb. salt between layers.
- Cover and let stand overnight.
- The next day place small amounts of vegetable mix in clean pillowcase (do not use your best—it will be stained green) and squeeze tightly until all juice is squeezed out.
- Mix sugar and spices together in another large container.
- Add vinegar and let come to a good boil.
- Add vegetables and let come to a roaring boil. Stir often and cook about 35-45 minutes.
- Taste largest piece of cabbage to see if its hot all the way through.
- Remove from heat and seal in hot jars.

SPECIAL NOTE: THIS WILL YIELD BETWEEN 2-3 DOZEN QTS. WE ALWAYS MADE THIS ON VACATION IN THE SUMMER WHEN THE TOMATOES AND VIDALIA ONION CROPS ARE THEIR VERY BEST.

Fr. Tom Fitzgerald

TURKEY STUFFING

EGG BREAD:

1 egg	1½ tbsp. melted shortening
1¼ cup meal	1 tsp. salt
1 cup buttermilk	½ tsp. soda
	1½ tsp. baking powder

- Bake in oven 300° about 30 minutes. Crumble the cooled eggbread
  and add:

2-2½ cups old bread or commercial stuffing (Pepperidge Farm)	Chopped onions and celery
	2-3 eggs
	½ tsp. pepper
4-5 cups turkey stock	1 tbsp. salt
½ cup melted butter	1 tsp. sage or poultry seasoning

- Mix and pour in greased 12 x18-inch pan. Bake 425° for 40 minutes.

Gerda B. Brown

VANILLA

2 vanilla beans	1 fifth vodka

- Split vanilla beans and scrape insides into the vodka, drop beans in Vodka.
- Store in cool place 1 month.
- strain through a coffee filter.

SPECIAL NOTE: YOU WILL HAVE VERY GOOD VANILLA.

Mrs. Robert W. Peters

Preserved Children

1 large yard
½ dozen children
2 or 3 small dogs
Pinch of creek
Some pebbles

Method: Mix the children and dogs well together.

Put them in the yard, stirring constantly.

Pour the creek over the pebbles, sprinkle the field with flowers; spread over all a deep blue sky and bake in the sun.

When children are done, set away to cool in the bath tub.

CLERESTORY WINDOWS

The clerestory windows, installed in 1969, were reworked from an earlier sanctuary window. They have an allover pattern of passion flowers.

The window on the Gospel side bears the dedication "To the Glory of God and in memory of Rebecca Isbella Wylly. Born March 9, 1843. Died May 7, 1912."

CLERESTORY WINDOWS

The clerestory windows, installed in
1969, were reworked from an earlier
sanctuary window. They have an allover
pattern of passion flowers.

On the Epistle side, banners are
emblazoned with the words, "Angels and
Archangels guiding loved one now.
Saints departed waving welcome
made glorious her coming into the
city of our Lord."

GLORIFIED ONIONS

5-6 jumbo Vidalia onions	1 tbsp. celery salt
½ cup white vinegar	1 tsp. cayenne pepper
1 cup sugar	1 tbsp. dried dill weed
2 cups water	1 cup mayonnaise (approx.)

- Slice onions thin. Mix vinegar, sugar and water. Stir until sugar is dissolved.
- Pour over onions. Soak, covered in refrigerator overnight.
- Mix mayonnaise with spices.
- Drain onions and pat dry as possible.
- Toss with mayonnaise mixture, refrigerate for about an hour.
- Toss again and put in bowl to be served over soda crackers.

SPECIAL NOTE: AN OLD VALDOSTA RECIPE SLIGHTLY IMPROVED! THERE WILL NOT BE ANY LEFT AT A COCKTAIL PARTY.

Serves 15-20   *Bunky and Belitje Bull*

BEEF VEGETABLE SOUP

2 lbs. stew beef	1 can small green lima beans
4 medium potatoes cut in chunks	3 cans tomatoes, cut up
	Any leftover vegetables
4 carrots, sliced	Worcestershire sauce to taste
2 ribs celery, sliced	Tabasco sauce to taste
1 medium onion, chopped	Salt and pepper to taste
1 can cut okra or fresh or frozen	½ cup catsup
1 can corn	Water

- Cut meat in small chunks. Discard fat and gristle. Brown in 4 qt. Dutch oven using small amount of oil.
- Add all other ingredients. Amount of water will depend on size of pot. I fill the pot. Bring to a boil then cover and simmer.
- Taste now and then. Season to taste.
- Cook 1 cup of rice. When soup is ready to serve, place two spoons of rice in the bottom of each bowl and then add soup.

SPECIAL NOTE: GOOD FOR THE FIRST COOL DAY OF FALL.

Serves 8   *Allen Burns*

BRUNSWICK STEW VIRGINIA STYLE

8 to 10 chicken breast halves
2 large cans Progresso tomatoes
2-3 large onions, chopped
3 large potatoes, diced
2 boxes frozen Green Giant baby limas
2 boxes frozen white shoepeg corn
2 tsp. sugar
Thyme, Worcestershire, salt and pepper to taste
2 slices raw bacon or streak of lean
½ stick butter

- Boil the chicken breasts, save stock. Remove chicken from bone, chop coarse. Reserve.

- To 8 cups stock add onions, tomatoes and juice, potatoes, bacon, seasonings and water if necessary.

- Boil until tender.

- Add lima beans, cook 25 more minutes.

- Add corn and cooked chicken and ½ stick butter. Simmer 30 minutes. Freezes well.

SPECIAL NOTE: THIS RECIPE CAME FROM WILLIAMSBURG, VA. OLD FAMILY RECIPE. THE ORIGINAL MEAT USED WAS RABBIT, SQUIRREL AND CHICKEN.

Serves 6-8

Bunky and Belitje Bull

JULIUS CAESAR'S 11.19 LB. LASAGNA

Brown 2 lbs. ground round (or horse) until all the water escapes. Add:

2 large cans peeled tomatoes (32 oz. each), 1 can tomato paste (15 oz.)
3 cloves garlic minced, 3 shakes Tabasco, ½ tsp. dried hot red peppers
2 tsp. sugar, 4 onions chopped and sautéed, 3 tsp. oregano (people have been arrested for omitting this ingredient), and 3 tsp. sweet basil.

Simmer the meat sauce for 1½ hours.

Boil 1 lb. lasagna noodles with water just to cover and 2 tbsp. oil to keep them from sticking. Remove after 20 minutes. Time this to have noodles done just before you're ready to assemble.

Grate (coarse) 2 lbs. mozzarella. Divide into 4 equal parts.

Add 1 beaten egg to 1 or 1½ lbs. ricotta cheese and mix. (Actually quantity depends on availability of goats.)

Grate ¼ lb. romano cheese or use pregrated, tax paid romano.

Oil a baking dish 3- x 15- x 8-inches, or 360 cubic inches. This is a minimum size. Deeper is better.

Assemble the lasagna according to the following order:

Noodles, sauce, mozzarella cheese, dabs of ricotta chieese, romano cheese. Should be 4½ layers if using dish size above.

Bake 350° for 45 minutes to 1 hour.

This dish serves 14 persons, or 5.3 centurians, or lasts for 20 minutes at an orgy.

KING'S ARMS TAVERN
CREAM OF PEANUT SOUP

1 medium onion, chopped	2 qts. chicken stock or canned
2 ribs of celery, chopped	chicken broth (or recipe
¼ cup butter	below)
3 tbsp. all-purpose flour	2 cups smooth peanut butter
	1¾ cups light cream
	Peanuts, chopped

- Sauté the onion and celery in butter until soft, but not brown.

- Stir in flour until well blended.

- Add the chicken stock, stirring constantly, bring to a boil.

- Remove from heat and purée in a food processor or a blender.

- Add the peanut butter and cream stirring to blend thoroughly.

- Return to low heat and heat until just hot, but do not boil.

- Before serving garnish with chopped peanuts. This is also good served ice cold.

Serves 10-12

Williamsburg Chicken Stock

Bouquet Garni:	2 medium onion
½ tsp. leaf thyme	3-4 ribs celery with leaves
1 small bay leaf	3-4 carrots, washed but unpeeled
½ tsp. leaf marjoram	2-3 leeks or spring onions
3 sprigs parsley	with tops
6 peppercorns	4-5 lbs. chicken necks, backs,
	and wings
	1 tbsp. salt
	1 cup dry white wine (optional)

- Prepare Bouquet Garni by tying the herbs in a cheesecloth bag.

- Cut the vegetables into 1-inch pieces.

- Put all the ingredients into a large soup pot with enough water to cover them by at least 2-inches.

- Bring to a boil over medium heat. Partially cover and simmer for 2-3 hours, or until the chicken comes easily from the bones. Remove the chicken (and bones).

- Leave uncovered and continue to simmer the stock over low heat until it is reduced to about 4 qts.

- Strain the stock, refrigerate and when cold, remove all fat.

SPECIAL NOTE: I BROUGHT THESE WONDERFUL RECIPES HOME FROM HISTORIC WILLIAMSBURG. THE STOCK CAN BE FROZEN IN CUBES FOR FUTURE USE.

Yields 4 qts. *John K. McEvoy*

BUTTERMILK BISCUITS

- Sift 3 cups of self-rising flour (I like Martha White) into a large bowl, one big enough to get both hands inside.

- Next cut in ½ to ¾ cup of shortening (I prefer Crisco). Work shortening in with a fork until flour is the texture of moist meal.

- Add 1½ cups of buttermilk and stir it in with a fork. Add another dash or two if dough isn't sticky. (The trick is to get dough just as moist and sticky as possible but not too sticky to work.)

- Work dough into a ball in the center of the bowl and sprinkle lightly with flour so it won't stick to your hands.

- Lift ball of dough out and knead gently on a floured dough board or smooth surface. (I simply fold the dough over in a clockwise manner with the right hand as I press it out with the left.) Don't over-knead—just to the point to where the dough is soft and consistent.

- Pinch off a golf ball size ball and press out between the palms to about a ¼- to ½-inch thickness and lay out on a slightly greased (with shortening) bread pan.

- Bake in oven, preheated to 425° for about 15 minutes.

SPECIAL NOTE: THE SECRET HERE IS TO LEARN, BY TRIAL AND ERROR, HOW TO GET THE DOUGH AS FULL OF BUTTERMILK AS POSSIBLE AND YET KEEP IT MANAGEABLE. THE NOSTALGIC, REAL HOMEMADE TASTE COMES FROM THE BUTTERMILK-SOAKED DOUGH.

Along with a slab of butter or a ladle of gravy, these substantial biscuits just about make a meal in themselves—the kind you can stick a hole in with your finger and then pour 'em full of syrup and eat like cream-filled bakery pastry. They used to be called "cat head biscuits," because you could butter one and lay it on top of your head and your tongue would beat your brains out trying to get at it.

Congressman Lindsay Thomas

FREEMAN'S QUAKER OAT BRAN MUFFINS

1	banana, mashed or ½ cup raisins	1	cup Quaker Oat Bran
2	tbsp. corn oil	1	cup cake flour
¼	tsp. spice (all spice, apple pie spice, ginger or cinnamon)	⅓	cup molasses (cane syrup, honey, brown or white sugar, OR 4 packages artificial sweetener [except Equal] with 1 tbsp. molasses for color)
2	tsps. baking powder		
1-1⅓	cups skim milk		
1	tsp. vanilla extract		

- Add oil to bananas or raisins.
- Combine bran and flour with spice and baking powder.
- Combine molasses (or other sugar), milk and vanilla.
- Add fruit mixture to bran mixture alternately with liquids.
- Spray muffin tins with Pam. Fill half full.
- Bake in a 375° oven for 22 minutes (more or less).

Yields 18 muffins   *Joseph J. Freeman*

APPLE PANCAKES

1	cup pancake mix	1	tsp. sugar
1	cup milk	1	tsp. cinnamon
1	egg	½	tsp. nutmeg
1	cup fresh sliced apples		Oil for frying

- Mix all ingredients.
- Prepare skillet and heat. Spoon ¼ cup of batter into heated skillet. Turn when brown on both sides.

SPECIAL NOTE: MADE UP BY CHRISTOPHER (AGE 10).

Serves 4   *Christopher Allen*

SPOON BREAD

1	cup corn meal	3	eggs
2	cups water	1	cup milk
½	tsp. salt	3	tbsp. vegetable oil

- Bring water and salt to a rolling boil.
- Remove from heat and immediately add corn meal while rapidly stirring with a whisk.
- Mix eggs, milk and oil together. Then add to cooked corn meal.
- Stir with a whisk to break up lumps.
- Pour into greased casserole. Bake at 400° for one hour.

John Hardee

WAFFLES

2	cups all-purpose unbleached flour	3	eggs, separated
3	heaping tbsp. yellow corn meal	1¾	cups milk
		3	tbsp. vegetable oil
1	tbsp. baking powder	1	tsp. lemon juice

- Whip egg whites.
- Mix dry ingredients in a bowl.
- Mix liquid ingredients separately then add to flour mixture.
- Stir until smooth then fold in egg whites.
- Cook in waffle iron coated with Pam.

John Hardee

ROMAINE AND MANDARIN ORANGE SALAD

½	bunch romaine, torn	**Dressing:**	
1	can mandarin oranges	¼	tsp. dry mustard
1	small Vidalia onion, sliced thinly, punched into rings (or 4 green onions. sliced)	¼	tsp. salt
		¼	tsp. black pepper
Sunflower seeds		2	cloves garlic, minced
		6	tbsp. olive oil
		3	tbsp. cider vinegar

- Rinse, dry and crisp the romaine.
- Combine with oranges and onions in a salad bowl.
- Sprinkle with sunflower seeds.
- Serve with dressing passed separately.
- Dressing: Combine mustard, salt, pepper and garlic in a small jar or cruet with tight-fitting lid.
- Add oil and vinegar, shake well. Refrigerate unused portion.

SPECIAL NOTE: DRESSING IS GREAT ON TOSSED SALADS AND AS A MARINADE FOR SHRIMP OR FISH.

Serves 2   *Charles Lamkin*

CAESAR SALAD

1	head romaine	1	egg
¾	cup olive oil	1	lemon, halved
3	tbsp. red wine vinegar		Freshly ground pepper
1	tsp. Worcestershire sauce	¼	cup grated parmesan cheese
½	tsp. salt		Garlic croûtons (recipe below)
¼	tsp. dry mustard	1	2 oz. can anchovy fillets
2	cloves garlic, minced		(optional)

- Wash romaine, dry and chill at least 2 hours in a plastic bag.
- Combine oil, vinegar, Worcestershire Sauce, salt, mustard and garlic in a jar. Cover tightly and shake vigorously.
- Coddle egg: carefully lower egg into rapidly boiling water. Turn off heat. Let egg stand 1 minute. Remove from water and set aside to cool.
- Tear romaine and place in large salad bowl.
- Pour half of dressing over and toss until well coated.
- Break egg over romaine; then squeeze juice from lemon halves over salad.
- Grind pepper to taste over salad and sprinkle with cheese. Toss lightly.
- Top with croûtons; garnish with anchovies (optional). Serve immediately.

Serves 4-6

Garlic Croûtons

3	tbsp. butter or margarine, softened	3	slices French bread (sliced ¾-inch)
		¼	tsp. garlic powder

- Spread butter over both sides of bread slices; sprinkle with garlic powder.
- Cut slices into ¾-inch cubes. Place on a baking sheet and bake at 350° for 15 minutes or until croûtons are crisp and dry.
- Let cool and store in an airtight container.

Charles Lamkin

FLOUNDER SUPREME

½ cup butter
2 medium onions, sliced thin
1 lb. flounder or sole fillet
  (fresh or frozen)
¾ cup mayonnaise

1 tsp. chopped parsley or
  parsley flakes
Juice of 1 lemon
¼ cup parmesan cheese

- Melt butter in oven-proof dish and place onions over the bottom.
- Place fish on top of onions.
- Mix mayonnaise, parsley and lemon juice. Spread over fish.
- Sprinkle parmesan cheese over the top.
- Bake in 350° oven 25 minutes.
- Sprinkle with toasted almonds after removing from oven (optional).

Serves 4   *Berrien Cheatham*

ARNAUD'S SHRIMP SAUCE

3 tbsp. vegetable oil
2 tbsp. olive oil
2 tbsp. vinegar
1 tbsp. paprika
½ tsp. salt

½ tsp. pepper
4 tbsp. creole mustard
½ small white onion, chopped
3 ribs of celery, chopped

- Mix ingredients in blender.
- Chill. Serve on shrimp.

Yields 1 cup   *Fred W. Collins*

SHRIMP PIE

Large sweet onion, chopped
3 tbsp. Worcestershire sauce
1 large can tomatoes, drained
8 slices white bread

2 cups cooked shrimp
Salt, pepper oregano to taste
Bacon slices to cover mixture

- Place halved bread slices in 9- x 13- x 2-inch dish.
- Sauté onion. Chop and add tomatoes, Worcestershire, seasonings, and shrimp. Heat.
- Pour this over bread slices.
- Top with raw bacon slices and bake at 350° until bacon is done.

SPECIAL NOTE: THIS IS AN EXCELLENT SUNDAY NIGHT SUPPER.

Serves 6   *Bob Amme*

BROILED LAMB STEAK

1-inch thick lamb steak
½ cup olive oil
1 mashed clove garlic

2-5 tbsp. parsley, minced
¼ tsp. black pepper
Salt to taste

- Have butcher cut 1-inch steaks from a leg of lamb between the shank and the aitch bone.

- Combine the olive oil and mashed garlic. Paint each side of steak. Place on a broiler pan. Broil 1-1½ minutes per side.

- Mix remaining olive oil with 2-3 tbsp. of minced parsley and ¼ tsp. black pepper.

- Place 1-2 tbsp. of the above mixture on one side of steak. Broil ½ minute.

- Turn steak. Repeat above step on other side.

- Serve immediately.

SPECIAL NOTE: AS OVEN TEMPERATURES VARY, BE CAREFUL NOT TO OVER-COOK. MEAT SHOULD BE SLIGHTLY PINK.

Serves 2 (if a large steak)　　　　　　　　　*Robert (Bob) McCauley*

PORK LOIN SOUTHERN STYLE

2½ lbs. fresh pork loin

Basting sauce:
3 cups catsup
2½ tsp. chili powder
1 tsp. prepared English
　mustard (your choice)
1 tsp. black pepper
¾ cup maple syrup

¼ lb. real butter
1 tbsp. Worcestershire sauce
1 clove garlic minced
1 medium yellow onion, halved
¼ cup lemon juice
1 bay leaf
¼ cup Italian or garlic salad
　dressing (made)

- Sauce: Mix all ingredients. Bring to a boil and simmer 1 hour.

- Remove bay leaf. May be served on anything.

- Loin: Place meat on roasting pan, brush with prepared sauce. Bake 350° for 1½ hours.

- Baste every 20 minutes until done.

SPECIAL NOTE: JUST DELICIOUS!

Serves 4-6　　　　　　　　　　　　　　*Bob Allen*

GRILLED LAMB

Leg of lamb, boned with all
fat and skin removed
1   cup olive oil
⅔   cup lemon juice
5   cloves garlic
2   bay leaves

6   sprigs parsley
2   tsp. salt
½   tsp. ground pepper
½   tbsp. sage
½   tbsp. rosemary
1   tbsp. thyme

- Combine oil, lemon juice, garlic, bay leaves, parsley, salt, pepper, and herbs. Marinate lamb in this mixture for 24 hours, turning occasionally.
- Drain meat, reserving marinade and place meat on a hot grill; sear each side.
- Lower the heat and cook 45-60 minutes, brushing frequently with reserved marinade. Do not over-cook. The inside should be pink.
- Before serving pour sauce over sliced meat.

Sauce for Grilled Lamb

½   tbsp. sage
½   tbsp. rosemary
½   tbsp. thyme
¼   cup red wine

½   cup beef stock
2   tbsp. chopped shallots
3   tbsp. butter softened
3   tbsp. chopped parsley

- Combine stock, wine, shallots and herbs. Boil and reduce to ½ cup. Remove from heat and swirl in butter and parsley.

SPECIAL NOTE: A FAVORITE OF OUR FAMILIES AND FESTIVE ENOUGH FOR COMPANY TOO.

Joe Bradford

BLUE CHEESE BURGERS

3   lbs. ground chuck
¼   lb. crumbled blue cheese
½   cup chopped green onions
¼   tsp. Tabasco sauce

1   tsp. Worcestershire sauce
2   tbsp. mustard
12 toasted hamburger buns
Salt and pepper to taste

- In a bowl, combine meat and blue cheese.
- Add chopped green onions, Tabasco, Worcestershire, salt and pepper. Toss together lightly.
- Cover and chill for at least two hours to blend flavors.
- Shape into 12 patties handling as little as possible.
- Broil or grill about 5 minutes on each side or until done to your liking.
- Serve on buns with your favorite topping.

SPECIAL NOTE: SO EASY TO PREPARE AND TASTY.

Serves 12

Bob Allen

CHIANTI BURGERS

Glaze:
1   large garlic clove, minced
¼   cup dark molasses
⅓   cup chianti wine

Toppers:
8   thin slices red onion
8   small slices mozzarella cheese

Combine for burgers:
2   lbs. ground chuck
½-1 tsp. salt (optional)
2   eggs (or Egg Beaters)
½   cup bread crumbs
½   cup chianti wine
½   tsp. oregano
½   tsp. basil

- Mix all burger ingredients together well. Shape into 16 thin patties.
- On 8 patties, place 8 thin slices red onion, 8 slices mozzarella.
- Top with the other 8 patties. Pinch edges to seal. *Chill one hour.*
- Broil (on grill) 10 minutes on each side, brush often with glaze.
- Serve on grilled buns, or French or Italian bread, buttered and grilled.

SPECIAL NOTE: THE BEST BURGER IN THE WORLD! WE'VE MADE THIS FAMILY FAVORITE FOR 30 YEARS.

Serves 8   *Pete Smith*

STUFFED CUBE STEAK

1½ lbs. cube steak
¼   cup finely chopped onions
½   cup chopped celery
3   tbsp. butter
2   cups cubed day old bread
½   tsp. salt

¼   tsp. sage
Dash pepper
1   tbsp. chopped parsley
1   tbsp. water
Flour and oil for frying
1   can cream mushroom soup

- Lightly cook onion and celery in butter until tender. Add bread cubes, seasonings, parsley and water.
- Cut meat into 4 pieces and spread with dressing mixture.
- Roll up and secure with toothpicks.
- Roll in flour, brown in oil.
- Dilute soup with 1 cup water. Pour over meat.
- Sprinkle with additional salt and pepper. Cover and simmer over low heat 1½ hours.

SPECIAL NOTE: MOTHER'S RECIPE.

Serves 4   *Phil Allen*

TEXAS BEEF BRISKET

1 fresh beef brisket, 2½ lbs. (not corn beef)	3 12 oz. cans beer or ale
1½ tsp. garlic powder	1 tbsp. salt
1 medium, coarsely cut onion	1½ tsp. black pepper
2 oz. Worcestershire sauce	6 oz. BBQ sauce (your choice)

- Put brisket and next six ingredients in a Dutch oven.
- Cover and bake at 220° for 8-9 hours.
- Carefully remove meat so it doesn't fall apart.
- Coat with BBQ sauce and place on hot charcoal grill.
- Grill each side 3 times allowing 2-3 minutes on each side and liberally basting with BBQ sauce.

SPECIAL NOTE: LEFTOVERS MAKE AN EXCELLENT SANDWICH. A FRIEND FROM TEXAS GAVE ME THIS RECIPE MANY YEARS AGO.

Serves 5   *Floyd T. Taylor, III*

BIRDS OF PARADISE

4 whole boned chicken breasts (8 pieces)	½ cup grated Parmesan cheese
2 eggs, beaten	½ cup butter
3 tbsp. milk	1 cup sherry or Madeira (not cooking sherry)
½ tsp. salt	

- Beat eggs, milk and salt together in small bowl.
- Place Parmesan cheese in another.
- Dip chicken first into egg mixture, then into cheese.
- Using an electric skillet, set at 300°, brown chicken on both sides.
- Add wine, cover and cook at 225° for 45-60 minutes.
- Serve on a bed of Uncle Ben's wild rice cooked according to pkg. directions. Spoon some of the wine/butter mixture over and surround with tomatoes Florentine or broiled tomatoes.

SPECIAL NOTE: THIS HAS BEEN A FAVORITE FOR MANY YEARS. A RECIPE GIVEN TO ME BY AN ATLANTA FRIEND AND ONE I HAVE NEVER FOUND IN PRINT.

Serves 8   *Berrien Cheatham*

CHICKEN POT PIE

2-3 lb. hen	1 can English peas and carrots
½ stick butter	1 cup chicken broth
1 chopped onion	1 tbsp. flour
1 cup chopped celery	Biscuit mix for 10 biscuits

- Boil hen until tender. Remove meat from bone and cut into small pieces.
- Melt butter in ovenware pan. Add onion and celery. Cook very slowly for 15 minutes.
- Add can of peas and carrots;
- Blend broth and flour. Add broth mixture, chicken, salt and pepper to taste.
- Top with biscuits and bake at 425° until brown.
- If desired, add ½ cup chopped bell pepper or can of mushrooms as onion and celery cook.

Governor Zell Miller

We thank you Lord, for bringing our friends to our table tonight. We haven't been together for such a long time and there's so much news to catch up on. We'll be talking 'way past midnight. But, Lord, before we dig into each other's lives, give us Your blessing through this beautiful meal before us. Let us be aware of Your presence here among us and let us feel Your hand in ours as we offer You our prayers and thanksgiving. Amen.

TABLE GRACE FOR OLD FRIENDS

COUNTRY CAPTAIN

2	large hens		Salt and pepper	
2	medium green peppers	4	cups canned tomatoes
2	small onions	3	4 oz. cans mushrooms
2	cloves garlic	½	lb. blanched almonds
2	tbsp. butter or margarine	½	lb. currants or raisins
3	tsp. curry powder		Cooked rice
2	tsp. thyme			

- Cut up chicken and steam until tender.

- While chicken is steaming, cut up peppers, onions, garlic and sauté in a frying pan until slightly brown, not done.

- Add curry powder, thyme, salt, pepper, tomatoes, and mushrooms.

- When mixture is well blended, add cooked chicken and half of blanched and toasted almonds, and half of raisins; cook together for 1 hour. (Do not thicken gravy.)

- When ready to serve, pour mixture over cooked rice, or place rice around it. Sprinkle with remaining almonds and raisins.

- Garnish with chutney, coconut, chopped peanuts, chopped onions, raisins, chipped bacon, other condiments.

(Note: Georgians claim this dish, insisting that a mysterious sea captain drifted into Savannah via the spice trade and entrusted his recipe to Southern friends. It was a favorite dish of General George Patton while stationed in Columbus, Georgia.)

Condiments are often referred to as "boys," because of Indian custom having servants bring in each condiment in single file. The more servants you have the higher your status, therefore, today's custom— "the more boys you have, the better the dish."

Serves 8-10   *Congressman Lindsay Thomas*

Aspirin Cake

Preheat oven to 375°. Turn down the TV, remove toys from countertops. Measure 2 cups flour, get baking powder. Remove Bobby's hand from the flour. Put flour, baking powder and salt into sifter. Vacuum mixture off kitchen floor (Bobby spilled). Get an egg. Answer phone. Separate egg and warm Ashley's bottle. Help Sue figure out new math problem—the old reliable way. Grease pan. Salesman at door. Take ¼-inch of sale from greased pan and look for Bobby. Put mess in wastebasket, dishes in dishwasher, call the bakery. Take 2 aspirins.

STUFFED PEPPERS

1 lb. ground beef	4 bell peppers
1 sweet onion, diced	¼ cup olivie oil
2 cloves garlic, finely chopped	
½ cup grated Parmesan cheese	Sauce:
½ cup cooked white rice	2 15 oz. cans tomato sauce
Salt and pepper to taste	1 tbsp. sugar
1 egg, beaten	⅛ cup red wine vinegar
Chopped parsley	1 tsp. oregano
¼ cup red wine	1 tsp. basil
½ cup bread crumbs	Salt and pepper to taste

- Sauté onions and garlic in oil until transparent.
- Combine onions, garlic, red wine, ground beef, Parmesan cheese, rice, parsley, egg, bread crumbs, salt and pepper.
- Cut tops off peppers, remove seeds and fiber. Stuff with above mixture, place in a stove top casserole.
- Mix all ingredients for sauce in pan and heat.
- Pour sauce over peppers in casserole.
- Simmer slowly in covered casserole for about 2 hours until meat is cooked and peppers tender. Baste occasionally.

Serves 4 (8 if halving large peppers)   *Bob McCauley, Jr.*

SPAGHETTI SAUCE WITH MEAT

5 lbs. lean hamburger	1 tbsp. white pepper
30 oz. tomato sauce	1 tbsp. salt
12 oz. tomato paste	2 tbsp. red peppers, crushed
8 1 lb. cans tomatoes	6 cloves garlic, minced
1 tbsp. chili powder	3 large onions (3 lbs.) chopped
1 tbsp. sugar	4 large bell peppers, chopped
1 tbsp. Italian herbs	2 tbsp. red wine (dry)
1 tbsp. black pepper	8 oz. chopped mushrooms

- Brown meat lightly in olive or vegetable oil.
- Sauté onions, bell peppers until somewhat translucent.
- Combine meat, onions, bell peppers and other ingredients, reserving wine and mushrooms until last.
- Cook slowly several hours, adjusting seasoning to taste.

SPECIAL NOTE: FREEZES VERY WELL.

Yields 30 cups   *Hubert Veal*

SPICY HOPPING JOHN

2	cups dried blackeyed peas	1	tbsp. salt	
8	cups water	2	tsp. chili powder	
8	oz. chopped ham	¼	tsp. dried basil, crushed	
1	16 oz. can tomatoes, cut up	1	bay leaf	
1	cup chopped onion	1	cup long grain rice	
1	cup chopped celery			

- Rinse peas. In kettle combine peas and water. Bring to boil; simmer 2 minutes, then remove from heat.

- Cover and let stand 1 hour. Do not drain.

- Add ham hock, tomatoes, onion, celery, salt, chili powder, basil and bay leaf. Cover and simmer about 1 hour until peas are tender.

- Add rice and cook 20 minutes or until rice is done. Remove bay leaf.

SPECIAL NOTE A MUST AT OUR HOUSE ON NEW YEAR'S DAY.

Serves 12   *Gene Palmer*

BÜLOW CAKE

1	lb. butter	1	tsp. vanilla	
5	eggs	1	tsp. baking powder	
2	cups flour, sifted	⅛	tsp. salt	
1½	cups sugar			

- Preheat oven to 325°. Butter and flour pans (2 loaf pans or 1 tube pan).

- Cream butter and flour.

- Beat eggs until foamy. Then beat in vanilla, baking powder, salt and sugar.

- Mix egg mixture with flour mixture, beat 2 minutes.

- Pour into pans, ⅔ full, and bake 1 hour and 15 minutes (check at 1 hour). Cool on rack.

Jack Hooton

DOUBLE CHOCOLATE BROWNIES

¾	cup all-purpose flour	1	12 oz. pkg. semi-sweet
¼	tsp. baking soda		chocolate chips
¼	tsp. salt	1	tsp. vanilla
⅓	cup butter	2	eggs
2	tbsp. water	½	cup chopped pecans
¾	cup sugar		

- In small bowl, combine flour, baking soda and salt. Set aside.
- In small saucepan combine butter, sugar and water; bring *just to a boil.* Remove from heat.
- Add 6 oz. chocolate chips and vanilla. Stir until melted and mixture is smooth.
- Transfer to a large bowl. Add eggs, one at a time, beating after each addition.
- Gradually blend in flour mixture. Stir in remaining chocolate chips and nuts.
- Pour into greased 9-inch square baking pan.
- Bake at 325° for 40-45 minutes.

Senator Sam Nunn

GOVERNOR'S CREME BRULÉE

12	extra-large egg yolks	2	tsp. vanilla extract
1	cup granulated sugar	1¼	cups light brown sugar
4¼	cups heavy cream		

- Heat heavy cream in a double boiler until hot.
- Beat the egg yolks and granulated sugar until thick and light in color.
- Slowly pour the heated cream over the yolk mixture, beating constantly. Return mixture to the double boiler and cook stirring constantly until custard coats a spoon heavily.
- Remove from heat and stir in vanilla.
- Strain into individual Ramekins or custard cups and chill thoroughly (at least 4 hours or overnight).
- Before serving, sift 2 tbsp. of brown sugar over each custard. Make sure that you have an even layer of sugar and then glaze one or two at a time underneath a preheated broiler or with a small propane torch on low flame.
- Serve within 15 minutes after glazing.

Yields ten 4 oz. custards

Governor Zell Miller

ONE EGG CAKE

1 cup flour
½ cup sugar
½ cup milk
1 egg
2 tsp. baking powder
3 tbsp. melted butter
½ tsp. vanilla

Sauce:
1 cup sugar
2 tbsp. flour
1 cup water
1 tsp. vanilla
2 tbsp. butter

- Beat egg with sugar. Add milk and flour that has been sifted with baking powder.
- Add butter which has been melted in pie dish.
- Pour mixture into dish. Bake in 350° oven for 25 minutes.
- Sauce: Combine flour and sugar. Add water. Boil until clear.
- Remove from heat. Add butter and vanilla. Pour over slices of cake.

SPECIAL NOTE: A QUICK, EASY AND DELICIOUS CAKE SERVED ON OCCASION BY MY MOTHER, ELIZABETH PALMER.

Gene Palmer

SWEET POTATO POUND CAKE

1 cup butter
2 cups sugar
2½ cups cooked, mashed
   sweet potatoes
4 eggs
3 cups flour
¼ tsp. soda
½ tsp. nutmeg
1 tsp. cinnamon
1 tsp. vanilla

½ cup chopped pecans
½ cup flaked coconut

Icing:
1 lb. box confectioner's sugar
Grated rind of one orange
Grated rind of one lemon
Juice of one lemon
Juice of one orange

- Cream butter and sugar; add sweet potatoes and beat until light and fluffy.
- Add eggs one at a time beating well after each.
- Combine dry ingredients and stir into creamed mixture.
- Add vanilla, nuts and coconut.
- Pour mixture into greased 10-inch tube pan and bake at 350° for 1 hour 15 minutes or until cake tests done.
- Spread with icing while warm.
- Icing: Combine all ingredients, slowly adding enough orange juice to make spreading consistency.

Governor Zell Miller

B-B-Q Sauce for Beef and Pork

2 tbsp. butter
1 medium onion
1 bay leaf
3 tbsp. molasses
1 clove garlic, chopped
½ cup celery, chopped
½ cup sweet pepper, chopped
1 1 lb. can tomatoes

1 can tomato sauce
2 tsp. dry mustard
1 cup red wine vinegar
¼ tsp. cloves
¼ tsp. allspice
1 lemon
1½ tsp. salt
2 tsp. Tabasco

- Sauté onion in butter
- Add sweet pepper, garlic and celery.
- Add remaining ingredients after vegetables are tender and soft.
- Simmer covered over low heat for 2 hours, stirring often.
- When cooked, purée in food processor.
- Strain into sterilized jars.

SPECIAL NOTE: SOME LIKE MORE VINEGAR, GO AHEAD!

Serves enough (maybe)

James D. Gould IV

Bar-B-Que Sauce

1 cup vinegar
¼ lb. margarine
2 tsp. Worcestershire sauce
2 tsp. chili powder
1 tbsp. paprika
1½ tbsp. black pepper
1½ tbsp. salt

1½ cups catsup
½ tsp. dry mustard
¼ cup water
1 tbsp. Tabasco
½ cup brown sugar (or molasses, honey, syrup)

- Mix together all ingredients and simmer for 15 minutes.

Joseph J. Freeman

Bobby's Barbecue Sauce

¼ lb. butter
1 cup catsup
2 tbsp. brown sugar
2 tbsp. Worcestershire sauce

20 dashes Tabasco
3 tbsp. vinegar
Juice and rind of 1 lemon
Salt and pepper

- Slowly heat above ingredients, until butter melts. Refrigerate

SPECIAL NOTE: KEEPS WELL. GOOD ON BEEF, PORK, CHICKEN AND SHELL FISH.

Bob Amme

DAD'S SALAD DRESSING

½ cup vinegar
4 eggs
1⅓ cups oil
4 cloves garlic

2 tsp. salt
1 tsp. pepper
3 tsp. Worcestershire sauce
4 oz. bleu cheese

- Mix all ingredients and store in refrigerator.

SPECIAL NOTE: STORES FOR AGES IN THE REFRIGERATOR. A GREAT DRESSING!

Bob Amme

MINCE MEAT

3 bowls beef or venison (boiled, no fat)
2 bowls cider
3 lemons (juice and yellow rind grated)
1 bowl suet, chopped
2 tbsp. cinnamon
1 bowl sugar (can use more)
5 bowls apples, chopped fine
1 bowl molasses

2 bowls raisins
1 tbsp. ground cloves
1 tbsp. pepper
1 bowl vinegar
1 bowl citron
1 tbsp. salt
3 nutmegs grated or to taste
Brandy and rum to taste

(Note: Bowl equals 1½ pints. Increase or decrease accordingly.)

- Cook on low to medium heat 'til apples are cooked and suet melted.
- Put in sterilized qt. jars while hot and seal with paraffin and then cap. In warm climate, refrigerate.

SPECIAL NOTE: CANDIED FRUITS MAY BE ADDED. A VERY OLD VERMONT RECIPE. WILL KEEP INDEFINITELY.

Yield: 1 qt. makes 2 pies

Bob McCauley

PEAR CHUTNEY

Hot mixture:
1½ qts. vinegar
2 lbs. white sugar
2 lbs. brown sugar
4 tbsp. salt
1 tbsp. chopped garlic
2 tbsp. mustard seed
1 tbsp. celery seed
1 tbsp. ground cinnamon

½ tbsp. ground cloves
1 tbsp. crushed red pepper or cayenne
Chopped:
4 lbs. hard pears, sliced, diced
6 medium onions, chopped
6 medium bell peppers, chopped
6 oz. crystallized ginger, chopped
1 lb. raisins

- Pour hot mixture over chopped ingredients using large glass bowls. Let sit overnight.
- Cook on medium heat stirring often until chutney is consistency of jam. (about 4 hours.)
- Put in pint or half pint jars and seal.

Yields 10 pints

Ronald F. Adams

Restaurants

ROQUEFORT-VEGETABLE SOUP

1	cup butter	3	qts. chicken broth
1	gal. chopped cabbage	1	qt. whipping cream
3	qts. chopped cauliflower	1	cup crumbled Roquefort

- Melt butter in a large soup pot and stir in cabbage until well coated.
- Cook, uncovered, over low heat for 10 to 15 minutes until cabbage is soft, stirring occasionally.
- Stir cauliflower and chicken broth into cabbage mixture.
- Bring to boil over high heat.
- Reduce heat. Cover and simmer about 30 minutes until cabbage and cauliflower are tender.
- Stir in cheese and cream. Heat through.
- Season with salt and pepper to taste. Garnish with croûtons.

Serves 24

Florence Packard Anderson

Irish Seven Course Meal

1 six pack beer (use Guiness!)
1 boiled potato

Open first beer. Wash potato well in a small pan of water and set water aside for later use.

Open second beer; then carefully remove potato eyes. Peel potato exactly 1/8 inch deep and put peels in pan of water you used to wash the potato, set on back of stove to simmer.

Open third beer. Place peeled potato in small pot; cover with water, add a dash of salt and cover with lid. Boil exactly 43 minutes; remove from heat and drain, retaining broth.

Drain potato skins, retaining broth.

Open fourth beer, then quickly put skins back on potato while they are still hot and will stick to potato.

Throw potato away, and drink remaining 2 beers. *Serves 1.*

Chelsea

TOMATO AND
ITALIAN SAUSAGE SOUP

½ lb. smoked bacon, small dice
1 lb. Italian sausage, ½-inch slice
2 cups leeks, ¼-inch slice (white part only)
1½ cups red plum tomatoes, peeled, seeded and chopped coarse

¼ cup basil, fresh chopped
Salt and freshly ground
Black pepper to taste
⅛ cup flour, all-purpose
3 cups rich chicken stock
¼ cup heavy cream

- Cook bacon in a heavy saucepan until crisp. Pour off about half of the grease.
- Add sausage and cook until half done.
- Add leeks and cook until soft.
- Add tomatoes, basil, salt and pepper. Simmer 10 minutes.
- Blend in flour to form roux. Slowly add chicken stock, stirring.
- Bring to a boil and immediately reduce heat to simmer 10 minutes.
- Stir in cream and serve.

Serves 8-10   *Chef Patrick Simpson*

The Cloister

CORN BREAD MUFFINS

¾ cup butter
½ cup sugar
4 eggs
¼ lb. bacon
1 12 oz. can corn, creamstyle
4 oz. cheddar cheese

4 oz. Jack cheese
1 cup flour, pastry
1 cup yellow corn meal
4 tbsp. baking powder
1 tsp. salt

- Use diced, rendered bacon. Shred all cheeses.
- Cream butter and sugar, add eggs, one at a time. Add remainder of ingredients and mix until well incorporated.
- Fill well-greased muffin tins half way.
- Bake in preheated 350° oven for approximately 20 minutes.

SPECIAL NOTE: DINING AT THE CLOISTER IS A TRULY ELEGANT DINING EXPERIENCE WHERE MERRY GUESTS ALSO COME FOR DANCING.

Louis Borochaner, Certified Pastry Chef

Royal Cafe

WHOLE WHEAT HOT ROLLS

1	lb. flour	11	oz. cold water
8	oz. whole wheat flour	¼	oz. salt
3	oz. oil	¼	oz. yeast
3	oz. sugar	3	oz. water heated to 110°

- Sprinkle yeast over 100° water. Do not use temperatures above 110°. Mix well, let stand 5 minutes.

- Place cold water in mixer bowl; add sugar and salt, stir until dissolved. Add yeast solution.

- Combine flour; add to liquid solution. Using dough hook, mix at low speed 1 minute or until flour mixture is incorporated into liquid.

- Add oil; mix at medium speed 10 minutes or until dough is smooth and elastic. Dough temperature should be 78° to 82°.

- Ferment: Set in warm place (80°) 1½ hours or until double in bulk.

- Punch: Divide dough into 3-4 pieces. Shape each piece into a smooth ball; let rest 10-20 minutes.

- Roll each piece into a long rope of uniform diameter. Cut rope into pieces about 1-inch thick weighing 1¾ oz. to 2 oz.

- Proof: At 90° until double in size.

- Bake: 15-20 minutes or until golden brown. Brush with butter wash.

SPECIAL NOTE: ELEGANT DINING IN THE HEART OF HISTORIC DOWNTOWN BRUNSWICK. THE UNIQUE AMBIENCE OF THE LANDMARK ROYAL HOTEL COMBINED WITH MODERN CUISINE.

Chef David U. Earl, C.E.C.

CHEESE-APPLE SALAD MAFOLIE

2 lb. apples	½ lb. sour cream
2 lb. celery	½ lb. mayonnaise
1 lb. cheddar cheese	Salt to taste
1 lb. pineapple	Lemon juice to taste
½ lb. plain yogurt	Sugar to taste

- Core and dice apples into ¼-inch cubes.
- Wash celery. Dice celery and cheese into ¼-inch cubes.
- Peel and dice pineapple into ¼-inch cubes.
- Prepare dressing using yogurt, sour cream and mayonnaise. Season to taste with salt, lemon juice, and sugar.
- Combine all ingredients. Fold in dressing. Adjust seasoning.

SPECIAL NOTE: BE CAREFUL TO DRAIN APPLES, CELERY AND PINEAPPLE OR IT WILL DILUTE DRESSING. IF APPLE SKIN IS VERY TOUGH, PEEL APPLES BEFORE DICING. SALAD CAN BE SERVED IN HOLLOWED OUT APPLE.

Serves 28   *Franz J. Buck, Certified Executive Chef*

CHICKEN SALAD IN MELON RINGS

3 tbsp. lemon juice	⅓ cup mayonnaise or salad dressing
4 cups cut-up cooked chicken	
1 cup sliced celery	1 cup seedless green grapes, halved
⅓ cup chopped onion	
1 tsp. salt	2 cantaloupes or honeydew melons
½ tsp. pepper	
1 2 oz. jar sliced pimiento, drained	Crisp greens or lemon leaves
¼ cup diced, roasted almonds	Clusters of grapes

- In medium bowl, pour lemon juice over chicken. Add celery, onion, salt, pepper pimiento, almonds, mayonnaise and 1 cup grapes. Toss, cover and chill.
- Slice off ends of cantaloupes. Scoop out seeds and membrane. Cut each cantaloupe crosswise into 3 even slices.
- To serve: place melon rings on greens. Spoon chicken mixture into centers. Arrange grape clusters around melon.

SPECIAL NOTE: CAN ALSO BE SERVED IN MELON BOWLS (CUT MELON CROSSWISE IN HALF).

Serves 6   *George Gould, Chef*

MARINATED CHICKEN SALAD

4	6 oz. chicken breasts	½	cup red wine vinegar
1	cup broccoli flowerettes	1	tbsp. soy sauce
½	cup cubed squash	½	tsp. ginger
½	cup cubed zucchini	1	tsp. chopped garlic
1	cup quartered mushrooms	½	tsp pepper
1	head iceberg lettuce		
1	bunch romaine lettuce		

Chopped pecans (optional)

Ginger and pepper to taste

Marinade for chicken:

¼	cup olive oil
1	tbsp. soy sauce
½	tsp ginger
1	tsp. chopped garlic

Pepper to taste

Vinaigrette for vegetables:

¾ cup olive oil

- Marinate chicken for 3 hours.
- Mix vinaigrette. Marinate vegetables in half of mixture 3 hours.
- Chop lettuce and place on 4 plates. Remove chicken from marinade and grill until done.
- Slice chicken, place warm chicken strips on lettuce. Top with marinated vegetables and remaining vinaigrette. Top with chopped pecans.

Serves 4   *Tim Wellford*

FREDERICA HOUSE COLESLAW

1¼ lb. shredded green cabbage	Herb seasoning
½ cup shredded purple cabbage	Seasoned salt
½ cup shredded carrots	Pepper
⅓ cup sweet relish	Garlic powder
Mayonnaise (don't over-do)	

- Mix all ingredients together and season to taste.

SPECIAL NOTE: RICHARD VARNEDOE IS ASSISTANT MANAGER. THIS IS HIS GRANDMOTHER'S RECIPE. FREDERICA HOUSE, BUILT OF AGED CEDAR AND CYPRESS WOOD, FEATURES COZY, INDOOR BALCONY SEATING.

Richard Varnedoe at Frederica House

TURKEY CURRY SALAD

4	cups turkey	1	tbsp. Roses lime juice
3	cups celery	1½	cups mayonnaise
3	cups apples	¼	cup curry powder
3	hard boiled eggs		Alfalfa sprouts
1	cup raisins		Shredded lettuce
1	cup cashews		Cashews

- Dice cooked turkey. Chop celery. Dice unpeeled apple.

- Coarsely chop hard-boiled eggs.

- Add remaining ingredients, mix and serve on a bed of shredded lettuce. Garnish with alfalfa sprouts and cashews.

Serves 12   *Florence Packard Anderson*

CRAB CAKES

1	lb. crab claw meat		Parsley for color
1	onion, finely chopped	2	eggs, beaten
1	green pepper, finely chopped	2	tbsp. Worcestershire sauce
2	ribs of celery, finely chopped		Tabasco sauce to taste

- Mix together and form into patties.

- Cook on grill until golden brown.

CRAB NEWBERG

1	lb. margarine, melted	2	tsp. Worcestershire sauce
1½	cups flour	1	tsp. hot sauce
1	qt. milk, heated	3	lbs. cleaned crab claw meat
1	tsp. yellow food coloring	¼	cup dry white wine, or to taste

- Melt butter. Slowly blend in flour over low heat, 3-4 minutes to cook flour.

- Gradually, add hot milk, stirring constantly until smooth and thicknened. Add seasonings, blend.

SPECIAL NOTE: FOR CRAB AUGRATIN ADD CHEESE TO ABOVE RECIPE AND MELT, OMIT WINE.

Serves 12-14   *Bennie Gentile*

DEVILLED CRAB

1	onion	Salt and white pepper to taste
2	bell peppers	Worcestershire sauce to taste
1	celery rib	1½ tbsp. dry mustard
4	tbsp. clarified butter	1½ pt. heavy cream
3	tbsp. flour	¼ cup parsley
2	lbs. lump crabmeat	

- Pick crabmeat carefully.

- Dice onion, bell peppers, and celery. Sauté in butter.

- Add flour and let simmer. Add heavy cream

- Into roux and crabmeat, add Worcestershire sauce, salt, white pepper, and dry mustard. Let simmer. May be thickened with bread crumbs if needed. Allow to cool.

- Fill clean crab shells, with crab mixture. Brush with butter. Sprinkle tops with bread crumbs, paprika, and butter.

- Bake in 375° oven for 10 minutes. Garnish with lemon star.

SPECIAL NOTE: FASHIONED FROM A BARN ONCE PART OF ANTEBELLUM RETREAT PLANTATION, THE SEA ISLAND GOLF CLUBHOUSE COMBINES EXCEPTIONAL DINING WITH HISTORIC PRESENCE.

Serves 4

Allegro

BAKED SALMON WITH TARRAGON PEPPERCORN CREAM SAUCE

8	salmon fillets, boned, skinless	1	cup mushrooms, sliced
3	tbsp. melted butter or olive oil	4	tbsp. melted butter or olive oil
4	tbsp. fresh tarragon (no stems)		Salt and pepper to taste
2	tsp. green peppercorns		1½ cup whipping cream
1	medium tomato		

- Oil a baking pan large enough to hold the salmon fillets. Place fillets in pan, brush with butter and bake in preheated oven at 450° for 8-10 minutes.

- Put butter/oil in large sauté pan. Add mushrooms and lightly sauté (about 2 minutes). Add tomatoes (peeled, seeded and chopped), green peppercorns and tarragon. Warm (about 1 minute).

- Add cream, reduce (about 3-5 minutes) to desired consistency. Salt and pepper to taste.

- Pour finished sauce over salmon.

Serves 8   *Allegro*

PAN-FRIED OYSTERS EN BROCHETTE

12 doz. oysters	1⅓ tbsp. pepper
4 doz. mushrooms	3 tsp. white pepper, onion
48 pieces thick bacon	powder, oregano, thyme
⅓ cups salt, garlic powder,	2 cups flour (to dust bacon)
paprika, and cayenne	

- Using six wooden skewers alternately thread 6 oysters, 2 mushrooms, and 2 pieces of bacon on each one.
- Combine spices, sprinkle the mixtue on the sides of each skewer.
- Dust the skewers with flour and fry until brown in bacon fat.
- Drain on paper towels and serve immediately.

Florence Packard Anderson

SWORDFISH PICATTA

2 lb. swordfish (or shark)	Lemon caper beurre blanc:
1 cup parmesan cheese, grated	Juice of 2 lemons
6 eggs	1 jar non-pariel capers
6 tbsp. flour	2 sticks lightly salted butter (cut
½ cup buttermilk	in cubes, room temperature)
	2 tbsp. heavy or whipping cream

- Combine eggs, buttermilk, flour and cheese in a bowl. Whisk until smooth.
- Slice swordfish ½-inch thick. In a large frying pan melt 2 tbsp. butter and add 3 tbsp. salad oil over medium heat.
- Dust swordfish with flour, shaking off excess, then place in the parmesan-egg batter.
- Transfer swordfish to heated frying pan and cook about 2 minutes on first side or until golden brown. Turn, cook one more minute.
- Place on heated serving platter, top with lemon-caper beurre blanc.
- Lemon caper beurre blanc: In a small stainless steel pan add lemon juice and 2 tbsp. brine from capers. Over medium high heat bring to a boil and reduce by half. Add heavy cream and reduce slightly. Whisk in butter gradually, not allowing the mixture to boil or cool (whisk non-stop while taking on and off heat) 'til sauce is thick and smooth in appearance.
- Sprinkle swordfish with capers with beurre blanc. Chopped parsley garnish and sliced lemons.

SPECIAL NOTE: A VIEW WHICH OVERLOOKS THE GOLDEN ISLES MARINA WITH EVENING NIGHTLIFE ALSO.

Serves 4

Oglethorpes, Sea Palms

VEAL D'ANGELI

7	oz. fresh veal cutlet	¼	cup julienne bell pepper
2	tbsp. clarified butter	¼	cup julienne zucchini
1	tsp. chopped garlic	1	oz. white wine
1	tsp. chopped eschallots	1	oz. beef stock
¼	cup sundried tomatoes		

- Dredge cutlet in flour and season with salt and pepper.
- Heat clarified butter in sauté pan. Sauté cutlet until golden brown. Remove from sauté pan.
- Sauté garlic and eschallots. Add sundried tomatoes, bell peppers and zucchini. Sauté . Season with salt and pepper.
- Add white wine and deglaze in pan.
- Add beef stock and simmer 1-2 minutes.
- Place veal cutlet on bed of fresh angel hair pasta and top with remaining ingredients.

SPECIAL NOTE: A SHOWCASE OF CULINARY DELIGHTS WITH MUSICAL ENTER-TAINMENT IN LOUNGE AFTER DINNER.

Serves 1   *Ralph J. Coughenour, Certified Executive Chef*

Jekyll Island Club Hotel, Radisson

CHICKEN AMERICAN

2	8 oz. chicken breasts	2	tbsp. sliced mushrooms
6	tbsp. flour	½	cup heavy cream
6	tbsp. honey	2	puff pastries
4	tbsp. white wine		Vegetable oil
2	tbsp. chopped green onion		Salt and pepper

- Skin and cut chicken into 6 even strips. Dust with flour. Place in hot sauté pan with vegetable oil. Cook on one side until brown and turn.
- Add onions and mushrooms. Deglaze with white wine and add honey and cream.
- Reduce flame and let simmer until chicken is completely cooked.
- Roll puff pastry ⅛-inch thick, cut into 2- x 3-inch boats. Brush with egg wash. Cook in 400° oven until top becomes very brown.
- Split puff pastry and serve chicken in the middle.

SPECIAL NOTE: THE ROCKEFELLERS AND VANDERBILTS DINED IN THIS DINING ROOM DURING THE FORMATION OF THE FEDERAL RESERVE.

Serves 2   *Earl Donivan, Executive Chef*

Cafe Frederica

CHICKEN MILANAISE

8	4 oz. boneless, skinless chicken breasts	2	tsp. fresh chopped parsley
½	cup fresh French bread crumbs	3	tbsp. olive oil
⅓	cup fresh grated Parmesan cheese		Lemon-Scallion Butter Sauce:
1	tsp. fresh chopped thyme	2	pencil-thin scallions, sliced
1	tsp. fresh chopped oregano	¼	cup fresh squeezed lemon juice
1	tsp. fresh chopped rosemary	½	cup heavy cream
		2	sticks unsalted butter, cubed

- Heat 1½ tbsp. olive oil in large sauté pan.

- Combine the bread crumbs, parmesan and herbs (If using dry herbs, use ¼ as much.)

- Press the chicken breasts in the herbed-crumb mixture, place in heated pan with the olive oil. Sauté over medium-low heat for 2½-3 minutes per side. Cook in 2 batches using the remaining olive oil in the second batch. (Allow the oil a minute to reheat.)

- Lemon-Scallion Butter Sauce: Combine the lemon juice and heavy cream in a stainless steel pan and reduce by half over medium heat.

- Stir in scallions and remove from heat. Add butter and whisk vigorously until butter has been incorporated.

- Slice chicken on the bias, two breast per plate, and lace with sauce.

Serves 4

Tom Delaney, Cafe Frederica

ST. SIMONS ISLAND CHICKEN

2	tbsp. white wine	½	cup seasoned flour
4	tbsp. lemon juice	5	mushrooms, sliced
6	tbsp. butter	4	oz. spinach, washed
2	cloves garlic, minced	2	tbsp. whipping cream
1	7 oz. chicken breast, boned and skinned		

- Cut chicken in half, pound gently. Dredge in flour.
- Heat 4 tbsp. butter in skillet and drop in floured chicken. Brown on both sides.
- Add garlic, wine and mushrooms. Let reduce until chicken is done (about 3-4 minutes).
- Add whipping cream and blend.
- In a separate pan add remaining 2 tbsp. butter, sauté spinach until tender (about 2 minutes).
- Serve chicken on top of spinach. Great with pasta or rice.

SPECIAL NOTE: THE KING AND PRINCE IS AN ISLAND TRADITION LOCATED ON BEAUTIFUL ST. SIMON'S BEACHFRONT.

Serves 1   *Rick Barnhart, Sous Chef*

BRAISED VIDALIA ONIONS

2	doz. vidalia onions	Salt, white pepper and mace
1⅛	cups chicken broth	1 pt. heavy cream
¾	cup honey	

- Slice onions in half, and then into ¼-inch slices.
- In a large sauté pan, melt butter over medium heat.
- Add honey and stir to dissolve. Add the onions, chicken broth, salt, pepper and mace and reduce heat to low.
- Cover and braise until tender, 8-10 minutes.
- Uncover and cook on high until all the liquid evaporates.
- Add cream and cook, stirring until most of the cream has been absorbed.

SPECIAL NOTE: SPOON ONTO PLATES AND TOP WITH VEAL SCALLOPS.

Serves 24   *Florence Packard Anderson*

POTATOES AND BEER

4	medium potatoes	2	cups beer
1	large onion	1	cup heavy cream
5	tbsp. butter		

- Thinly slice the potatoes and the onion.
- Overlap the potatoes and onions in a buttered casserole dish.
- Dot with butter and sprinkle with salt and pepper.
- Pour beer over all and cover with foil. Bake at 350° for 30 minutes.
- Uncover, pour on heavy cream and return to oven for 30 more minutes.

Serves 6   *Florence Packard Anderson*

BARLEY CASSEROLE

½	lb. mushrooms	1	tsp. salt
¼	cup butter	½	tsp. ground pepper
1	large onion, finely chopped	2	cups chicken stock
1	cup pearl barley		

- Slice mushroom caps thin and chop stems.
- In a large skillet melt the butter, add the onions. Sauté 3-4 minutes until tender. Stir in mushrooms, cook 4-5 minutes.
- Mix in the barley, salt and pepper. Brown lightly, mixing well with the onions and mushrooms.
- Transfer the mixture to a four cup casserole. Stir in the stock.
- Cover and bake at 350° for 25 minutes.

Serves 6   ·   *Florence Packard Anderson*

BLANCHE'S BREAD PUDDING

1½ qt. milk	½ tsp. salt
½ stick margarine	½ tsp. cinnamon
6 eggs	½ lb. raisins
1 cup sugar	6-8 cups stale bread

- In a sauce pan scald, milk and margarine.
- In a bowl combine eggs, sugar and spices. Add scalded milk.
- Place bread in a baking dish with raisins.
- Add egg-milk mixture, saturate.
- Bake in 300° oven in water bath for 45 minutes or until firm and dry.

SPECIAL NOTE: UNIQUE BAYOU-VICTORIAN ATMOSPHERE COMPLEMENTS AN ARRAY OF DELICIOUS ENTRÉES AND DESSERTS.

Pat. Benton

Frederica House

CHOCOLATE PEANUT BUTTER PIE

3 lb. softened cream cheese	5 large boxes Jello instant chocolate pudding mix
40 oz. Jif peanut butter	
16 oz. Cool Whip	10 prepared chocolate graham cracker crusts
3 cans sweetened condensed milk	

- Mix cream cheese, peanut butter and condensed milk.
- Fold in Cool Whip.
- Fill crusts ⅔ full.
- Mix Jello pudding following directions on box.
- Pour over above mixture.
- Freeze and thaw as needed.

SPECIAL NOTE: ASSISTANT MANAGER, RICHARD VARNEDOE'S OWN CREATION.

Yield ten pies (each serves 8)   *Richard Varnedoe*

MILLION DOLLAR CHOCOLATE PIE

2	chocolate crumb crusts	6	eggs
1¼	cup butter	3	tbsp. cognac
1⅓	cup sugar	2	cups walnuts, finely chopped
4	1 oz. squares baking chocolate	1	pt. heavy cream, whipped
			Semi-sweet chocolate curls

- Cream butter and sugar.

- Add melted chocolate. Stir.

- Add eggs one at a time beating 3 minutes after each egg.

- Add cognac and nuts and pour into the pie shells.

- Top each with whipped cream and curls and refrigerate 3 hours.

Serves 16   *Florence Packard Anderson*

Common Market

COLORADO COWBOYS

½	lb. margarine	½	tsp. baking powder
1	tsp. vanilla	½	tsp. salt
1	cup white granulated sugar	2	cup quick oats (not old fashioned)
1	cup brown sugar		
2	eggs	6	oz. chocolate chips
2	cup flour	1	cup chopped pecans
1	tsp. baking soda		

- Cream first 4 ingredients with an electric mixer.

- Add the eggs one at a time, blending well each time.

- Mix flour, baking soda, baking powder, salt, quick oats, chocolate chips and pecans.

- Add dry ingredients to egg mixture.

- Drop by large spoonfuls 2-inches apart on non-stick cookie sheet.

- Bake at 325° for 15-20 minutes. Will harden as they cool so remove from oven even if they seem soft.

ORANGE-RHUBARB PIE
WITH APRICOTS

1¾ cups sugar
1   2-inch piece vanilla bean
½   orange with peel, in chunks
20 oz. frozen rhubarb
½   cup cranberries, coarsely
      chopped
½   cup dried apricots, thin
      sliced

¼   cup flour
2   9-inch pie crusts

Topping:
1   cup sour cream
2   tbsp. brown sugar
½   tsp. grated orange peel

- Preheat oven to 400°.
- Combine sugar and vanilla bean in food processor and blend until bean is finely chopped.
- Add orange and process until orange is finely chopped.
- Transfer to bowl. Add rhubarb, cranberries, apricots and flour and toss.
- Press one crust into a 9-inch pie pan. Trim leaving a ¾-inch overhang.
- Cut remaining pie crust into ½-inch wide strips.
- Spoon rhubarb mixture into crust.
- Place strips across pie forming a lattice. Seal and crimp edges.
- Bake in a 400° oven until crust is golden and filling begins to bubble.
- Serve warm with sour cream topping.
- Topping: Combine sour cream, brown sugar and orange peel.
- Will keep in the refrigerator for 2 days.

Serves 8   *Florence Packard Anderson*

Allegro's

BOURBON PECAN CHEESECAKE

32 oz. cream cheese, softened	Crust:
1¼ cups sugar	1½ cups Graham cracker crumbs
1 cup pecans, chopped	1 cup melted butter
½ cup quality bourbon (Jack Daniels, Black Label)	
4 large eggs, room temperature	

- Crust: Mix crumbs and melted butter.

- In a 10-inch springform pan pour Graham cracker crumb mixture, pressing around edges about ½- to ¾-inch high, and pressing smooth on bottom. Bake at 350° for 15 minutes.

- While crust is baking, cream the cream cheese and sugar with electric mixer.

- Add the pecans and bourbon; mix until homogenized.

- Add the eggs one at a time (not adding another until the first is completely absorbed).

- Pour cream cheese mixture into finished crust.

- Place pan into larger pan holding 1-2 qts. water. Bake at 350° for 1½ hours.

- At the end of the 1½ hours turn oven off and crack door for 1 hour.

- Let cheesecake sit at room temperature for 30 minutes and refrigerate for at least 4 hours or overnight.

- Remove cheesecake from pan by opening the latch slightly and running a knife around the circumference of pan.

SPECIAL NOTE: CULINARY SPECTACLES NIGHTLY THAT COMPARE TO FINEST RESTAURANTS IN ATLANTA AND NEW YORK.

Serves 12   *Allegro*

Café Frederica

PRALINE CHEESECAKE

1½ cups Graham cracker crumbs
3 tbsp. sugar
3 tbsp. melted margarine
24 oz. cream cheese
2 tbsp. flour

3 eggs
2 tsp. vanilla
½ cup chopped pecans
¾ cup brown sugar

- Mix Graham cracker crumbs, melted margarine and sugar. Pat crust into 8-inch springform pan. Bake in 350° oven for 10 minutes.

- Beat cream cheese until smooth, gradually add brown sugar and flour, mix well. Add eggs one at a time.

- Stir in pecans and vanilla.

- Pour into crust. Bake in 350° oven for 40-45 minutes.

SPECIAL NOTE: I SPRAY PAN WITH BAKER'S JOY.

Serves 10   *Cindy Bearse*

The Fourth of May

GEORGIA PEACH CHUTNEY

2 lbs. peaches, peeled, sliced
1 cup onions, diced
1 cup green peppers, diced
1 cup red peppers, diced
1 cup vinegar
1 lb. brown sugar

2 tbsp. red pepper flakes
2 tsp. ground ginger
1 tsp. salt or to taste
1 box chopped dates
1 box raisins

- Sauté the onions and red and green bell peppers in a little oil until soft.

- Add remaining ingredients and bring to a boil.

- Refrigerate.

Serves 8   *Florence Packard Anderson*

The Cloister

SAVORY CHEESECAKE (APPETIZER)

1 lb. cream cheese
1½ tsp. salt
¾ cup sour cream
2 eggs
2 egg yolks
½ cup heavy cream

Bread Crumb Base:
1⅓ cups bread crumbs
2-3 tbsp. butter, melted
Garnishes: ham, smoked salmon,
olives, herbs

- Blend the cream cheese with mixer until smooth.

- Add salt, blend in.

- Add sour cream and blend. Scrape bowl and blend.

- Add eggs and blend. Scrap bowl and blend.

- Add cream and any chopped garnish desired: ham, smoked salmon, herbs, olives.

- Pour mix into 8-inch cake pan the bottom of which has been spread and packed down with bread crumb base.

- Bread Crumb Base: Combine butter and bread crumbs until crumbs hold together lightly when squeezed in your hand. Spread crumbs evenly on bottom of cake pan and pack down with your fingers. Bake for 15 minutes before filling.

- Bake at 300° in a water bath until center is firm, but springy (as for a custard).

- Allow to cool thoroughly, then refrigerate before unmolding (2 hours).

- To unmold: Put cake pan in sink fulled with 2-inches hot water.

- Leave for 30-45 seconds.

- Invert pan onto cardboard cakeboard.

- Cover the bottom with another cakeboard, then turn upside. Remove cakeboard from topside.

- Serve as is, or slightly warmed. Serve accompanied by water crackers, fruit, or pickled vegetables.

SPECIAL NOTE: THIS IS NOT A DESSERT.

Franz J. Buck, Certified Executive Chef

Olde Time

Hand Soap Recipe

Wash and measure the fat

- Mix 7 lbs. (2½ Crisco cans) of waste fat (which you have rendered from cooking and saved in the refrigerator) with 3 times its volume of water. Add 2 tbsp. salt, 1 tbsp. baking soda and bring to a rolling boil for 5 minutes.

- Set aside to cool.

- The fresh clean fat will rise to the surface and can be skimmed off.

- Measure 6 lbs. of fat (2 Crisco cans) discarding the dirty bath water.

Mix the lye solution

- In a large glass container, mix 5 cups of cold water with a can of red devil lye and quickly stir with a wooden spoon until the two are combined. *(Be careful not to breathe the fumes or splash the solution.)*

- Cover the opening to contain the fumes and let cool to room temperature.

Add the lye solution to the fat

- Place the washed fat in a large enamel basin *(no aluminum)*.

- Using a wooden spoon, begin to stir in the lye solution starting with only **a drop at a time** and making sure the liquid is absorbed by the fat before adding more.

- Work patiently as if you were making mayonnaise, and gradually increase the solution additions until the fat has accepted all of the liquid and the mixture becomes too thick to stir.

- Turn the soap out onto a cloth lined box or pan to harden and age a minimum of 3 weeks.

- Cut into squares or soften in a warm oven and press into balls.

- The soap is soft and gentle and still full of its natural oils which will not dry your skin.

Betsy Enney

Recipes of Mrs. John Couper
(1775-1846)

Rebecca Couper was a Maxwell, the daughter of a prominent Scottish family who had settled in Massachusetts early in the 18th century and later moved through Pennsylvania, South Carolina to Liberty County, Georgia where she met John Couper after the Revolutionary War. They were married in 1793, moving to St. Simons Island in 1794. The Coupers were famous for their entertaining, especially sumptuous dinners. Mrs. Couper was responsible daily for the selection of meats butchered by the staff, fish caught by the fishermen and vegetables grown in the gardens. However, most certainly she supervised the preparation and serving of the foods with the help of Sans Foix, the Couper's French trained chef.

Oyster Soup (Hand written)

- 6 qts. of oysters, yoke of 18 hard boiled eggs, 1 tea cup of cream small lump of butter, 1 onion stuck with cloves and a little mace, small bundle of herbs.

- Stew your oysters gently for a few moments, then rinse them out into a clean pan, let the liquor settle from it gently off into the pan with the oysters., being careful not to include the sediment.

- Return the oysters and the liquor, together with the onion and the herbs, into the liquid now cleaned from the sediment. Let the whole stew gently until the oysters are _____ . Strain the oysters from the liquor, which again sat in the boiler. Break the yolks of the eggs, together with the cream and butter on a marble mortar and mix gradually with the liquor to thicken your soup. Take great care not to burn the oysters to the bottom of your boiler. Salt and pepper as fancy or taste is added.

Cure for Dysentery or Diarrhea

- Boil 1 tea cup of logwood chips in 1 pint of sweet milk, add 1 tea cup loaf of sugar and boil another 10 minutes. Then cool and strain. Take 4 tablespoons of Brandy, put it into a saucer and set it on fire. After burning what it will, stir it into the mixture and it is ready for use.

- Give 1 tablespoon 3 times a day the first day to an adult. If a cure is not affected give it only twice the second day and only once the third day.

- Let the patient eat nothing unless it may be a little rice, milk, porridge or toast and take very little if any drink.

- Give only half the quantity to a child.

Orange Drink

- Put into three qts. of brandy the chips of 18 Seville oranges, and let them steep a fortnight in a stone bottle. Close the stopper. Boil 2 qts. of spring water with a pound and a half of the finest sugar, near an hour very gently. Clarify the water and sugar with the white of an egg. Then strain through a Jelly-bag, and boil it nearly half away. When it is cold, strain the brandy into the syrup.

Martha Washington's Boston Cream Pie

1 cup sifted cake flour
1 tsp. baking powder
Dash of salt
2 eggs, separated
1 cup sugar
1 tbsp. butter or margarine
½ cup hot milk

- Sift flour, baking powder and salt together. Beat egg whites until stiff. Beat egg yolks until thick and lemon-colored. Fold yolks into whites and beat together. Add sugar gradually, beating constantly. Fold sifted dry ingredients into mixture. Melt butter in milk; stir into mixture and blend thoroughly. Turn into greased and floured 8-inch round pan. Bake at 350° for 25-30 minutes. Cool. Cut in half crosswise. Spread filling between layers. dust top with confectioner's sugar.

Yield: 6 portions

Cream Filling
⅔ cup sugar
¼ cup flour
2 tbsp. cornstarch
Dash of salt
2 cups scalded milk
1 egg, beaten
1 tsp. vanilla

- Mix sugar, flour, cornstarch and salt. Stir in milk. Cook in top of a double boiler until thick and smooth, about 10 minutes, stirring frequently. Stir a little of mixture into egg, return to double boiler and cook 2 minutes longer. Cool. Add vanilla.

Yield: 2 cups filling

Helpful Hints

Substitutions

1 whole egg, for thickening or baking: 2 egg yolks. Or 2 tbsp. dried whole egg plus 2½ tbsp. water

1 cup butter or margarine for shortening: ⅞ cup lard, or rendered fat, with ½ tsp. salt. or 1 cup hydrogenated fat (cooking fat sold under brand name) with ½ tsp. salt.

1 square (oz.) chocolate: 3-4 tbsp. cocoa plus ½ tsp fat. For semi-sweet, add 3 tbsp. sugar

6 ozs. semi-sweet chocolate: 2 ozs. unsweetened chocolate, 7 tbsp. sugar and 2 tbsp. fat.

1 tsp. double-acting baking powder: 1½ tsp. phosphate baking powder. Or 2 tsp. tartrate baking powder.

Sweet milk and baking powder, for baking: Equal amount of sour milk plus ½ tsp. soda per cup. *(Each ½ tsp. soda with 1 cup sour milk takes the place of 2 tsp. baking powder and 1 cup sweet milk.)*

1 cup sour milk, for baking: 1 cup sweet milk mixed with one of the following: 1 tbsp vinegar. Or 1 tbsp. lemon juice. Or 1¾ tsp. cream of tartar.

1 cup whole milk: ½ cup evaporated milk plus ½ cup water. Or 4 tbsp. nonfat dry milk plus 2 tsp. table fat and 1 cup water.

1 cup skim milk: 4 tbsp. nonfat dry milk plus 1 cup water.

1 tbsp. flour for thickening: ½ tbsp. cornstarch, potato starch, rice starch, or arrowroot starch. Or 1 tbsp. granulated tapioca.

1 cup cake flour for baking: ⅞ cup all-purpose flour.

1 cup all-purpose flour for baking breads: Up to ½ cup bran, whole-wheat flour, or corn meal plus enough all-purpose flour to fill cup.

1 tbsp. cornstarch: 1½ tbsp. flour

1 cup corn syrup: ¾ cup sugar plus ¼ cup water

1 tbsp. tomato paste: 1 tbsp. tomato catsup

3 tbsp. chopped fresh parsley: 1 tsp. dried parsley flakes

1 tbsp. prepared mustard: 1 tsp. dry mustard plus 1 tbsp. vinegar

1 cup buttermilk: 1 tbsp. vinegar or lemon juice plus milk to make 1 cup

1 tbsp. fresh herbs: ½ tsp. dried herbs

1 clove fresh garlic: ¾ tsp. garlic salt or garlic powder

1 tbsp. active, dry yeast: 1 pkg. active dry yeast or 1 compressed yeast cake

Food Weights

2 slices bread=1 cup soft crumbs
Eggs: 5-6 whole = 1 cup
12-14 yolks = 1 cup;
8-10 whites = 1 cup
Flour: 1 lb. all-purpose = 4 cup
Lemons , med. size:
Juice of 1 – 2-3 tbsp.;
1 rind (lightly grated) = 1½-3 tsp.
Pasta, uncooked: 1 lb. = 5 cup
Pecans: 1 lb. shelled = 4 cups meat
Meat, ground: 1 lb. = 2 cup

Oranges, med. size:
Juice of 1 = ⅓ - ½ cup
Rice, uncooked: 1 lb. = 2⅓ cup
Shortening, solid pack:
1 lb. = 5 cup
Sugar: 1 lb.granulated = 2 cup
1 lb. brown = 2¼ cup (packed firm)
1 lb. confectioners = 3½ c (sifted)
1 lb. powdered = 2⅓ cup
Shrimp, in shell:
1 lb. = 2 cups cooked and peeled

Food Measurements

Sugar: 1 tsp. = 15 grams
Flour: ¼ cup = 240 grams
Salt:
1 tbsp. – 35 grams;
1 cup = 140 grams

Rice: 1 cup = 240 grams
Butter: 1 tbsp. = 15 grams
½ cup = 125 grams

Equivalents

3 tsp = 1 tbsp.	2 cups = 1 pt.	32 ozs. = 1 qt.
4 tbsp. = ¼ cup	4 cups = 1 qt.	8 ozs. liquid = 1 cup
8 tbsp. = ½ cup	16 ozs. = 1 lb.	1 oz. liquid = 2 tbsp.

(For liquid and dry measurements use standard measuring spoons and cups. All measurements are level.)

Abbreviations

tsp. = teaspoon(s)	qt.(s) = quart(s)	lb.(s) = pound(s)
tbsp. = tablespoon(s)	gal.(s) = gallon(s)	pkg.(s) = package(s)
pt.(s) = pint(s)	oz.(s) = ounce(s)	° = degrees

Oven temperatures are preheated unless otherwise stated.

Bar Set-up

2 qt. scotch
1 qt. bourbon
2 qts. vodka
1 qt. gin
1 gallon punch (serves 20)

Mixers:
1 soda water(large)
2 gingerale
2 tonic water

Cut limes and lemons, 1 lb. ice per person

Index

Christ Church, Frederica Cookbook
6329 Frederica Road
Saint Simons Island, GA 31522

Please send _____ copies   @ $ 20.00 each _____

Postage and handling   @ $ 5.00 each _____

TOTAL ENCLOSED $ _____

Name_____

Address_____

City_____ State _____ Zip_____

Phone Number_____

Email: _____

- -

Christ Church, Frederica Cookbook
6329 Frederica Road
Saint Simons Island, GA 31522

Please send _____ copies   @ $ 20.00 each _____

Postage and handling   @ $ 5.00 each _____

TOTAL ENCLOSED $ _____

Name_____

Address_____

City_____ State _____ Zip_____

Phone Number_____

Email: _____

- -

Christ Church, Frederica Cookbook
6329 Frederica Road
Saint Simons Island, GA 31522

Please send _____ copies   @ $ 20.00 each _____

Postage and handling   @ $ 5.00 each _____

TOTAL ENCLOSED $ _____

Name_____

Address_____

City_____ State _____ Zip_____

Phone Number_____

Email: _____